FORM AND VITALITY

Form and Vitality
in the World and God

A CHRISTIAN PERSPECTIVE

Trevor Williams

CLARENDON PRESS · OXFORD

Oxford University Press, Walton Street, Oxford OX2 6DP
Oxford New York Toronto
Delhi Bombay Calcutta Madras Karachi
Petaling Jaya Singapore Hong Kong Tokyo
Nairobi Dar es Salaam Cape Town
Melbourne Auckland
and associated companies in
Beirut Berlin Ibadan Nicosia

Oxford is a trade mark of Oxford University Press

First published 1985
First issued as a paperback 1988

British Library Cataloguing in Publication Data
Williams, Trevor
Form and vitality in the world and God:
a Christian perspective
1. Theology I. Title 230 BR118
ISBN 0–19–826671–5
ISBN 0–19–826698–7 (Pbk)

Library of Congress Cataloging in Publication Data
Williams, Trevor, 1938–
Form and vitality in the world and God
Bibliography: p.
Includes index.
1. Apologetics—20th century 2. Jews—History—To 70 AD
3. Jesus Christ—Person and offices
4. Christianity—Essence, genius, nature
I. Title BT1102.W543 1985 230 85–323
ISBN 0–19–826671–5
ISBN 0–19–826698–7 (Pbk)

Printed in Great Britain
at the University Printing House, Oxford
by David Stanford
Printer to the University

In memory of my Father and Mother
A.M.W.   M.E.W.

Foreword

THEOLOGIANS often shirk writing theology. Scriptural exegesis, history of doctrine, and philosophy of religion are necessary constituent parts of theological work. Because they are more circumscribed in character, it is both easier and safer to confine one's approach to one such area. Broader theological treatments can easily appear arbitrary or platitudinous. Not infrequently they are one or the other. So it is an unusually courageous enterprise to undertake to write theologically on so broad a canvas as Mr Williams has chosen to do, especially for a first book. I think his courage has paid off. His book helps us, as few theological writings do, to look at the Christian tradition in a way that is both positive in its approach and also takes full account of a contemporary understanding of the world and of human knowledge. It is not just one more book on theological method. It is a work of theological substance in its own right. It deserves to be widely read and carefully pondered.

MAURICE WILES

Preface

THERE were rare moments in my undergraduate days when I thought I had had a new idea, but one kind friend was almost invariably able to remind me of the book in which I must have found it.

In the intervening years he has not been at hand to perform this invaluable service. I can only acknowledge that I owe a far greater debt to many more people than the footnotes or the limited bibliography included here would suggest. I owe as much besides to the stimulus of tutorial discussion and reactions to talks and sermons, as over the years I have tried to see how the extraordinary claims of the Christian faith can be maintained in the sort of world we live in now, and with the understanding we have of it.

This enterprise has drawn me into many different fields and areas of expertise to a degree that must seem foolhardy, if not presumptuous, to scholars on whose territory I have trespassed. I certainly cannot claim to have covered all the literature. But my aim as a systematic theologian has not been to take issue with specialists on their own ground, but to draw on the fruits of their labours, to see how things might fit together, and how the picture that emerges might bear on our lives.

I do not therefore address theological experts or even Christians particularly, but anyone who might be wondering how the Christian faith can be interpreted today and what vision of life it can offer. For this reason, I have tried not to assume a familiarity with Christianity and its origins, or with the Bible, which cannot be taken for granted even among professed Christians nowadays. If the amount of background information given proves tedious at times to those already in the know, I hope they will be tolerant. For those who want more, I have drawn attention in each Part to major works in which a much fuller treatment and comprehensive bibliographies may be found.

Apart from the wider debt which I have acknowledged, I owe much to others—too many for me to mention by name, but of whose kindness and assistance I need no reminder.

Among students and colleagues, I am particularly grateful to Kim Richardson, Stuart Williams, Simon Fisher, Robert Morgan, James Barr, and Maurice Wiles. Without their critical comments and advice, there would be many more mistakes and obscurities than may still be found. Responsibility for these is mine.   .

My gratitude is also due to Anne Ashby, Audrey Bayley, and John Waś of Oxford University Press for guiding this book through the final stages of preparation; to Mrs Joyce Reid for her painstaking scrutiny of the final text; to numerous secretaries in my college who over the years struggled to impart coherent form to my anarchic handwriting; to Stella Wood, particularly in the early stages, and to Pat Rogers, who put it all on disks.

Lastly, I must thank my wife, Sue, and daughters, Rebecca and Catherine, for letting me take so much time that I might otherwise have been able to spend with them.

T. S. M. W.

Trinity College, Oxford
June 1984

Contents

Part III. God's Relatedness in Jesus

Part IV. The Response to Jesus Worked Out in History

Part V. Implications

CONTENTS

Introduction

WE live in an age in which believing in God has become increasingly difficult, if not impossible, for a great many people. The dividing line between believers and non-believers is not as simple and clear-cut as is often supposed. Many professed believers experience the difficulties of belief and in their heart of hearts wonder if they are merely keeping up a pretence. Many non-believers are by no means hostile to religion; they wish they could believe, but what they are asked to believe too often seems incompatible with or completely irrelevant to that understanding of the world by which they live. In order not to deny this world, they are driven to deny God.

Is it possible to believe in God, in particular, is it possible to be a Christian believer, without hypocrisy, without the sacrifice of integrity or reason, without being forced to live in two separate worlds simultaneously?

I could not be a Christian if a positive answer could not be given to this question. If my attempt to discover where and how a positive answer is possible helps anyone else both to affirm the world and to believe in God, the main purpose of this book will have been served.

The first Part is somewhat theoretical in approach, because my aim has been to provide a framework within which a modern understanding of evolutionary existence and Christian belief in God can be integrated. I hope this theoretical form will be vitalized by the more substantive discussions that follow in the later Parts. So if some readers find portions of Part I hard to swallow, if not positively indigestible, I can only beg them to press on to the main courses without worrying too much about what has had to be left on the side of the plate. Some of it may prove easier to absorb in retrospect.

One thing, however, must be explored further at this stage, as it is fundamental for understanding all that follows. This is the concept of 'polarity'.

To explain. Our lives are set within a framework of complementary opposites, such as individual/society, subject/
object, order/freedom, continuity/discontinuity. The word
'polarity' is now commonly used of such paired concepts.[1]
In this book the polarity of form and vitality[2] will be used as
an interpretative model or perspective from which to explore
the conditions of existence in our world and in relation to
God.

The complementary character of polarities suggests that
they should balance each other, and that the overemphasis
of one at the expense of the other might be expected to have
a distorting and harmful effect. This happens if too much
emphasis is placed on society, for example, at the expense of
the individual, or on order at the expense of freedom, or vice
versa. In the extreme case, this amounts to treating a partial
truth or good as the whole, the penultimate as the ultimate,
the less than absolute as absolute. In traditional language
this is the offence of idolatry, treating what is less than God
as God. According to the Judaeo-Christian tradition, idolatry always has disastrous consequences. Putting it differently, one might speak figuratively of a limited good
claiming to be the absolute good and thereby giving rise to
evil. One is reminded of the belief that the Devil was originally an angel who only fell after attempting to usurp God's
throne.[3] Hence the word 'demonic' has been appropriately
introduced to describe the disordered and destructive consequences of polar imbalances.[4]

The character of a polar relationship may be illustrated
by the analogy of the two touch-lines on a football pitch.
Neither is dispensable; together they define the field of play.
The action can develop between them in an infinite variety

[1] Cf. P. Tillich, *Systematic Theology*, i (London, 1978), 198.
[2] Cf. R. Niebuhr, *The Nature and Destiny of Man*, vol. i (New York, 1964);
chapter 2 is entitled 'The Problem of Vitality and Form in Human Nature'. Cf.
also Tillich's use of 'form and vitality' (or 'dynamics') in *Systematic Theology*, i.
178 ff. and ii. 64. Both authors have contributed to the ideas developed here.
[3] 2 Enoch 29: 4–5 (in R. H. Charles, ed., *The Apocrypha and Pseudepigrapha of
the Old Testament in English* (Oxford, 1913), 447). Cf. Niebuhr, 192.
[4] Tillich, *Systematic Theology*, i. 140, '. . . the demonic is the elevation of something conditional to unconditional significance'. See also id., *Dynamics of Faith*
(London, 1957), 11 f., 109.

of ways, though the nearer one approaches either touch-line, the less room there is for manoeuvre.

In the same way, the polarity of form and vitality may be seen as defining the field of evolutionary and historical play. The two poles do not exist independently, but define the sphere in which things can happen. Their dynamic interplay is what will be meant here by the phrase 'polar dialectic'.

It will be argued that the polarity of form and vitality represents a necessary condition of evolutionary existence. But just as different games can be played on the same pitch, but according to different rules—soccer, rugger, hockey— so can different ways of living develop under the same basic conditions of existence. We must make a distinction, then, between natural rules and man-made rules. What human beings cannot do is override the natural rules of life in our world; the attempt to do so leads to frustration and injury in sport and, on a larger scale, to man-made disasters and ecological crises. To discover and to formulate the natural rules is therefore of vital importance, if human goals are to be realized.

On the other hand, man-made rules can be changed. Every game must have its rules, but without our freedom to change old rules and invent new ones, there could not be any games or sports at all. This illustrates again the interplay of form and vitality.

One further point needs to be made. Various sports are of necessity mutually exclusive, but there is no need for a hierarchy of merit. As long as the rules of the game do not defy the natural rules of existence, each sport can have its own particular value for those who engage in it and accept its objectives. If, then, no single sport can claim to be the ideal, no more can one particular experience of the possibilities of human life claim to be the ideal.

What will be opposed in the pages that follow is the imposition of any fixed form or ideal on the creative scope of human existence. It will be argued, however, that the polar dialectic itself defines all fields of play and is thus the underlying condition of sport and of every other human enterprise—cultural, political, or religious—and that failure to recognize this condition results in disorder and the loss of creativity.

The analogy of touch-lines has, it is hoped, served to show that the relationship between apparent opposites is not necessarily one of contradictions. The opposing terms may be distinguishable and even mutually exclusive (the right touch-line cannot at the same time and for the same person be the left touch-line); nevertheless, it is only when their dynamic—dialectical—interrelationship is accepted that the business of playing football or living life can proceed. In fact, as far as life is concerned, it proceeds that way whether the dynamic interrelationship is openly accepted or not.

It remains to be said that whatever value the polarity model may have, it is not intended to serve as a key to unlock all the mysteries of the universe; that would be too much to expect of such a simple formula. Nor, it should be emphasized, is it the aim here to establish a logically compelling argument on the basis of first principles, of such a kind that a logically weak link at any point would break the whole chain. My hope is rather to provide a coherent interpretation of Christian origins and attitudes within the framework of modern thought, using the polarity of form and vitality as an interpretative model. The success of the enterprise will depend on the plausibility of the model itself, and on the extent to which it allows us to organize and interpret the phenomena of life and experience in general, and of Christian life and experience in particular, in a way that rings true. Proof is not claimed, nor perhaps is it necessary or possible.

The task, then, may be summed up as follows: first, to establish the view that human life can plausibly be understood to be set within the polar relationship of form and vitality; secondly, to show that belief in God is not unreasonable, and that if God exists, then it is reasonable to suppose that humankind's relationship with him is set within the same polar relationship; thirdly, to show that accounts of God's relationship to the world and to human beings which do not rest on this basis are in practice distorting and potentially destructive; fourthly, to show that the account of God's relationship that derives from Jesus does conform to this polar pattern and reinforces it, and is creative in effect.

In other words, it will be argued that this account marks out the pitch within which the possibilities for human beings of right relationship with God, each other, and the physical world, can be realized creatively in many different but not mutually exclusive or mutually devaluing ways. Fifthly, it will be suggested that the polar character of the relationship between humanity and God is well expressed in the symbol of the Trinity, even if that is not the usual interpretation of it, and even though it has all too often been interpreted in such a way as to lose its creative power. Sixthly and finally, it will be argued that in the light of this approach certain clear conclusions can be drawn in respect of a number of practical problems facing the Churches today internally, in relation to each other, in relation to other religions, and in relation to political life and secular ideologies.

I

THE WORLD WE LIVE IN
AND GOD

INTRODUCTION

THIS book is addressed to those who share one basic assumption and who ponder one fundamental question.

The assumption is that we live in an evolutionary world, of which the sciences have given us a far more accurate understanding than was ever achieved before our age, even if the scientific account is still by no means complete.

The question is, 'Does life have meaning?'

Human beings seem to be driven by a powerful impulse to integrate the whole of reality as they encounter and experience it. This, perhaps, is the penalty of rationality. One consequence is that if a positive answer is given to the question of meaning, a further question imposes itself. How does the reality of meaning relate to the reality of the world which we observe and experience, and of which we see ourselves to be a part? In short, how does meaning relate to being? This may be seen as a restatement of the age-old question, 'How does God relate to the world and humanity?'—since whatever else the word may signify, 'God' is taken here to stand for that which is the source or ground of meaning.

Many people, it is true, hold that there is no ultimate answer to the question of meaning, and hence that there is no God. They are still left with the apparent meaningfulness of human relationships and ideals. If such experienced meaningfulness is judged to have no ultimate ground, two courses lie open. Either it will be treated as illusion and dissolve into nothingness, or it will be acknowledged as real but as an unintegrated anomaly of life.[1] In the former case, the consequences are demonstrably destructive for individuals and society. The alternative is inherently unstable. The anomaly is liable to give way to the consistency of nihilism, or to provoke a renewed search for an answer to the question of meaning.

In this direction innumerable possibilities lie open. The word 'God' may be employed in widely differing senses or avoided altogether. In every case, however, the question can and must be asked, 'How does meaning as you conceive of it relate to being as we all observe and experience it?'

Those who profess to see in the story of Jesus the answer to the question of meaning are as much obliged as anyone else to face up to this question. They must show, or attempt to show, how the meaning found in Jesus relates to the being not merely of themselves, but of all human beings and their world, not least of those who do not see things that way.

What follows is an attempt to respond to this demand. It begins with the being we all share, as evolutionary creatures in an evolutionary world. It rests on the supposition that such existence is meaningful, in other words, that God is real; he is the ultimate ground of meaning for us, and can be that precisely because he is at the same time the ultimate, eternal, and creative ground of our being. This means that he is the ground not merely of human being in isolation, but of the being of the universe of which we now recognize ourselves to be a minute but integral part.

That God is real cannot be proved, but some attempt will be made below (chap. 2, sect. 1) to show that this belief is not unreasonable. For God to be the ground of meaning and being requires not only that he be related to the world and to us, but also that he should in some sense be knowable in this relationship; otherwise he could not be the ground of meaning for the rational, conscious creatures that we are.

Our task now is to examine further and to spell out some of the implications of these basic assumptions: that we live in an evolutionary world, that God is real and is related to our world and is in some sense knowable. We begin with evolution.

---

[1] See H. Küng, *On Being a Christian* (Glasgow, 1976), 70-9.

1. Evolution

I. THE EMERGENCE OF HUMAN BEINGS AS SYMBOL-USERS

(a) Evolutionary conditions

DESPITE recurrent disputes between so-called 'creationists' and Darwinists, no serious case has yet been raised against the general theory of evolution as the basis for understanding the origin and development of life on earth.[1] Not surprisingly, Darwin has proved to have been wrong in respect of certain details. His own account of the mechanisms of evolution may be inadequate, and evolutionary developments may not have occurred gradually and continuously but in a series of dramatic leaps. Issues of this kind, however, do not affect the basic theory, which is that higher forms of life, including human life, have evolved from lower forms of life over millions of years.

Acceptance of the general theory of evolution carries with it certain other assumptions about the sort of world in which evolution can happen. First, there must be an environment characterized by some sort of order, so that evolutionary adjustment to it can serve a purpose and improve a creature's chance of survival. Secondly, the possibility of change must be built into that environment, or else adjustment to it (or of it) would be neither necessary nor, of course, possible. As things are, change and adjustment are both possible and necessary. At the same time, they are limited by the structures of earthly existence.

To be in an evolutionary world is, then, to exist within a framework marked out by continuity and discontinuity, order and freedom, form and vitality. The polarity of form and vitality will serve in what follows to represent the fundamental polar relationship which defines the context of evolutionary existence.

In the light of contemporary scientific understanding of

---

[1] See L. R. Godfrey, ed., *Scientists Confront Creationism* (London and New York, 1983); P. Kitcher, *The Case against Creationism* (Milton Keynes, 1983).

the physical universe, we can now recognize that not only human life, nor just evolution on this planet, but all that exists—the universe as a whole—stands within this fundamental polar relationship. Nothing in the universe is pure form—absolutely unchanging or unchangeable. Nothing that is new is totally unrelated to what was before, or to the larger whole within which the dynamic interaction of form and vitality is continually expressed. Concrete forms are at the same time manifestations of energy or vitality, and energy can only be encountered in some form.

Within this evolutionary world, an extraordinary creature has emerged which not only exists under the same conditions as everything else, but which can talk about them, and superimpose its own conditions. A complete account of this remarkable evolutionary phenomenon, the human being, is not possible here, but since the intention is to take seriously our present understanding of ourselves and our world and to explore our relationship to God in the light of this, we must say something about human beings as evolutionary creatures and about their ability to talk about their world and themselves.

Whatever we say about our primitive ancestors must remain somewhat speculative, as we cannot put ourselves alongside them and observe them directly. Nevertheless, we can assume in the first place that the same basic rules of existence governed their lives as ours, even if they were far from possessing our understanding of them, and even if our present understanding of them is still far from perfect. In the second place, scientific research in various fields, particularly the study of fossil remains, primate behaviour, human psychology, and learning and communication processes, has presented us with a broad picture of human evolutionary development. This may be accepted as reasonably accurate, and therefore to be taken into account in our examination of the relationships between God and ourselves and our world, in relation to the past as well as to the present.

If the evolutionary account of human origins is accepted at all, it would seem impossible to deny that the human infant, from the first moment when any primate infant could be called human, would discover himself in relationship with

others of his kind—mother, father, siblings, and the family
or tribal community. However far removed he may have
been from our present self-conscious awareness of ourselves
as persons, he would have emerged into conscious awareness
within significant, life-giving relationships of a kind inherited from a distant primate past, but becoming known to
human consciousness in a new way. This knowledge would
have had two components. First, there would have to be a
cognitive content, namely, a conscious awareness that within
a specific, definable set of relationships lay security, the basic
provisions of life, and protection against enemies, such as
was not to be found in other definable groups or anywhere
else. Secondly, there would have to be the inner conviction
that these things were so. This knowledge would rest not
merely on such statements as might possibly have been
made, but on the experience of acceptance, of being the
object of protection and care, in short, on the experience of
belonging and being known by others of one's kind and of
being able to exist in their presence. Perhaps it is a vestige
of our prelinguistic past that this knowledge is at once so
important to us still, and at the same time not only capable
of being grasped without words, but incapable of being put
totally into words. It is disclosed within the experience of
relationship, as the wordless human infant demonstrates beyond all reasonable doubt, and can never be translated completely into statements *about* persons or relationships.

The significance of this kind of personal knowing within
the experience of relationships will be explored further below (chap. 2, sect. 2). First we must consider the other kind
of knowing, which can and must be talked about.

If survival in an evolutionary environment depends on a
right response to prevailing conditions, it is clear that creatures which developed the capacity to identify these conditions, and to react appropriately, would gain an
evolutionary advantage. The capacity to identify and respond may be seen in simple or complex forms, from the
automatic response to touch of a sea anemone to the exercise
of a wide range of responses to various sense perceptions in
the higher mammals. This creates a situation where it is
possible to speak of choice, though not yet of self-conscious

choice. It is obvious that a wide range of sense perception would serve no purpose where the ability to differentiate and correlate the incoming sense data had not developed. It is not surprising, then, that creatures with various highly developed senses have relatively large brains. Human beings share a wide range of senses with other mammals but have exceptionally large brains. It now seems likely that the increase in human brain size was closely linked with the evolution of another faculty, the power of speech, for which the evolution of speech mechanisms in the throat was as necessary as brain enlargement.[2] Though some capacity for communication is present in other creatures, it is the degree of development in human beings that renders their position unique.

It is clear that a creature capable of receiving a wide range of different environmental signals, and of differentiating, interpreting, storing, and retrieving the information received so as to be able to picture different situations and possibilities of action, would maximize its power of choice. It would, within limits, be free to act to its best advantage and hence have an exceptional evolutionary advantage. But these capacities did not develop in human beings in isolation but in communication and hence in a social context. Humans emerge with the advantages conferred not only by their individual faculties but by their social context. Within that setting, it is possible for valuable information to be received at second hand, without depending on the time-consuming and perhaps dangerous process of direct experience. At the same time, the power of speech and the power of choice make it possible for individuals to co-operate with others of their kind to their mutual advantage. Our next task is to examine more closely this new tool that human beings have at their disposal—the power of communication—and to consider what difference it makes to them as evolutionary creatures.

(b) The invention of symbols

The development in humans of a unique ability to handle a mass of complex data seems to have been intimately connected with their ability to make and to distinguish between

    [2] E. H. Lenneberg, 'Brain Correlates of Language', in F. O. Schmitt, ed., *The Neurosciences Second Study Program* (New York, 1970), 361.

a wide range of noises. They learned how to correlate certain sounds, whether made by themselves or others, with certain occurrences, things, or purposes, and hence could represent them at one remove from the original source. In short, they could use certain sounds as symbols to signify different things disclosed through their senses, such as what was good or bad, what was specific or recurring, and also what to do about it. Thus, out of the vast range of human vocal possibilities, certain sounds by common consent (significantly, different sounds in different communities) were appropriated to serve specific symbolic functions, as words.

The purposes which words could serve were, and are still of course, extremely varied. Vocal symbols could be employed to identify not only particular things but also classes of things or characteristics of things, or socially desirable or undesirable attitudes or rules of behaviour. With the emergence of a wide range of sound-symbols, there developed also the means of correlating them with each other by the use of further special symbols. This made it possible for the overall environment encountered by an individual to be represented symbolically to himself and others, without the whole having to be present to them concretely.

To be sure, the total environment could not disclose itself to the first human beings in an instant. Their capacity to perceive what was there through their natural senses was very limited, and so accordingly was their range of symbols. Thus, their symbolic representations were rudimentary in the extreme compared with the complexity of what was there, and what was there was itself caught up in the dynamic process of evolutionary change. Nevertheless, we may attribute to our early ancestors a sense of the larger whole which they could represent to themselves and others symbolically like a map, and once even the most rudimentary map was conceived the possibilities of enlarging it and improving it would open up. In time, symbolic signs—writing—would become an important adjunct to symbolic sounds, opening up even greater possibilities of communication and symbolic representation. In time, too, the question of what was there would be followed by other questions: 'Why was it there?' 'Who put it there, and to what purpose?'

(c) *The implications of symbols*

We find human beings emerging as creatures discovering themselves in relationship to their own kind, and in relation to a wider and often mysterious environment, and able, even if only imperfectly, to represent their world to themselves and to communicate with others of their kind.

We must now look at some of the consequences which befell these symbol-using creatures, in respect of their own understanding of themselves and their relationship to their world. The power conferred on human beings by the use of symbols to transcend their world was at the same time the power to transcend themselves. Self-consciousness emerged—the most awesome development in the course of evolution. But if self-consciousness set human beings at the highest point of the evolutionary process, it also set them on the edge of a terrifying abyss. If a person could picture himself in his world, what could prevent him picturing his world without himself? To see himself there was also to see that he was not necessarily there—to picture the world 'without me in it'—to become aware of the possibility of self-negation.

The price of self-consciousness in the early human being, as in a growing infant, would seem, then, to be the realization of death. Thus, the discovery of self and of the possibility of self-negation may be regarded as among the first distinguishing features of humanity's unique evolutionary status.

The questions posed by death have preoccupied human beings from the beginning. Much energy has been devoted to the search for a route through the limitations of finitude[3] disclosed from the mysterious, transcendent vantage-point in self-consciousness. However, human beings could not live permanently on the edge of the abyss. The more immediate demands of everyday life, such as the provision of food and shelter, required attention. It was in the context of having to meet these needs that we have supposed the human power to communicate and symbolize to have developed, and this

[3] J. Bowker, *The Sense of God* (Oxford, 1973), 66–85.

capacity continued to provide humans with a practical evolutionary advantage. The conceptual maps that they constructed would, as we have seen, not only serve to disclose the overall environment within which they stood and various things within it, but would provide a basis for further exploration. Such maps would allow movement from the familiar to the unfamiliar, and so enable the unfamiliar to be related to the familiar and given a place in the conceptual whole. Well-known landmarks would play an important part in helping the adventurous to keep their bearings as they headed out towards unknown territories. Various things they saw around them could serve as useful landmarks, but one familiar to all would have been the experience of existing in relationship with other human beings.[4] It would not be surprising if this inner point of reference served as a guide to the understanding of the relationship of human beings to other mysterious phenomena. We may suppose, then, that as human beings mapped out their world, they interpreted the phenomena within it, and their relationship to them, both in terms of the knowledge of what was not human as well as in terms of the experience of being human. In other words, they might see things in personal and/or impersonal categories, without necessarily drawing any hard and fast distinction between the two.

It remains possible that the experience of being human is as good a clue to the way things are as the many impersonal alternatives offered today. This does not settle the question of whether the reality outside ourselves is in the last resort rightly to be thought of as personal or impersonal. A distinctive characteristic of human beings as evolutionary creatures is that they can ask this question.

Another distinctive feature is that humans exist not only in direct relationship to their immediate environment, but in relation to their own conceptual creations—the symbol-systems or images which mediate between them and their environment. The question of the relationship of symbols to the symbol-users and to that which is symbolized—the total

---

[4] Cf. J. Bowlby in R. Harré, ed., *Personality* (Oxford, 1976), 15 f., on 'working models' in child development.

environment including ourselves—has been a source of fascination, debate, and dispute among human beings for millennia. It needs to be considered here, if only briefly, for two reasons. In the first place, my own attempt to map out our situation in the world involves, like any other communication, the use of a particular symbol-system, and the critique of others. To judge the issue, we need as clear an idea as possible of the nature and function of symbols. Secondly, the use of symbols raises an important theoretical question in relation to the polarity model itself, which cannot be ignored.

2. SYMBOLIC FORMS

It is as symbol-users that human beings create under conditions of evolutionary existence a new kind of form, the symbolic representation of the concrete conditions in which they find themselves. Thus, we may speak of 'symbolic forms' in contrast to the 'concrete forms' of physically existing phenomena. Symbolic form, while strictly applicable to any kind of pictorial representation, will be generally understood here to refer to words, whether considered singly or, more usually, in structured combinations.

A distinction needs to be drawn between the symbolic representation of conditions (the way things are) and the symbolic representation of purposes (what ought to be done). Their interrelationship is of the closest possible kind. It is the stimuli of immediate conditions that provoke responsive action in all creatures. Just as a slate beetle scurries for cover when it senses exposure to light, so I may head for shelter when I feel the first drops of rain. However, I may risk getting wet, if my purpose is to reach the shops before they close. It is the unique capacity of human beings to transcend their immediate conditions, to envisage the consequences of their reactions, and the different conditions that different responses might give rise to, that makes the conscious choice of purpose possible for them. Their freedom of choice also includes the possibility of surrendering this advantage and relapsing into spontaneous response to stimuli, regardless of consequences. Whether the advantage of reflective decision is abandoned or not, purposes remain governed by conditions; where this advantage is not abandoned, purposes will be governed by envisaged conditions as much as or even more than by immediate conditions.

Thus, in the close relationship of conditions and purposes the priority of conditions emerges. To be sure, actual life is complicated by the conflict between rational and subrational, instinctive reactions, and conflicting goals. But ideally, for a thinking creature, the awareness of the way things are or might be determines the course of action to be taken, whether in the defence of what is, or in pursuit of what is envisaged and desired. The way in which the desired condition or goal is defined will determine the kind of action to be taken in pursuit of it. The more clearly defined the goal itself, the more clearly defined will be the actions directed to its attainment.

Since, then, we must ask about the way things are before we can decide what to do about them, the main emphasis in this stage of our inquiry will be on symbolic forms functioning as representations of the way things are.

(a) Symbols and meanings

Symbols, as we have seen, transcend the immediacy of any given situation and so stand outside the ebb and flow of concrete existence. Pictures, including verbal pictures, stay the same, it seems, whatever happens in the scene depicted. This raises the question of whether symbolic forms, in virtue of their transcendent character, are exempt from the polar dialectic of form and vitality which, we have argued, embraces all concrete forms. In other words, do symbolic forms after all provide us with instances of changeless realities occurring within the context of evolutionary existence, contrary to the rule put forward above that nothing that is completely unchanging can exist in our world?

It will be argued here that the rule is not broken, and that though the polar dialectic does not apply to symbolic forms (verbal pictures) in the same way as it applies to concrete forms (tangible things), the former are not exempt from it, and to imagine otherwise will have disordering and harmful consequences.

In pursuing this issue, we must first distinguish between two separate questions. The first is whether a verbal symbol—word—is in itself, in its visible or audible manifestation, a changeless form (without regard to what it might symbolize); the second question is whether a symbolic form might correspond to, disclose, or serve as evidence for the existence of some unchanging static reality beyond and apart from the symbol in which it is represented.

The first question can be easily disposed of. Apart from the fact that the phenomenon of symbols divorced from the function of symbolizing is of little interest to anyone, it is clear that a symbolic sound is transitory in the extreme in itself; under worldly conditions, it can never be repeated in identically the same form. Written symbols, on the other hand, are as contingent and changeable as the material on which they are drawn, whether that is paper or rock.

In practice, slight variations in the repetition of a symbol in audible or visible form do not matter, as long as they fall sufficiently within an agreed range of usage to convey the same meaning. (Foreign accents and untidy writing are hard to understand when they fall outside the agreed range.) At this point the question shifts from the possibility of changeless symbolic forms to the possibility of changeless meaning. To be precise, the question is whether the intended meaning which stands behind the symbolic forms remains constant, even if the symbolic forms employed to convey it vary, whether the variation is slight, as in the way described above, or almost total, as when different words are used in different languages to convey what is intended to be the same meaning.

Two problems face us here: first, whether the notion of the same meaning standing behind different symbolic forms can be properly maintained; secondly, whether, even if it can, this provides an instance of changeless reality existing within our evolutionary world.

To deal with these basic issues it will be necessary to look again at the evolutionary setting of the human symbol-user and to make some further important distinctions.

Symbols, as we have seen, are both evidence of our human capacity to transcend ourselves and our world, and the means

by which we do so. They function in relation to conditions
and purposes within the environment as set in time and
space, but also serve to replicate those conditions outside
their immediate setting in time and space, as a map stands
outside the terrain it represents. In order to utilize symbols
at all, human beings need to know what conditions and purposes they serve to represent, and hence in what circumstances their use is appropriate. They are then able to
envisage to themselves, and to communicate to others, possible conditions and purposes, *whether these actually prevail
on the ground or not.*

From this account we can draw a number of conclusions.
Where certain conditions prevail in the actual environment
(for example, it is raining), or certain purposes are intended,
specific symbols (including recognized alternatives as used
in different languages) can always be used to represent them,
as long as the conventions for their use are recognized and
accepted by those wishing to communicate. It follows that
symbols can be used to represent these conditions and purposes (or any others), whether these prevail in actuality or
not. Thus, a correlation is established between symbols and
conceivable conditions and purposes; in other words, a correlation between symbols and meanings can be recognized,
which does indeed transcend the material conditions of evolutionary existence and is not subject to the polar dialectic
in the way that affects all concrete phenomena existing in
time and space.

It does not follow from this admission, however, that symbolized meanings are totally exempt from the dialectic of
form and vitality, still less that they serve in themselves to
disclose changeless realities beyond and apart from the symbol and its meaning. In the first place, not only can the
conventions of use change, as, for example, in the case of the
word-symbol 'gay', but complete languages can be and have
been forgotten. In the second place, meanings depend on
symbol-users, who themselves stand within the polar dialectic and do not transcend time and space. The choice of
symbol to convey a particular meaning depends on the individual wishing to communicate. The appropriateness of
his choice depends on the accuracy both of his awareness of

the current conventions governing the use of symbols, and of his perception of the conditions about which he wishes to communicate. Equally, the meaning conveyed depends on the interpretation placed upon a symbol by the person to whom it is communicated and the accuracy of his understanding. Where the correlation of symbol and meaning is well established through repeated usage and simplicity of reference (i.e. where there are familiar words for familiar things), the variations of interpretation may be minimal, but where symbols are applied to what is new, complex, or not open to public scrutiny, the correlation of symbol and meaning is far less stable. Furthermore, in so far as meaning is acquired from the circumstances in which symbols are used, then, since every individual's experience of their use is different, different meaning resulting from different associations of usage will arise. This will be greatest where the difference of experience has been greatest, or where the reference of a given symbol is least open to public gaze and hence to public consensus concerning the conventions for its use. Words about what is mysterious will be the least constant or precise in meaning.

We may therefore conclude that even if it were argued that an absolute and perfect correlation between symbol and meaning might be possible in some cases at a given time, it is not possible for all times and never in all cases. An absolute correlation of meaning would require an absolute correlation in understanding between persons communicating by means of symbols; this, in respect of many important areas of human concern, remains a practical impossibility.

It remains true that the conventions for the use of a great many symbolic forms are sufficiently clearly established for at least a very high degree of correlation between symbol and meaning to be acknowledged, so that these symbols in various combinations can convey clear meanings whenever they are employed, as long as the conventions for their use are known and observed.

(b) Symbols and reality

However close the correlation between meaning and symbolic form may be, this offers no answer to the question of whether what is symbolized and rightly understood actually exists. I have no doubt about the meaning of the statement 'It is raining', but that does not tell me whether it is or not, and it is the question of the correlation between symbolic forms with their meanings and the way things actually are or might be which is crucial for human beings as evolutionary creatures faced with the problems of living. What is at stake is not only the interpretation of symbols, but their applicability. Is the map accurate, and therefore trustworthy? Can it remain so for ever, without change or modification? That will depend on what is mapped, and not on the map itself.

Such a remark may seem to be too obvious to be necessary, and yet the contrary view is often held, that the way things are expressed in speech makes them what they are. But this can only be true in so far as words make things what they are for the speaker (and those who accept his words). This is important inasmuch as a person's symbolic representations determine his actions. He may interpret internal pain as cancer and plan to commit suicide. What matters then is to discover whether things really are as he says they are. A strange phenomenon in human history—to which we must return—has been the tendency to suppose that old maps cannot be wrong—in the face of overwhelming evidence to the contrary. Religions, including Christianity, have played a major role in preserving the use and application of symbolic forms in relation to the world, long after the understanding of the world which previously made their application seem appropriate has been superseded. But whatever authority may be claimed for saying how things are, saying it does not make it so. What really matters is whether the map does in fact correspond to the terrain; only then will it provide useful guidance.

This needs to be said as much to the proponents of new accounts of reality as to the defenders of the old. The mere fact that the world and the conditions of existence can be construed and represented symbolically in a radically new way is obviously in itself no reason whatsoever for supposing that the new representation is superior to the old. It may correspond more closely to things as they are, but it may not. New maps are not necessarily more accurate than old ones; new scientific hypotheses are not always correct; the fact that radical transformations of society can be envisaged does not guarantee their superiority; new religions and new theologies are not necessarily nearer the truth. In any case, to suppose that the new or the old is true and definitive for all time must be wrong, as we shall be arguing below in the cases of Judaism and Christianity, and other religions and ideologies.

It remains true that while human intentions are governed by conditions as they are conceived to be, their outcome is governed by conditions as they really are. So whatever symbolic representation of the conditions of existence is accepted, it will have very serious practical consequences, for good or ill. A bad map is likely to lead to confusion and disaster, whatever the publisher's claims.

In the case of reality as a whole, one more point must be made. If the possibility of change is built into it, then an adequate symbolic representation will represent that possibility; it will disclose not only what is but what might be. By disclosing accurately the underlying conditions of existence, it can point to as yet unrealized but possible new conditions and so generate viable new purposes.

We have to accept, however, that some of the most important questions we ask about the way things are or might be cannot be so easily decided as the question of whether it is raining. To imagine that the sense perceptions which have evolved in human beings are adequate to penetrate any phenomenon which they may encounter is presumptuous, to say the least. To suppose that the symbolic forms which have developed in conjunction with their sense perceptions are sufficient to replicate every mystery they encounter, or to lay open to the mind the totality of existence, or all possible conditions of existence, verges on the absurd. So that for anyone to assume that the meaning he associates with his symbolic forms is the norm of all meaning and is able to determine all that is really there, rather than dimly mirroring a small part of what is there, would be unbelievable if it did not happen so often.

We may now sum up the conclusions we have reached in response to the questions raised at the beginning of this section concerning symbolic forms. First, they are not in themselves instances of changeless realities. Secondly, though they may serve to symbolize conditions in a way that transcends the immediate conditions of time and space, the symbolic meaning they convey is dependent on the human user who exists under evolutionary conditions, and it is those conditions which determine their applicability. Hence they cannot of themselves serve to disclose changeless realities, unless such changeless realities are already there to be appropriately symbolized as such. We have already ruled out the possibility of the concrete existence of pure form, or of any changeless concrete phenomenon, as incompatible with an understanding of evolutionary existence in a universe where nothing is absolutely unchanging or unchangeable.

Two problems remain. How, on the one hand, are the extremes of relativization to be avoided? This may still be a problem, even though it has been argued that a high degree of correlation between symbol and meaning is possible in some cases. On the other hand, at the opposite extreme, why have symbolic forms come to be treated historically as representing changeless realities in a way that is incompatible with evolutionary existence and destructive in effect? A further question will be how this can be avoided.

3. ALIENATED FORMS

I have argued that no specific, concretely existing phenomenon within the universe is or can be totally unchangeable. The question, then, is whether the symbolic forms, in which our world is represented to our minds, convey no more than a changelessness of meaning in the terms we have already discussed. In so far as they appear to represent change-lessness in the world itself, are all such forms deceptive and illusory? We are not, in fact, driven to this conclusion.

It has been argued that the applicability of symbols depends on what is really there, and not merely on their meanings, and that no specific concrete phenomenon in our evolutionary world is in fact changeless. Nevertheless, the capacity of the human mind to differentiate between different things allows it also to distinguish between different aspects of different things. We are thus able to see that certain things are in certain respects unique, while certain aspects of them are recurring. We can also recognize certain features of our environment to be variable, and others to be invariable.

That which is symbolized by the term 'gravity' is, we now realize, a constant feature or natural rule of the universe as we know it, governing the existence of all things in all times and places, which we must take into account whatever we plan to do. It is not a thing by itself in a particular time or place. Similarly, other underlying conditions of existence have been discerned which can be represented symbolically and which cannot be thought of as not being applicable to the universe, so long as we conceive of it in the way we do. It is in these terms that the polar dialectic itself is presented here. It is neither a changeless object nor free from the limitations governing all symbolic forms, but the phrase is offered as a symbolic representation of an underlying condition of existence. It can be appropriately applied to the way things are *if* that is the way things are but not otherwise. Our judgement on whether we think it is in fact applicable will be governed by the same considerations which determine the use of any symbolic forms, but above all by the consideration whether its application illuminates and ties in with other things which our world has disclosed about itself to our senses, and which we have replicated as appropriately as we have been able to in our symbol-systems. On this basis, we maintain that certain characteristics and features of our world are constant and can therefore be symbolically represented as such, while denying that any single object, or creature, or complete structure, that exists under evolutionary conditions is in itself unchanging. There cannot be pure form unrelated to vitality, any more than one touch-line without another. Least of all can form or vitality exist as concrete independent phenomena.

The language of polarities has the advantage of allowing the differentiating characteristics of the dynamic whole within which we exist, and of which we are a part, to be identified and mapped out, without attributing to those conceptualized aspects of it any misleading notion of separate

independent existence. Because of this, it does not matter
very much if different words are employed to designate the
polar relationship. Indeed, a variety of terms may better
convey the meaning intended, where the narrow, conventional connotations of one or two would be misleading.

Whatever terms or symbols are used, they need to be
constantly re-evaluated in the light of what is disclosed by
the world we live in, but some at least may prove their
adequacy. However, when we turn to a total or complex and
detailed symbolic representation of the world as a whole,
and to the purposes determined by such a representation,
the case is very different. To say that any representation of
the world or reality as a whole is totally adequate, and hence
never to be changed or enlarged, would not only be presumptuous but incompatible with our understanding of
evolutionary existence. A detailed symbolic representation
of our world may at best be more or less adequate at a given
moment, but cannot remain so when the scene as a whole
stands within a process of movement and change. If the
symbolic representation of conditions as a whole cannot remain valid, it follows that the actions determined by such a
representation will not be appropriate when the underlying
conditions have changed. Winter coats are not appropriate
on summer days.

The fact remains that symbolic representations of reality
have been in the past, and still are today, often treated as
changeless in themselves and as representing a changeless
state of affairs, to which all purposes should be conformed,
regardless of present experience and understanding. Some
account is now needed of this strange development, which
in effect subordinates the terrain to the map, instead of the
map to the terrain.

As we have seen, the symbolic structures which human
beings have created, and the maps which they have made,
do indeed in their visible form stand outside the immediate
conditions of concrete existence. In doing so, they give evidence of the human ability to transcend the immediacy of
the environment and experience within it, and also enable
human beings to relate to it in various ways and for different

purposes. Not only are they enabled to adjust to their environment in a more appropriate and generally more successful way than other creatures (for example, in the pursuit of longer-term goals); they are able also, within limitations, to adjust it to their purposes and needs, and to relate individual and social existence to the total conceptual representation of the world.

On the basis of this interpretation of the threefold relationship between symbol-systems, their human creators and users, and the environment to which they relate and within which they exist, some further points need to be made.

First, the preliminary observation may be made that the continuing value of any map will depend on its being kept up to date. New discoveries will need to be entered in, or it may need to be revised to conform to changes in the familiar environment which has already been mapped out. As long as its function and relationship to its user and his setting are not lost sight of, this creative activity would not seem to pose any problem.

However, the extent to which problems can arise has been illuminated in recent years by sociologists of knowledge, such as Peter Berger. He argues that all human societies are engaged in the process of world-building.[5] They are engaged not only in mapping out their physical environment, but in constructing a world of meaning within which the phenomena, experiences, and values of life—individual and social—will form a coherent whole. Each individual is born into such a world of meaning, a combination of conditions and purposes. It confronts him as an objective reality, a world picture, which transcends his immediate existence, conveying value and demanding assent. As long as its origins in the creative activity of human beings are remembered, and the inner dialectic is maintained, whereby it serves to give shape to existence, but is at the same time open to enlargement or modification in the light of experience, all is well.

[5] P. L. Berger, *The Social Reality of Religion* (London, 1969), 3. Cf. P. L. Berger and T. Luckmann, *The Social Construction of Reality* (Harmondsworth, 1967).

The problem arises when the source of a given world-picture, or cognitive structure, is forgotten; when it confronts people not just as an objective reality but as an autonomous objective reality, isolated from the dynamic interaction of form and vitality, no longer seen by them as of their own making, and hence alien. The state of alienation arises when human beings mistake their own creation for their creator. This projection, with its transcendent quality, long established as the source of meaning and value, the basis of social structure, now confronts them as the independent source of their world and themselves and no longer in any way as a product of it. It acquires the attributes of God. Hence it appears that it cannot be subject to change, least of all in reaction to actual conditions in the world, which now appears as a derivative, secondary phenomenon. If one wonders why this should happen, part of the answer may be that any given world-picture is a basic source of security. It not only tells us where we are but who we are. To admit change is to risk one's own being. To ascribe it to God would seem to guarantee our security.

However, a changing world will correspond less and less to any once-given account of it. The map becomes increasingly out of date, and will cease to provide a faithful guide to existence under concrete evolutionary conditions. By virtue of its supposed inherent changelessness, it cannot admit anything that might emerge from the enlargement of human understanding and insight. The claim of any map or cognitive structure to permanent validity can only be defended at the price of denying anything in the world or human experience that appears to contradict its claim. Thus, alienation gives rise to a dualistic world-rejecting attitude, within which human creativity is repressed with disastrous consequences.

In conclusion, in the light of this examination of the relationship between symbolic forms and concrete existence and its underlying conditions, we should be on our guard against the misapplication of representations of reality in symbolic form. We should be prepared to acknowledge the value, but also the provisional status, of such representations

in a changing world and in relation to our changing understanding of it. The subordination of all symbolic forms
to things as they are must remain our guiding principle. If
things as they are remain mysterious in many respects, we
should be humble enough to accept the fact, but not so
humble as to deny what we can perceive and understand.

Adopting this attitude may mean that we can no longer
accept without criticism the symbolic representations of
reality handed down from the past, whether by priest or
politician. If that is so, then neither can we accept without
question the practical conclusions and the definition of purposes which rest on these ancient interpretations as their
premiss. It does not follow, however, that antiquity alone
rules out the possibility of genuine insight or perception
into the way things are. In particular, a perception of the
underlying conditions or rules of human existence may be
valid, even if the symbolic representation of the world as a
whole is highly inaccurate. If any perception is accurate, it
will never prove to be incompatible with any subsequent
accurate perception of the conditions of existence. Truth has
nothing to fear from truth.

What has been said holds good whatever particular
symbolic forms have been employed to represent the conditions of existence, not excluding the symbolic form or word
'God'. That symbol has perhaps been harder to correlate
with a specific clearly accepted meaning than any other.
The reasons for this are the same as for any symbol that
stands on the edge of the mysteries of existence or experience. Nevertheless, present convention associates the word,
or perhaps name, 'God' with the ultimate ground and arbiter
of the way things are and of the purpose of existence. In so
far as he is related to our world and ourselves, any change in
our account of our world and ourselves must have implications for our account of the relationship between those
things and God. Just as our reason requires that our understanding of reason itself, of language and thought, be tied in
with our view of ourselves as evolutionary creatures, in the
same way reason requires that our understanding of the symbol 'God' be tied in with our understanding of evolutionary
existence.

The fundamental issue, however, is not how our symbols and their meanings may be related to each other, but how that which is called God, if he exists, relates to our universe and our existence, as we now conceive of and experience it. This is the basic question concerning the conditions and purposes of existence, and it cannot finally be evaded. Yet while it may be true that new insight concerning our world could not leave our understanding of its creator's relationship to it unaffected, the prior question is 'Why should anyone suppose or assume that such a Creator, Arbiter, or God, exists at all?' If his existence cannot be reasonably supposed, then obviously the question of his relatedness need not be raised, and the question of the conditions and purposes of existence would have to be approached in very different terms.

4. THE SYMBOL 'GOD'

It was argued in the introduction to this chapter that if God exists, who is the eternal and creative ground of all that exists, the source of being and meaning, then this God can and must have made himself known to humankind. We are not committed here to prove the truth of these propositions, nor indeed is that possible; but an attempt will be made to give some indications why they are not unreasonable, and to show what their implications are in the light of the present approach.

Our discussion so far has been concerned with the conditions of existence, actual or envisaged. Human beings have been portrayed as uniquely able to represent to themselves the actual conditions of existence in symbolic form, and as a result able to envisage how they might be otherwise. The awareness of such things comes to a person within the actual experience of existing, of finding himself in the context of significant human relationships and encountering mysterious forces and energies which affect his existence for good or ill. It is here that his awareness of different possible conditions confronts him with the possibility of his own non-existence—death. But the ability to envisage death allows another possibility to be envisaged, that of transcending the limitations of death.

The ways in which the transcending of limitation can be envisaged are infinitely varied. The mere fact that they are envisaged does not of itself establish their validity, since, as we have previously argued, the validity of a symbolic representation depends on things being that way or being possible in practice, and not merely on the possiblity of envisaging them that way. But where a person subordinates his own purposes to anything (family, country, party, or ideals) which transcends his own immediate existence, to the point of risking death, to that extent he transcends at least his own death as the limiting factor of his existence. A range of purposes can then be entertained which are not determined in the last resort by the factor of one's own death, but by an understanding of the way things are in which one's own death, acknowledged as a fact, is not accorded the ultimacy over existence which appears to be its prerogative. Any such understanding of the conditions of existence may or may not be ultimately valid, but what is clear is that whether a person envisaged things that way or not would bear strongly on his choice of purposes or goals. Even if not all human beings are or have been existentialists—dwelling consciously on the fact of death—it remains implicitly or explicitly a radical challenge to any understanding of the conditions or purposes of human existence.[6] There cannot, in fact, be many human beings who have never been confronted with the question of what it might be necessary to die for, the converse of which is 'What is worth living for?' This can be expressed in contemporary terms as the question of the meaning of life. There are two sides to it. First, what is the true meaning of life? What conditions and purposes, actual or envisaged, truly conform to the way things are? Secondly, does this meaning match up to our deepest aspirations as human beings, to the extent that its realization can negate the negation of death, and transcend the limitations of finitude in all its dimensions?

Once posed, the question of whether life has meaning is open to only a very limited number of possible answers. Either it has not, or it has, or we can never know (but the last is effectively the same as the first). To deny that life has

---

[6] See M. Heidegger, *Being and Time* (Oxford, 1962), 293.

any meaning is at once to rule out the possibility of God, but at the same time it rules out the validity of the vast range of activities and pursuits which human beings profess to find meaningful. Such a judgement, far from being a rational conclusion derived from all available evidence, has the appearance rather of an irrational assumption based on some of the evidence, and maintained in the face of what is at least conflicting evidence. The contrary assertion, that life has meaning, is open to different levels of interpretation. In the first place, it is possible to acknowledge various things in life, various activities, goals, and purposes, to be meaningful to varying degrees and so to be sources of meaning; but inasmuch as they lie on the near side of the limiting factor of death, they cannot ultimately offer a positive answer to the question of whether life has a meaning which transcends the limitation of death. That which transcends an individual's death, such as his community or even the world he lives in, may offer a partial solution or even appear to offer an adequate solution. However, once the possible or inescapable negation of that which is supposed to confer meaning is envisaged, its power to confer meaning in the face of death is lost, and the question of meaning arises again with greater force. It has particular force today, when for different reasons the negation of individual life, of all human life, of the planet earth, and of at least the solar system—if not the universe itself—cannot only be envisaged but has to be acknowledged as inescapable in purely physical terms.

There would seem to be only two possible positive answers to the ultimate question of meaning. On the one hand, it may be maintained that the evolving universe, which encompasses all existence in itself, bears its own meaning within itself, which human beings can discover and with which they can align their own existence. (As argued above in the case of God, to assert a meaning to be there but beyond all human grasp would be almost self-contradictory as an answer to the question of whether human life is meaningful.) However, the disclosure of the universe to human minds has not in fact revealed a positive meaning unambiguously. It would only seem possible to affirm it (as to deny it) in the face of what is at least conflicting evidence. In our world, the problem of good stands alongside the problem of evil, and the ambiguities of existence do not provide a firm ground for either affirming or denying meaning in existence, nor are they resolved by merely asserting one or the other to be the case. As assumptions, and they are no more than that, both answers lack rational cogency; neither would have any right to lay the burden of proof on any alternative answer, while refusing to bear it itself.

Another possibility does exist in response to the question of the meaning of life. It is that meaning is conferred on existence within the universe from a source outside the universe, not spatially distant, but transcending the structures of the universe. The symbol conventionally employed to designate this transcendent ground of meaning is 'God'. To postulate God is not to prove his existence, any more than the use of any symbol creates conditions to which it is applicable. But if God is postulated, the way may be opened up towards a resolution of the ambiguities of existence, which the universe on its own leaves unresolved; and a ground of meaning is offered which by definition transcends the limitation of death. It is no more possible for human beings within their present limitations to prove the existence of God than it is for them to prove his non-existence. To assume the existence of God is no less rational than assuming his non-existence. In fact, if life is for any reason believed to be meaningful, the conjunction of that belief with the assumption that God exists is less irrational than its conjunction with the assumption that God does not exist.[7]

On such grounds, we proceed on the assumption that God does exist, who is the ground of all that exists and the source of meaning for human existence in particular. This last remark entails the further idea that God is apprehensible to human beings, otherwise he could not be the source of meaning in human life in practice. If he is apprehensible at all to human beings, then in principle at least the possibility is open to them of representing him, in so far as he is apprehensible, in symbolic form, and communicating about him to each other. This is no problem. Problems only arise

[7] See above, p. 8 n. 1.

over the choice of symbols, the conventions governing their use, their adequacy, and applicability. The appropriateness of all symbols depends on what is there. Ways of representing God symbolically cannot of themselves establish what he is or that he is. Still less can the conventional and therefore constant meaning of a symbol be assumed to disclose what is eternally the case with God. What that is depends on God, and is not determined by any symbol applied to God. He owes nothing to any symbol. This does not mean that a symbolic representation of what he is like cannot in principle correspond to him at all. On the contrary, the correspondence may be very close if he happens to be like that. The real problem is not how or whether he can be symbolized or talked about at all, but how human beings may come to perceive the way he is, apprehend what he is really like, and so choose and utilize appropriate symbols, establishing the right conventions for their use and eliminating the wrong ones. These issues, as we shall find, lay at the heart of the conflict between Jesus and his contemporaries. They remain the major point at issue between Christianity and other religions, a topic we shall pursue further in chap. 8, sect. 3 below.

One further consequence follows from the assumption that God is real, and is the ground of all that exists and the source of meaning for all that exists, including human existence. Since human life is personal, it follows that the source of meaning for that mode of life—the ground of personal life—must in some sense be personal. If the ground of existence is not in any sense personal, then the human experience of being a person would have no ultimate ground or meaning, and so would have to be judged illusory, as it is in some parts of the world. But social relationships were the very context and condition of the evolution of human beings as such, and no account of the meaning of our existence which disregarded or controverted our origins would seem to me satisfactory. The alternative conclusion is therefore preferable, that God is the ground of persons and therefore personal. So the assumption with which we shall proceed is that a personal God is the ground of all that exists.

God, who is ground of all, must of necessity be the ground

of all things as they really are, and not as they may be wrongly thought to be. In the light of science, we understand better than any previous generation how things really are in the universe. The implications are twofold. First, if we have the courage of our convictions, we cannot rest content with the account of God's relationship to the world as conceived by pre-scientific generations. If they were right about God being in relationship, they could nevertheless be very wrong about the world, and hence about some at least of the terms of that relationship. Secondly, however provisional the scientific account may be, reason cannot tolerate a blunt contradiction between the scientific and the theological accounts. Each may have distinctive concerns, but demarcation into completely separate spheres of interest is no solution.

If, then, God is the ground of the world that discloses itself to science and human understanding, and is himself apprehensible to human beings, then our symbolic representations of the world and of God respectively must correlate,[8] if they are to be judged adequate to their objects. An inherent contradiction between the two symbolic representations would disclose the inadequacy of one or other (or both), or undermine the claim that God is the ground of the world as it really is. This would controvert the symbol 'God' itself.

So, in conclusion, the word 'God' is taken here to be the symbol for the mysterious but personal source and ground of all that exists—the whole of creation. As such, he must be thought of as relating not just to a part but to the whole of creation, to the total, complex, dynamic, evolving reality of which we are aware, of which we now understand ourselves to be a part,[9] and of which we can give a not wholly inaccurate account. This means, in the present context, that he must relate to, and we must be able to represent him as relating to, each and every term of the polar relationships that define evolutionary existence. Above all, it is necessary to show how God is related to, or conversely, is revealed

---

[8] See Tillich, *Systematic Theology*, i. 59–66. I acknowledge the value of his 'method of correlation', though I do not employ it in exactly the same way.

[9] A. R. Peacocke, *Science and the Christian Experiment* (London, 1971), 33, 'We are, as it were, like adopted children, suddenly aware, after years of ignorance, of who their parents really are.'

in or through, that polar relationship which appears to be constitutive of evolutionary existence, form and vitality.

The challenging question for Christians is how the God, whose supposedly special self-disclosing activity is located two thousand years ago in a pre-scientific age, can be thought of intelligibly as relating to our scientifically conceived and evolutionary world. The aim here will be to present a way of understanding God's relatedness to the world which it is hoped will not be unintelligible or fail to do justice to Christian belief about God. It will also be argued that to a considerable degree the insights of the sciences, natural and human, so far from raising greater difficulties, in fact enable us the better to grasp how God relates to his world, precisely because they have given us a clearer picture of it. The same scientific insights may also help us to see more clearly now how the Church, not only in the past but in the present, has continued to convey a badly distorted picture of this relationship, with the harmful results that follow any attempt to force reality into the picture one has of it, instead of allowing the picture to be conformed to the reality. In particular, all too often in the thought of the Church God has been related too closely to one or other polarity of existence and excluded from the other. This error might result in part from understanding polar terms to be opposed to each other absolutely rather than dialectically, so that the affirmation of one term seems necessarily to contradict and exclude the other (see above, p. 4). But such a misunderstanding of the nature of the polar relationship is serious if, as we hold, the isolation of any one polarity has destructive, demonic consequences.

2. Revelation

WE have spoken of God's activity in relating himself to the world, and of the ability of human beings to apprehend God in this activity, and to picture or represent it to themselves and its implications for themselves. Revelation involves all these things, but the word itself can be ambiguous, since its emphasis may be particularly on the activity or on the representation, without the distinctions being made explicit. We here take the primary meaning of revelation to be the activity of God in relating, but it is the picture, or rather the various ways in which this activity can be pictured, which we must discuss, because it is only as pictured that revelation can be discussed.

Revelation involves some kind of disclosure and hence leads to some kind of knowledge. This could be conceived in different ways, according to whether that which became known in revelation was a thing, a fact, or a person. A different kind of relationship between the knower and what was known would be established in each case. Whatever other theoretical possibilities exist, our concern is with a personal relationship of some kind, with a personal God's relating to and becoming known by personal subjects.

It was argued in chap. 1, sect. 1 that personal relationships involve two kinds of knowing—a knowing about, which can be put into words, and also an immediate experience of knowing and being known, which can never be put entirely into words. Therefore, any account of revelation that reduced God's relatedness exclusively to what can be known about God, and be represented in symbolic form, would be inadequate. Yet the mere admission of the possibility of an immediate personal knowledge of God would not, on our present argument, provide for an adequate idea of revelation.

It was argued in chap. 1, sect. 4 that God is the ground of

all that is as it is. In that case, if the polarity model is valid, God must relate to both poles—form and vitality—and also embrace the polar dialectic itself. In other words, he cannot be rightly represented as relating to humankind and the world in terms of either pole exclusively, or in terms of both in mutual isolation. This will be the basis for the critique in due course of ideas of revelation in Judaism, Christianity, and the other religions. One must add that just as an isolated polarity unaffected by the polar dialectic is a practical impossibility, so also is knowledge of persons not possible in one mode exclusively. To be adequate, therefore, the idea of revelation must preserve the polar dialectic and admit a knowledge of God in both modes of knowledge. This will not imply a division of the underlying divine reality, any more than a division is implied in the dynamic whole of the universe when it is seen in terms of the polar relationship of form and vitality.

The polarity model can serve as the basis for categorizing different ideas or theories of revelation, according to whether their emphasis lies towards the polarity of form or of vitality.[1] A great many different positions are possible between the two wings. At different times and in different cultural, ecological, or political circumstances, one or the other may be developed in a given community and be particularly appropriate for it. We shall consider some of these possibilities later, but the main issues with which we are concerned here can best be clarified by a theoretical examination of the two opposing extremes. The characteristics of revelation in the formal mode will be considered first in the following section, with a distinction being made between revelation in concrete and symbolic form.

It will be argued that revelation must have a formal mode if the fact of God's relatedness is to be grasped consciously,

---

[1] Ideas of transcendence and immanence would be applicable to both poles. A typology on this basis may therefore have advantages over one based on the contrast between transcendence and immanence, as proposed by J. Macquarrie, *Principles of Christian Theology* (2nd edn., New York, 1977), 167. See also E. P. Sanders, *Paul and Palestinian Judaism* (London, 1977), 215 (attacking the view that, in Judaism, God is remote and inaccessible), 'The truth is that the terms transcendence and immanence lead to misunderstanding and are not really appropriate. In particular, they do not respond to the question of God's accessibility.'

but that it cannot be reduced exclusively to this mode or be divorced from the polar dialectic. Secondly, it will be argued that attempts to claim too much for formal revelation have destructive consequences (inside and outside Christianity). Thirdly, it will be argued that this conclusion, which follows from the present argument, can be reinforced on traditional theological grounds. Revelation in the mode of vitality will then be examined in a similar way in the subsequent section. The conclusion will be maintained that revelation conceived of exclusively in terms of one polarity, or with too much emphasis on one polar extreme or the other, is destructive and life-denying in its effects, and therefore cannot be regarded as true revelation of the life-giving God; but that where the two modes are held in dynamic polar relationship, creative and, it might be said, divinely creative possibilities exist.

I. FORMAL REVELATION

We begin with revelation in terms of *knowing about* God, that is, with ways in which he may be perceived or represented in visible, publicly accessible, and communicable terms—in other words, in concrete or symbolic forms. This is what is meant here by revelation in the formal mode, and the question that faces us is how adequately the relationship of God to the world and humankind can be expressed in this mode. Although revelation in concrete form and revelation in symbolic form belong in the same general category of formal revelation, it will be necessary to draw some distinctions and to consider the adequacy of each in turn.

(a) God and conrete forms

The first question is whether God can be represented totally and exclusively in concrete form, i.e. as a tangible object. This possibility can be ruled out at once on two counts. Whatever it was that confronted a person concretely, it would have to be identified for what it was, and hence be represented to the human mind symbolically. Thus, even if the 'whole of God' was encountered in concrete form, that form would have to be mediated through symbolic forms if

what was encountered was to be apprehended as God. But
the 'whole of God' could not be encountered in concrete
form, since that would place God alongside other things
under evolutionary conditions, in contradiction of our
understanding of God as the transcendent ground of these
conditions.

We are left with the possibility that God might be represented in, but not exclusively in, a given concrete form,
with the appropriate symbolic forms in its service to identify
it as a representation of God. Such a form, whether a seemingly natural phenomenon, such as a stone, plant, animal, or
person, or a man-made image, could then be seen as the
revelatory focus of the presence or activity of divine reality,
which was not, however, to be thought of as concentrated
there alone. The adequacy of such a form and of the interpretation placed upon it would depend in the last resort
on what God is really like, and on how far the form in which
he was represented and interpreted was not only *believed* to
conform to the truth about him, but actually conformed to
what he was and is in reality.

A fundamental question, however, and one to which we
must later return, is whether any concrete form can be
thought adequate at all to represent God. A central theme
in the Old Testament is the almost total rejection of this
possibility, witnessed to by the prohibition against images
of God (Exod. 20: 4; Deut. 5: 8) and the attack on idolatry.[2]
This attack may in part have been misplaced, in so far as it
supposed that idol-worshippers identified the concrete image and divinity to a degree which, we may be sure, they
never entertained. Nevertheless, the total rejection of such
identification, to the point of rejecting any concrete portrayals of God, remains a major landmark on the road
towards achieving an understanding of God as transcending
worldly existence. The only exception which justifies the
reference to 'almost total rejection' above is to be seen in the
readiness of the Old Testament writers to picture God as a
man, or, in technical language, to speak of him as an active
personal agent in anthropomorphic terms. The difference
between God and man is repeatedly emphasized in the Old

[2] e.g. Deut. 4: 15–24; Ps. 115: 3–8; Isa. 44: 9; Jer. 10: 1–16.

Testament, but the readiness to employ this human imagery is of some significance.

It remains the case that an emphasis on God as transcendent is likely to call in question the adequacy of any representation of him in concrete form. The alternative, if he is to be known about at all, is his representation in symbolic form, and it is to the adequacy of revelation in this form that we must now turn.

(b) God and symbolic forms

Whereas concrete forms could serve to represent God only in conjunction with symbolic forms, symbolic forms would seem able to stand alone, except for the sensory medium which is necessary to their expression in speech or writing. That exception is not unimportant, since the actual location of a symbolic representation of God is as important as the location of a concrete representation would be, if a right knowledge of and hence a right response to God is to be possible. Thus, the place where a comprehensive symbolic representation of God is located will acquire sacred significance as a source of revelation, whether that place is an accredited spokesman or a written record. Reliance on symbolic form (e.g. a revelatory book) is likely to be all the greater when the possibility of God's representation in concrete form has been ruled out for whatever reason. Hence it is not altogether surprising that the Old Testament, which ruled out that possibility so radically, should itself have come to be relied upon increasingly as the source of the only adequate and true representation of God. Yet how adequate can its representation or any other symbolic representations of God be judged to be?

It has already been argued that symbolic forms stand at one remove from any encountered reality. If this is true of the mysterious phenomenon of the world, it is equally true in principle of the mysterious phenomenon of God, whatever differences must thereafter be maintained between God and the world. This should put us on our guard against imagining that there can ever be a direct correspondence between or even identification of God and the representation of him in symbolic form, any more than there can be complete identification between God and any representation of him in concrete form.

The revelatory value of any symbolic form remains dependent in practice on two contingent and interrelated factors: first, on the appropriateness and adequacy of a conventionally recognized symbol for the hidden reality which it is intended to make visible; secondly, on the adequacy of the interpreting mind to receive that which the symbol is intended to communicate.

The creative powers of the human mind can in fact both enhance the resources of symbols and increase the problems they pose. Human creativity makes it possible in the first place for conventional symbols to serve as vehicles for unconventional meanings, that is, meanings that break through the face value of the symbol or symbols employed. The dynamic terminology of model, myth, metaphor, analogy, allegory, and symbol itself serves to illustrate this point. Without such devices and the creativity they witness to, it would be scarcely possible for new ideas or concepts to be incorporated into language at all, let alone for the inner personal feelings and experiences of human beings to gain any expression.

However, it is precisely the openness in which the creative potential of language lies that poses the problem. The price of openness is ambiguity, and the possibility that not only true but false meaning may be conveyed. Where the concern is with what is really there, and not merely with what is thinkable or envisaged, it becomes necessary and important to differentiate correctly between those symbols, with their various possible meanings, which point in the right direction to the true character and quality of what is there, and those which do not. The correctness of the judgement made depends ultimately on what is there and not on the sincerity or reputation of those making that judgement. Nevertheless, the responsibility for making such judgements rests with those able to use symbols and to whom symbols and, in particular, symbolic representations of God are communicated. Their responsibility and also their limitations are inescapable. For this reason symbolic forms can at best mediate between the known and what is there to be known;

they cannot correspond exactly to any thing, still less to a personal being, and least of all to God.

It follows that even if it is supposed that God could express himself directly in human speech it would not be *God himself* who would be thus expressed without qualification or re-mainder. He would rather be witnessed to in words only more or less adequate to their purpose, chosen for the pur-pose of communicating with human beings under evo-lutionary conditions, from the limited stock of human word-symbols and concepts on which human beings them-selves might draw in order to speak for or about God. But whoever it is that speaks, the free and creative response of the receiving human subject, with all his limitations, cannot be entirely overriden (short of actual destruction of the per-son), however strong the external constraints upon him may be. In most religious traditions, the existence of God is not postulated at the expense of the existence of those to whom he is revealed, though some accounts of revelation come dangerously close to negating the humanity of those to whom revelation is supposedly made.

Even if such limitations are admitted as to the possibility of God's self-representation in visible form, or in respect of the human capacity to picture God, it might nevertheless be argued that at least God's will can be made known directly to human beings and that therefore total conformity to it is required of them, and no qualification can be permitted. However, qualification cannot in fact be avoided. Even com-mands have to be interpreted by those commanded, and are subject to the inescapable changes influencing the de-velopment of language and affecting the situation in which they are given and received.

Furthermore, an important distinction needs to be made between two kinds of command. First, there are those which derive from the very meaning of the word 'God'. If by de-finition it means 'the ultimate', then, if the word is rightly understood, it means 'that which is to be obeyed or con-formed to'. To believe in God is to accept this obligation, whether God is portrayed as personally commanding it or not. It is not surprising, then, that very different religions have a common language of obedience or surrender to God, but the commands which spell out the basic attitude required towards God say nothing in themselves about the nature or character of God himself, or how a right attitude and response is to be lived out in practice.

We come, then, to the second category of commands, those which spell out the practical implications of conformity to God in terms of particular things to be done, which will count publicly as evidence of a right response to God. Convention may establish a relatively fixed and stable form and interpretation of such commands. In other words, codes of law or morality are attributed to God. It can then be argued that, since these are God's commands, they are eternally binding as God is eternal, even if their purpose is unknown or at least uncertain, and even if attempts to picture God himself are recognized to be imperfect and only provisional.

However, this distinction between binding commands and merely provisional representations of God cannot stand. The commands and the God who gives them cannot be divorced from each other. If, on the one hand, the commands are accepted as evidence for a particular understanding of God (which it is hard to deny when their binding character implies that they correspond to something which is eternal in God), then they are subject to the limitations already described, which govern any representation of God. If, on the other hand, it is argued that the practical commands of God can be known and are binding, but that he who gives them is not disclosed in or through them, but remains unknown and unknowable in himself, then the idea of one God revealed to humankind is itself negated. In effect, the commands are deified in themselves, and in their visible form become objects of total commitment such as is due to God. Yet in that visible form they in fact remain subject to the limitations described that render total commitment misplaced. Meanwhile, that which is called God, if he cannot be known in his commands, recedes into total unknowability, unintelligibility, and irrelevance. In practice, an idea of what is there is presupposed in every rational activity; and human beings cannot banish their reason entirely from their activity without surrendering their humanity. And so, as has been previously argued, our primary concern remains with representations of what God is. Representations of his will or purpose or law are subsidiary to the question of his being, though able to serve as evidence for a particular understanding of this.

To conclude. Creative freedom in pursuit of elusive meaning generates both the excitement and the dangers of human intellectual life, which is integral to, though not the whole of, our spiritual life. Human representations of God in relation to the world, and the understanding of the practical implications of this relationship, may be as true as possible, but can never be free from limitation. The unconditional character of the command to love and obey God might seem to be an exception to this rule. However, without interpretation and practical application it goes no further than defining the meaning of the word 'God'. With interpretation and application in terms of specific actions, the commands of God are brought within the sphere and limitations of creaturely existence, where the attributes of God himself, such as immutability and eternity, cannot be properly ascribed to them. Such attributes are the negations of creaturely limitation, and are predicated of God to signify his transcendent being. They cannot be properly transferred to creaturely, symbolic representations of God or of his will, not even if these representations are believed to originate from God himself. Some symbolic forms, as also some concrete forms, may in principle be more rather than less adequate to their purpose, but they are incomplete by themselves and imperfect in themselves. Too much should not be expected of them.

(c) Over-expectations

It remains the case that historically too much has been expected of revelation in the formal mode. Representations of God, or of the practical commands attributed to him, have been treated as normative and binding for all time and in all places, however far removed in time and place from the situation in which they were first formulated.

Berger's analysis summarized above offers one interpretation of the underlying causes that lead to extreme claims for revelation in the formal mode. In the light of it, we may better understand why an inherited account of divine reality and of divine law may come to be treated as absolute and immutable, whatever the cost. God himself is not necessarily excluded from the scene or from the interpretation of it on Berger's own admission.[3] He is not necessarily absent from the mysterious phenomenon of existence which humans actually encounter, and to which they try to give symbolic form in their cognitive structures. He is not necessarily absent, even when the account of his presence is more or less distorted. But if it is more distorted, and this distortion is pursued, however sincerely, as the source of truth about God, the tragic result will be that God is missed, and whoever conforms to the distorted form will be deformed accordingly. It would be important, not only for humanity but for God if he cares for humanity, that distortions be corrected. It remains true that the absolutization of forms may occur without reference to God, and also for less than the highest and purest motives, as when vested interests of race, class, or party are legitimated by appeal to an unchanging and unchangeable order of being, whether divinely grounded or not. Our concern here, however, is mainly with human intentions at their best, not their worst.

Our conclusion is that no account or symbolic representation of God can come to human beings without their own mediating, interpreting, and constructing activity. Our picture of God cannot correspond exactly to what God is. To suppose it can amounts to the divinization of human projections, the absolutization of partial truths—in traditional terms idolatry, in contemporary terms alienation. The destructive and demonic consequences of this in both ancient and modern times are apparent.

The mistake is to fail to distinguish between God and human accounts of him. When that distinction is made, not only is much needlessly bitter dispute avoided, but, more importantly, the phenomenon of which it is a symptom, the alienating impulse in religion, is held in check.[4] Criticism

---

[3] P. Berger, *A Rumour of Angels* (Harmondsworth, 1970), 10.
[4] I take issue with Berger here. He argues (*Social Reality*, 96-101) that religion,

of human inadequacies can be more readily accepted than criticism of God himself.

With the acknowledgement of the human creative role in the picturing of God comes the recovery of our creative freedom to advance towards a better understanding of what God is, and so to a better grasp of what a right relationship with him will mean in experience and practice. This is to be seen as happening in the context of God's activity of relating himself to human beings, with a corresponding openness on their part towards such a personal God. So the fear need not arise that the understanding arrived at is merely a human invention, any more than the world which we picture to ourselves is our own invention.

The position we have advanced on the basis of a contemporary understanding of ourselves and our world may finally be reinforced by more traditional theological arguments. In the first place, the doctrine that God is inexpressible in words (ineffable) should stand in the way of excessive claims for revelation in the formal mode. God transcends all human speech. In practice, however, the caution which the doctrine of ineffability should induce is all too often overridden by a misplaced over-confidence in human language, to which various theories of inspiration can give rise. The validity of such theories, in whatever form they occur, within Christianity or elsewhere, will be critically examined below (chap. 6, sect. 4, and Part V).

In the second place, traditional Christian doctrines about God and Jesus stand in the way of any notion of revelation exclusively in the formal mode. The necessarily static character of formal revelation taken in isolation is incompatible with an evolutionary understanding of the world and human existence, and with the polar dialectic. The notion of anything existing changelessly in history can only be

though often a source of alienation, may serve to overcome alienation, as, for example, when mystical religion relativizes and so 'de-alienates' alienated institutions. However, on his own argument, the transcendent God of mystical religion is liable to be a human projection and so an instance of alienation in itself. If lower-order alienations are simply 'de-alienated' by higher-order alienations, no real solution to the problem of alienation emerges. Oriental, mystical, and even biblical religions, as Berger presents the case, are not therefore so readily vindicated as agents of de-alienation as he would imply.

defended by isolating it from the dialectic of form and vitality. But this is to isolate it from history and in effect to deny the significance of physical and historical existence. No doctrine of God as creator and no Christology that takes Jesus' human life seriously can tolerate this. To present people with God *or* the world as mutually exclusive alternatives is an offence against both. Neither choice on these terms offers creative possibilities.

2. SUBJECTIVE REVELATION

We must now consider the other mode in which God relates to the world and humankind. In terms of the polarity model this could be described as revelation in the mode of vitality. What is meant is the free, unformalized, immediate, intuitive, subjective apprehension of the reality and presence of God; knowing God in contrast to knowing about God; the personal knowing that belongs to an experience of relationship, an awareness that is open-ended in character and incapable of being fully articulated in verbal or any other objective form, without the loss of its distinctive quality.[5]

This experience would probably not be described by any two people in the same way, which may make discussion difficult but at the same time proves the point. What we wish to examine is precisely that dimension of God's revelatory activity, his being in relation, the experience of which seems to be a possibility open to human beings but which is unique to each individual in the immediacy of his own awareness, whether he be mystic or motor mechanic, high, low, inside or outside the official structures of the Church or of any religious movement.

Such an awareness of God may not be as real and vivid to some as to others. It may not always be unmediated, but come through being known as a person by another person who knows God in this way. The possibilities of such mediated knowledge of God, its community setting and a community's potential for realizing it, are of great importance, but cannot be explored further here. Whatever the source,

[5] R. Bultmann, *Faith and Understanding* (London, 1969), 53, 'It is as impossible to speak about God as it is about *love*.'

the experience of being known as a person remains quali-
tatively different from the mere recognition that facts about
oneself are known; and Christianity has always taught that
the possibility of knowing God and being known by him in
a personal way is available to those who place themselves
in relationship to him through Jesus. The claim to such
immediate experience of God is certainly not exclusive to
Christianity, and the questions this raises will be examined
later (chap. 8, sect. 3).

Given the diversity and essential mystery of the phenomenon we are considering, the use of any single term to
describe it is liable to be misleading. We might sometimes
describe it as relationship in the spirit, though the present
intention is to avoid where possible terms heavily laden with
dogmatic preconceptions. To speak of revelation in the mode
of vitality would fit our model, but might not always sound
appropriate.

In the first section of this chapter the emphasis fell on
human beings in society and on revelation as public knowledge. Here it falls on the individual as the experiencing
subject. For that reason it may be convenient to speak of
revelation in the 'subjective' mode, or of 'subjective
revelation'.

It is neither necessary nor perhaps possible to explore
what it may feel like to know God in this revelatory mode.
What is significant is that this experience is claimed and
widely recognized as an important element within human
relationships to God. The key question is whether it can be
defended as the only important element. The immediate
answer is that revelation exclusively in the subjective mode
is not so much all-important as impossible. It is doubtful on
psychological and philosophical grounds whether one can
ever speak of pure experience, emotion, or feeling, un-
informed by any interpretative act. Just as pure, changeless
form cannot exist physically, so neither it seems can pure,
formless feeling exist psychologically. Feeling, consciously
experienced, comes with interpretation of some sort. Certainly no experience could be received, let alone described,
as an experience of God, unless some concept of God in

some form was available as an interpretative resource.[6] We
find here again the inescapability of the polar dialectic, and
the impossibility of one term in the polar relationship existing autonomously in the world.

The distinguishing feature of subjective revelation is the
emphasis placed on personal experience, and the recognition
that, even if it is interpreted, it is somehow more than and
other than the interpretation, and indeed that it neither need
nor can be fully articulated verbally or in any other objective
way. This conception poses little difficulty for persons who
experience for themselves both the reality and the mystery
of close personal relationships. Of importance here is the
weight attached to revelation in this subjective mode and to
the related interpretations of it. As in the previous case,
while revelation in this mode cannot in fact be exclusive,
the attempt may be made to render it so, or at least to
overemphasize its significance. The question now is what
follows from such overemphasis and what problems are
posed.

The first and most obvious problem is how any claim to
have had an immediate experience of God can be validated.
How can the subject know that the experience he has had
was of God? How can anyone else know? As argued above,
such a claim presupposes a concept of God in some form
which allows an experience to be interpreted in this way,
and which may indeed impart a particular quality to the
experience in the first place. In either case, then, even if in
fact the source of an experience is God, for a right interpretation to be placed upon it the subject must have
achieved a right conception of God. Where does this come
from? How can the subject or anyone else know it is correct?
If it is not, then not only will the understanding and account
of the experience be more or less distorted, but so will the
course of action it gives rise to. Whether this is the case or
not will not be open to discussion, because in the extreme
case under consideration the subject recognizes no external,
objective norm over against which his own claims can be
tested.

[6] See Bowker, *Sense of God*, 149.

A limited number of courses are now open to the individual who lays claim to an immediate revelation of God as sufficient in itself without external reference. First, he may keep silent and treasure it alone. This way he can make of it what he likes without fear of conflict, but at a price. The silence may have to be total, extending not only to words but to actions. For if the impact and interpretation of the given experience call for any practical response, a change of behaviour or a reorientation of life, then the subject will almost inevitably come into conflict with existing interpretations of divine reality and the related social structures and practices which have shaped the life of his society and of himself hitherto. Alternatively, he may come into conflict with other individuals who claim a similar immediate experience of God, but who interpret it and its practical implications differently. Ultimately, silent enjoyment may be possible only in complete privacy. This may be achieved either in literal isolation from the world of other people or through the isolation of God and the experience of God from any practical consequences in the world.

In the first case, the practical consequences of God's relatedness are restricted to a tiny fragment of the world. (The world-denying withdrawal envisaged here is not to be confused with the world-affirming withdrawal which has a positive place in many religious traditions. The former more or less excludes the world at large and ordinary human intercourse from God. The latter would comprehend it.) In the second case, the experience of God would have no bearing on what a person did or on what happened in the world, and what happened there would have no bearing on the experience of the divine. Yet if what happens in the world has nothing to do with the divine, then the world itself and history can have no real significance one way or the other. This retreat from the world, which preserves the appearance of remaining in it, is in fact more fundamental than the literal retreat of the hermit into the seclusion of desert or forest. However, it has already been argued that total world-renunciation for any reason is incompatible with any concept of God as the ground of all that exists. That may not be a concept of God which our hypothetical subject held in the first place, but then he has no grounds apart from himself for any alternative view, and no generally accepted basis against which to test or justify his views. That is excluded because merely human opinion would be irrelevant and no external, divinely authoritative, revealed criterion is acknowledged. Whereas in the previous case the constructs of society were divinized, here in effect the individual's constructs are divinized; or, to express it differently, the deification of society is matched by the self-deification of the individual.

This brings us to a third possibility open to the subject who claims immediate experience of God. He may maintain that the true interpretation of it has been given with the experience, and that its authority therefore transcends his individuality and should be acknowledged as binding on others as well as himself. He may succeed in transmitting this view by force or persuasion to others, but for them it then becomes a new formal revelation received from outside, though with certain possible qualifications. Where a person's revelatory authority continues to be recognized, there will theoretically be no limit to his formalization of revelation during his active life. In other words, he may add to his revelatory pronouncements or even contradict them, depending on whether a higher degree of revelatory value is attached by himself or by others to the speaker or to what is spoken. Whichever is the case, the possibility of enlargement or modification of the revelatory whole persists only while the revealer is alive. Where revelatory authority is identified with a single human being, scope for enlargement ends with his death, at which point revelation through him becomes a fixed datum of history and hence revelation in the formal mode.

However, where the source of subjective revelation is not identified exclusively with a single human being, but with some suprahuman spiritual reality, then a wide range of possibilities opens up. On the one hand, revelatory authority may continue to be ascribed more or less exclusively to the one person regarded as the unique mouthpiece of the spiritual source. The more exclusive the claims made for this person after his death, the more this approach will verge on formal revelation.

On the other hand, someone else might claim to speak at a later date in the name of the original human revealer, or independently in the name of that subjective source which inspired him—his God.

In the latter case, the basic problem pertaining to subjective revelation recurs. Since in principle the claim to validity remains unverifiable in relation to publicly acknowledged forms, it is liable to come into conflict with any number of other claims and interpretations. It is in these circumstances that new religions fragment into numerous independent sects after the death of the founder. In the competition between them, the success of one or other will be affected by a wide range of different factors, social, economic, political, and such like, as well as by different presuppositions concerning the legitimate possibilities of revelation.

In the former case, where formal revelation is derived from a uniquely regarded single source of subjective revelation (which may be termed subject-dependent formal revelation), the same criticisms will apply as outlined in the preceding section. The so-called true, final representation of God offered at a given time cannot, in its exclusiveness, correspond to the God who is the ground of evolutionary existence. It fails both on the count of its fixed character and because it implies the absence of God's revelatory activity in other forms and experience, again depriving God of his world and vice versa.

It appears, then, that any attempt to interpret revelation exclusively in either the formal or subjective mode is beset with problems, and is incompatible with any doctrine of God as the ground of all that exists. The negative and destructive consequences are further evidence that such representations of God do not truly represent the creator God. For if the outcome of attempting to isolate revelation in the formal mode is tyranny, the outcome of isolating revelation in the subjective mode is anarchy. Revelation must be expressed in the dialectical interplay of both modes together.

A swing to one extreme is always liable to provoke a reaction towards the other, though the extent to which one or
other seems to pose a threat in any given historical situation
will be governed by sociological and political factors,
amongst others. In the most general terms, one might expect
that in a loosely organized society, where a relatively high
level of freedom and responsibility has been accorded to the
individual, as amongst nomads, the fear of tyranny would be
greatest. In a highly complex and hierarchically structured
society, as in almost any urban situation (though not exclusively in urban settings), anarchy might seem to pose the
greatest threat. This is also likely to be the case whenever
external enemies appear. The history of human societies can
be seen to a considerable extent as the history of attempts to
achieve the balance between form and vitality appropriate to
prevailing environmental and social conditions. Such attempts are constantly dogged not only by conflicts between
vested interests, but by changes in prevailing conditions
which render what was appropriate once less appropriate at
another time.

3. THE POLARITY MODEL AND HISTORICAL INQUIRY

Before the conclusions reached in the foregoing sections can
be tested in relation to the Judaeo-Christian tradition, both
historically and in the present day, it is necessary to attend
to one further theoretical issue. This concerns the bearing
of the polarity model on the activity of historical inquiry
itself. It is important to recognize that this model applies not
only to the content of historical inquiry, but to the approach—to the way we look as well as what we look for. We
must therefore consider the methodological implications of
this approach for the historian.

The complex story of the past reaches us from outside
ourselves, from many different sources and in different
forms, though for the most part and most importantly in
written form. The sources as such are communications in
the formal mode, and are thus the same for all and available
to public scrutiny. However, our own standing within the

polar dialectic of form and vitality lays upon us the inescapable freedom and responsibility of personal reaction to
what confronts us individually from outside, whether that
reaction is negative or positive. This freedom is not of course
absolute. It is conditioned not only to a greater or lesser
extent by genetic or environmental factors of various kinds,
but also by previous experience and its interpretation.

Together these factors create for each individual a unique
perspective, within which he exercises his creative freedom
to interpret the objective evidence which confronts him and
others. It is within this polar dialectic that the creative originality of the rigorous scientific historian has its ground.
Only if the dialectic is broken will objectivity appear to be
incompatible with creativity. In practice, any act of formal
communication is two-sided, as has already been argued.
The writer or speaker can only offer. The recipient takes
what till then was not his, but in doing so makes something
of it for himself, which is never identical with what was
offered and may sometimes be very far removed from it (as
any teacher or preacher knows). The past speaks to each
generation in a new way; its message can never be fixed and
unchanging, even if the past as such cannot be changed.

Communication at any level, then, has an outer and inner
dimension, a formal and a subjective character. It might,
however, appear that the actual content of historical inquiry
is exclusively of a formal kind, in that only that which is
external, concrete, and in principle publicly verifiable can
provide the content of historical inquiry. This is true only to
a limited extent and subject to two important qualifications.
First, if the polarity model is accepted as valid, that is, if this
way of depicting the conditions of evolutionary existence
does correspond to the way things are, then it must hold true
for all events and conditions in the evolutionary world, in
the future, present, and past (just as the earth was round in
the past, even if people thought it was flat). This allows us
to affirm the reality of subjective experience in the past and
its constant interaction with the forms of existence, even if
in principle only the latter are available for scrutiny, and
the former is in principle inscrutable. Even such limited
acknowledgement is significant when we investigate the past.

It will prevent the giving of undue emphasis to what simply happens to be more open to objective scrutiny. Such emphasis tends to result in the significance of impersonal forces and statistical patterns being exaggerated, and the creative role of persons being undervalued.

However, we are not in fact restricted to the mere acknowledgement of subjective experience. In itself, this can never be totally isolated from formal expression, and, short of the extremes of privacy mentioned above, it is often the acknowledged source of purposeful action.[7] Hence, in the practical consequences of the experiences which persons in the past or present claim to have had, and indeed in the interpretations which they themselves have placed upon them, which have helped to shape these experiences in the first place, we can draw close to the subjective dimension of experience. It is therefore not totally hidden from the historian's gaze, even if never totally visible to it.

The polar dynamic conditions our approach to the subject-matter of history in one further important way. It prevents us supposing that anything exists or has existed in the world in purely objective form, unrelated to, uninvolved in, or unconditioned by the dynamics of evolutionary existence; equally, pure subjectivity is ruled out, whatever claims to the contrary are made and have been made in history in either case. This will bear on our treatment of the objects that lie at the centre of world religious movements, as well as the experiences claimed within those movements.

This has particular relevance for our understanding of Jesus. If, as is assumed here, he lived a fully authentic human life in history, then in his own person he experienced the dialectic of form and vitality, and this must be recognized in our understanding of him. Secondly, as a person he stood within the wider dialectic of form and vitality in the evolutionary world within which his own life was set. In other words, he cannot be understood in isolation, least of all as an isolated revelatory datum. He was what he was in relation to the past that formed the conceptual and practical framework of his existence, in relation to the present in terms of

[7] See R. Harré and P. F. Secord, *The Explanation of Social Behaviour* (Oxford, 1972), chap. 6, 'Why not ask them . . .?'

his reactions to the circumstances of his life, to the future in terms of the reactions of others to his life. In anticipation of the inquiry to be pursued, it might be said that his life gave expression to creative freedom in relation to the form of Judaism of his day, and gave form to the recovered freedom of his followers. He was the freedom of Judaism, the form of Christianity, but is certainly not to be isolated from the form of Judaism nor from the freedom of Christianity.

II

GOD'S RELATEDNESS IN
JUDAISM

INTRODUCTION

THE next stage in this undertaking is the application of the
polarity model to the account of God's relatedness (i.e., ideas
of revelation) to be found within the Judaeo-Christian tradition. An important question will be how far the movement
centred on Jesus of Nazareth should be distinguished from
its Jewish origins. The polarity model may suggest a way of
answering this question, on the basis of which the more
general issue of the distinctiveness of Christianity in relation
to other religions and quasi-religions[1] today can be tackled
in Part V. That will have to be preceded by an examination
of the origins and development of Christianity itself in the
light of this model.

In the course of the inquiry a number of points will emerge
which will have wider application than the particular issue
under discussion. However, it seems preferable to allow
these points to arise in the course of practical investigation,
rather than to try to anticipate in theory every possible per-
mutation. So we turn now to the historical circumstances in
which the Christian account of God's relatedness had its
origin.

[1] See P. Tillich, *Christianity and the Encounter of the World Religions* (New York,
1963), 5.

3. Israel and the Creation
of the Torah

INTRODUCTION

IT follows from what has previously been argued that the inquiry into the origins of Christianity should not begin with Jesus himself, but with the historical developments that lay behind him and which helped to shape the situation into which he was born and also the course and character of his own life and ministry. In particular, we must view in terms of the polar dialectic the specific understanding or understandings of God's relatedness which arose within the tradition he inherited, and which were later current within his own society. Space will not allow a comprehensive survey of Israelite history or permit a full evaluation of the sources and the problems posed by source-criticism; nor can we hope to do justice to the experience of God found in the Jewish tradition in all its depth and variety. The aim in this section will be simply to outline the pattern of development and shifts of emphasis in the Israelite or Jewish understanding of God's relatedness from the period of settlement in Canaan up to the time of Jesus, in the light of the available historical evidence and relying on the studies of scholars in this particular field.[1] Some misrepresentation is perhaps the inevitable price of any attempt at simplification; one can only hope it is kept to a minimum.

The survey will reveal a shift from an uneasy but creative tension between formal and subjective revelation in early Israel towards an increasing emphasis on formal revelation, and a consequent weakening of the polar dialectic in Judaism

---

[1] The main works drawn upon in this section are: J. H. Hayes and J. M. Miller, eds., *Israelite and Judaean History* (London, 1977); S. Herrmann, *A History of Israel in Old Testament Times* (London, 1975); H. Jagersma, *A History of Israel in the Old Testament Period* (London, 1982); R. de Vaux, *Ancient Israel, its Life and Institutions* (London, 1961); M. Hengel, *Judaism and Hellenism*, 2 vols. (London, 1974) (page references are to vol. i).

after the exile, and more especially after the Maccabean rebellion.

I. BEFORE AND AFTER THE BABYLONIAN EXILE

(a) *Unresolved tensions*

We may begin our survey of Israel's experience of God's relatedness with the arrival of the Israelites in Canaan (later called Palestine). It is now widely accepted that the book of Joshua, with its story of swift and decisive conquest, is a later stylized account. Most probably the ancestors of the Israelites were nomads or semi-nomads, who infiltrated the country from different directions and assimilated with much of the local population over a long period of time (*c*.1300–1100 BC). One group may well have come up from Egypt and shared the tradition of its 'exodus' (Gk. 'going out') with its later tribal neighbours.[2]

In the earliest period of the settlement in Palestine, before the monarchy, Israel appears to have consisted of a loose confederation of tribes with a relatively unstructured social organization[3] and, correspondingly, with a relatively unstructured relationship with God. There seems to have been no organized basis for concerted action against any external threats which might arise. According to the biblical record, when a crisis developed some individual on whom the spirit of the Lord descended, and who appeared to have no other particular qualification, took the lead. After victory, he would continue to exercise authority in his lifetime. These leaders were called 'judges'.[4] The events portrayed in the book of Judges in the Old Testament mostly occurred in the northern region. It has been suggested that the accounts we have of them may have been coloured by the ideas and interests of the spirit-possessed leaders of later generations, namely the prophets,[5] who may also have combined what were originally two distinct roles of deliverer and judge.[6] It

---

[2] Herrmann, chaps. 2–4; Jagersma, 19–22, 41.
[3] Herrmann, 112.
[4] Judg. 2: 16–19; cf. also 4: 4; 8: 22; 11: 2.
[5] Hayes and Miller, 310.
[6] Ibid. 321.

is likely that the original deliverers only acted on a clan or tribal basis and for as long as an emergency lasted. Either way, the idea of God's involvement in the affairs of men, and especially in warfare in that period, is strongly attested; and whatever the later prophetic interest, there seems little ground for doubting that military success at the time would have been taken as evidence of divine authorization of the leader. The picture given is of a very unformalized concept of authority, which could appear to derive directly from God.

The prophets themselves seem to have emerged after the time of the judges. They witness to another kind of direct relationship with God, acting as his mouthpiece rather than as the extension of his fighting arm, though these roles were not necessarily exclusive. The debate concerning the precise meaning of the words which can be translated as 'prophet', and the origins of those so described, need not be entered into here,[7] but clearly they antedated the institution of the monarchy in Israel. The existence of seers—prophets—before that time is witnessed to in the story of Saul visiting Samuel to inquire about his lost asses (1 Sam. 9) and in the description of his encounter with a band of prophets (1 Sam. 10: 10) after his anointing by Samuel. Samuel himself is variously depicted in the roles of priest (apprentice to Eli), judge, and prophet and seer.[8] It is also worth noticing that the possibility of an immediate relationship with or at least direct approach to God was open to ordinary men and women, if the story of Hannah's solitary and silent prayer in the Temple at Shiloh can be taken as evidence (1 Sam. 1: 13).[9]

The distinction between the role of prophet and priest in the early period does not seem to have been absolutely clear, as seen above. Prophets could build altars and conduct sacrifices,[10] and priests gave oracles.[11] But a priest appears to

---

[7] See J. Lindblom, *Prophecy in Ancient Israel* (Oxford, 1962).

[8] 1 Sam. 2: 18; 7: 6, 17; 9: 9.

[9] See R. E. Clements, *Prophecy and Tradition* (Oxford, 1975), 25-6, for the evidence of the psalms.

[10] e.g. Elijah (1 Kgs. 18: 20 ff.).

[11] Deut. 33: 8-10. The sacred lots, Urim and Thummim, are assigned to Levites. According to de Vaux (p. 343), there is no evidence of their use after the reign of David.

have had the specific function of serving at a sanctuary, and in this respect to have expressed a more formalized mode of relationship to God. To quote de Vaux (p. 346), 'In Israel the priesthood was not a vocation, but an office. The texts speak of a man being called or chosen by God to be a king or prophet, but they never use the term of a priest.' However, in this period the order of the priesthood was not yet highly formalized. A man of Ephraim could appoint his own son, even if he preferred to have a Levite.[12] To quote de Vaux again (p. 345), 'The priesthood properly so called did not appear until the social organization of the community had developed considerably. Then certain members of the community were entrusted with special tasks of looking after the sanctuaries and of performing rites which were becoming ever more and more complicated'. One might add that at that point, too, full-time kings took over from part-time judges to manage the affairs of State and defence. The threat posed by the Philistines may well have necessitated this development, and given rise to a stronger sense of identity among the Israelite tribes.[13]

For a historical inquiry into the development of Israel's understanding of God's relatedness, the key question is not so much who could enjoy an experience of God's reality and presence (as did Hannah), but who or what could represent God to the community in a form that would shape and influence the community's understanding of God and the demands of a relationship with him. During the period of the monarchy (both before and after the empire created by David was divided into the kingdoms of Samaria and Judah), God's relatedness was not conceived of in terms of one exclusive mode, formal or subjective; nor was the authority to represent God concentrated in one form; rather, it was recognized in the three forms we have already discovered, king (in place of judge), priest, and prophet. The terms in which their authority to represent God was conceived changed under the monarchy with, ironically, the king's position becoming weaker.

[12] Judg. 17: 5-10. For the tradition ascribing the priestly office to the sons of Levi, see Exod. 32: 29.
[13] Jagersma, *History*, 76.

Each of the three could in different ways lay claim to divine legitimation, that is, they could claim to be God's authorized representatives and express their special status in such symbols as son[14] or servant. They were, perhaps not surprisingly, as often in conflict as in harmony, or engaged in shifting alliances against one or other.

The position of the king depended on a combination of related factors: physical power, public consent, and religious legitimation. With regard to the last, the immediate charismatic but *ad hoc* authority of the judge was an insufficiently firm basis for the king, who required recognized, institutional authority if any stability was to be achieved. Charismatic leadership gave way to kingship 'by the grace of God'.[15] But that grace, it seems, lacked the strength of the charisma. The institution of kingship as such was a relatively late innovation in Israel, and this fact was never forgotten. Hence its claims could not be sustained by appeal to the most ancient and sacred traditions which constituted the community's identity.[16] This inherent weakness remained, even if with the passage of time the weight of tradition behind the institution of kingship would increase. Individual kings were inevitably even less secure than the institution, since in the nature of the case their authority could not be vested in the past and had to be legitimated in a derivative manner.

In fact both king and kingship could derive legitimation only at second hand. As it was not available from the sacred voice of the past (tradition), it could only come from those whose claim to speak for God in the immediacy of the present was recognized, namely the prophets. These must be treated more fully below, but in terms of leadership they were as much the true successors of the judges as were the kings.[17] What they could make, they could also break. The Old Testament, even if it reflects the bias of a later age, nevertheless witnesses both to a continuing critique of the

[14] 2 Sam. 7: 14. Cf. Hayes and Miller, 371.

[15] Ibid. 367.

[16] The exception in Deut. 17: 18 is more apparent than real. The king's authority depends on divine choice and on his observance of God's law. Deuteronomy is in any case a late work (see below, n. 35).

[17] Hayes and Miller, 307–8.

institution of kingship as such[18] and to recurring conflicts between kings and prophets,[19] and often the successful over-throw of the former at the instigation of the latter (2 Kgs. 9–10). The position of the king was far less stable in the Northern Kingdom of Samaria than in the Southern Kingdom of Judah. Obviously there were many variables in the circumstances of the two kingdoms, but the comparative stability of kingship in Judah would seem to have owed much to the fact that in Judah the house of David, and not just David himself, received prophetic legitimation from Nathan.[20] In other words, the dynastic principle was consecrated in a way it never was in the North, which reverted to a more charismatic form of leadership.[21] To this may be added the continuing alignment with the Davidic dynasty of the great prophets such as Isaiah, and the fact that Judah lay at a greater distance from the storm-centres of great-power politics of that period.

The legitimation of priests rested on different grounds. Even if here too the bias of a later age has superimposed subsequent developments on the past, there can be little doubt that the priesthood during the monarchy could claim a foundation in antiquity. Later tradition vested its institution firmly in the foundation of the Israelite community,[22] in a way that was never conceded to kingship. It is not necessary to pursue the history of the priesthood in detail here, though mention should be made of certain serious conflicts and tensions within it, as between the Jerusalemite priesthood and the country priesthood, and between the descendants of Zadok and of Abiathar.[23] Both had served David as priests, but the former took first place in Jerusalem under Solomon, while the latter was banished to Anathoth (1 Kgs. 2: 26),

[18] Ibid. 384. Cf. 1 Sam. 8; 12; Hos. 8: 4.
[19] See the stories of Ahab and Elijah in 1 Kings.
[20] 2 Sam. 7: 12–16. Hayes and Miller, 363; de Vaux, 97.
[21] Hayes and Miller, 385, 'Israel . . . rejoiced in her freedom. The charismatic ideal was given real political value and Yahweh was accorded a free hand, as it were, to bring a *homo novus* to the throne as he once had done with Saul.' Cf. de Vaux, 96. We may notice that kings, unlike judges, were legitimated indirectly through prophets, and not by a personal divine call—a division of labour that would be a further source of instability.
[22] 1 Chron. 6 (probable date, c.300 BC).
[23] de Vaux, 372 ff.

whence later Jeremiah emerged as the relentless critic of the priesthood in Jerusalem. The cases of Jeremiah, who came from a priestly family, and of Ezekiel, who was himself a priest, show that, although the priesthood had become strictly hereditary, the distinction between priest and prophet was not absolute. The co-existence of priest and prophet proves that the legitimating power of tradition was not yet overriding. However, the general point is that the priests were associated most closely with the accounts of God's relatedness inherited from the past. It was their task to teach and apply the rules governing the relationship between God and his people.[24] Their legitimation in sacred tradition was bound to inhibit their freedom to embark on a creative reinterpretation of their understanding of God's relatedness. A radical critique of the authority of tradition would have put their own status as guardians of tradition in question.[25]

While these divisions and constraints ought not to be exaggerated, nevertheless an important distinction in principle remains between those who echoed the voice of God which had spoken in the past and those who gave utterance to God's voice in the present. In the former case, the message once uttered and recorded was publicly available, and thus falls within the category of revelation in the formal mode. It remained in the care of those who, by virtue of physical[26] descent, could claim to be one with their ancestors who first witnessed and communicated the revelatory content. In the latter case, revelatory authority was not grounded in a past revelatory act of God but in the immediacy of the present moment and present experience, free from the formulations of tradition and free from the controls of lineage (though free to emerge within any lineage, including the priestly). The speaker of the new word could employ ancient formulations and abide by them to a greater or lesser degree, but they rested on a new authority. It is those who could thus claim to speak freely for God in the present who are known as prophets.[27]

[24] Ibid. 355 f.
[25] Cf. de Vaux, 375, '. . . the religious reforms were introduced by the kings, not by the priests'.
[26] Ibid. 359.
[27] For a full account of the prophets, see Lindblom; also Clements.

The prophets emerged within a community which as a whole was constituted by its acknowledgement of the inherited formal representations of God in his relatedness, but which at the same time acknowledged the relatedness of God in the immediacy of present and personal experience. Further, and most importantly, this community allowed sufficient weight to revelation in the subjective mode to permit the reformulation of the terms of God's relatedness. Such reformulations drew naturally and inevitably on past representations. However, the prophets not only modified or developed them, but could on occasion explicitly break with them under the overriding impact of what they took to be an immediate experience of God.[28] Such developments certainly did not occur without conflict. The prophet was liable to be strongly opposed by priest or king or both, or even, though not in fact surprisingly, by other prophets.[29] The divergent claims to revelatory authority left many unresolved problems and tensions. Yet, one might well believe, it was the very absence of consolidated divine authority which was the necessary condition for the emergence of the great prophets—a development of momentous significance for both Israel and the world. One might even say that, despite Jeremiah's anguished denunciation of them (Jer. 5: 30-1; 28), if there had not been room for false prophets in Israel and Judah, there could never have been true prophets. But despite the opposition encountered by the great prophets, the continuity of prophetic activity and the survival in written form of their message proves in itself that their claims to represent God were acknowledged within their community.[30] Hence the continuing dialectic between formal and subjective revelation, between tradition and experience, was preserved.

It is interesting to consider what particular circumstances in Israel made possible this combination of revelatory modes, which for all the parties concerned contained such a dynamic potential. An answer may suggest itself based on the theoretical point made at the end of chap. 2, sect. 2 and

[28] See Amos 5: 18, where the 'Day of the Lord' is radically reinterpreted.
[29] 1 Kgs. 22: 5-28; Jer. 20: 2; Amos 6: 10-13.
[30] See Clements, chap. 4.

on the specific historical conditions just outlined. In the first case, we noted that more loosely organized societies such as nomads, where a relatively high level of personal responsibility is recognized, are more likely to react against the threat of tyranny, while complex city cultures are more likely to react against the threat of anarchy. The period we are considering saw the Israelites move from a nomadic or semi-nomadic rural culture to one in which city life and complex social structures developed under a newly instituted monarchy. Evidence of tension is hardly surprising.

We have already found the Israelite kings to be hampered in their attempts to secure complete control of their society by their lack of either independent or traditional legitimation. The extent to which they attempted to control the cult is significant in this respect. Saul in his day was severely handicapped by Samuel (1 Sam. 13: 8-14), and even David was restrained by the prophet Nathan (1 Sam. 7) when he wished to build a Temple for the ark. 'Solomon built the Jerusalem Temple without asking any questions, and he did it accepting many Canaanite theological elements.'[31] He also performed priestly functions, such as sacrifice and blessing. His dismissal of Abiathar, the representative of the traditional priestly line, and his favouring of Zadok, would have strengthened his position, if one theory concerning Zadok's origins is correct. According to this, he was a priest of the sanctuary of El Elyon in Jerusalem when David captured the city.[32] If so, he may have represented a Canaanite tradition which accorded the king a far higher cultic status than could be found in Israelite tradition. Whatever the truth of that supposition, the fact that the office of priest was by royal appointment would give the king a means of control.

The priests themselves were guardians of the cult and of the traditions which conferred on it sacred legitimation. Recent studies on the place of ritual in society suggest that rituals develop where social boundaries are significant and well defined, and that they perform an important social function in cementing the structures of society; conversely, an emphasis on ritual is symptomatic of a strong group-identity

[31] Hayes and Miller, 368.
[32] de Vaux, 374.

and of a highly structured society.[33] On this view, one would expect ritual and cult to play an increasingly important part in Israelite society as it became increasingly urbanized and organized as a kingdom. In so far as the king controlled the cult, he controlled the acknowledged and divinely legitimated source of formal authority; the greater the emphasis on this mode of divine authority, the less the risk from such independent spokesmen of God as the prophets.

However, while there can be little doubt that the priesthood welcomed the higher status which these conditions and royal patronage secured for it, there remained a point of conflict. There is evidence to suggest (despite the problems of dating Old Testament material) that a priestly tradition from pre-monarchical times survived in Israel, which maintained a concern for more than just detailed regulations for the cult.[34] Some at least of the priestly guardians of that tradition were not, it seems, prepared to sacrifice the ancient understanding of the terms of God's relatedness to the immediate interests of the king. To be sure, those priests who found themselves already out of favour had less to lose by opposing royal interests, and the possibility of this occurring in the Southern Kingdom has been shown, with the example of Jeremiah.

If the origin of the book of Deuteronomy is correctly located in the Northern Kingdom in the seventh century BC,[35] then we have evidence there also to suggest that some priests at least were on the side of the prophet Amos, and not Amaziah, priest of Bethel, who told him to go home and earn his living in Judah (Amos 7: 12). The question of the relationship between the authors of Deuteronomy and the prophets is of great interest but hard to resolve. The book itself certainly witnesses to a spiritual openness which can accept and give expression to new insight into the relationship between God and humanity, without by any means refuting ancient tradition, but also without relying exclusively on

[33] M. Douglas, *Natural Symbols* (London, 1970), 14, 73 f. (see above, p. 61 n. 13).

[34] de Vaux, 354.

[35] Ibid. 338; Herrmann, 267. See also A. D. H. Mayes, *The New Century Bible Commentary: Deuteronomy* (Grand Rapids and London, 1979), 81 ff.

it.[36] Deuteronomy itself was to have its greatest impact in the South, if it is rightly identified with the book of the law which gave such impetus to King Josiah's reform some time after 633 BC (2 Kgs. 22: 8). Its origin in the North and acceptance in the South would suggest a continuing tradition of priestly loyalty to Yahweh (revised spelling of 'Jehovah', God of Israel), which persisted whether the king was loyal or not, and which one might describe as a priestly opposition movement which acted to some degree as a constraint on the power of the king.

Thus, the combination in Israel's historical experience of nomadic and urban conditions, monarchical and non-monarchical forms of rule, produced a complex and dynamic interaction between different values, interests, and demands. The unresolved tensions provided conditions for creative insights into the nature of God's relatedness.

Within all this we may see the continuing operation of the polar dialectic. Given representations of God's relatedness shaped the interpretation of the experience of God in new circumstances. Under the impact of new circumstances and experiences, new representations superseded or radically qualified the older forms. Though different forces pulled in different directions, God's relatedness was not restricted to form or to experience exclusively, nor was one subordinated to the other.

(b) Formal revelation in the ascendant

We come now to the point in Jewish history when a significant shift of emphasis within the polar dialectic occurred, with a swing towards formal revelation. This came about in two stages. It was set in motion by the exile of the Jews to Babylon (in present-day Iraq) and the circumstances of their return, which we consider first. It was taken to the limit by the outcome of the Maccabean rebellion, which is the subject of the following section. It is significant that these revelatory shifts were occasioned by extreme challenges to the Jewish

---

[36] de Vaux, 144, 'This code [Deuteronomy] seems designed to replace the old code by taking account of a whole social and religious evolution; it also reveals a change of spirit by its appeals to the heart and by the tone of exhortation in which its prescriptions are often couched.'

community's understanding of itself and God. Whatever judgement one might form of the outcome, the very positive religious impulse behind it must be recognized.

In pursuing the story, we shall find that the two motifs, which we have already seen interacting so significantly in Israel's history, continue to feature in it—the prophetic and the priestly.

In 586 BC the Babylonians under Nebuchadnezzar destroyed Jerusalem and its Temple and took the leading citizens into exile.[37] The remarkable capacity of the Jewish people to survive such a disaster was, it may be argued, due to two things. In the first place, the great prophets made it possible for the people to recognize that their defeat was not necessarily God's defeat. In the second place, the priests strove to preserve the identity of this people in their relationship to their undefeated God.

The particular contribution of the prophets to the understanding of God's relatedness lay in their interpretation of it in ethical rather than in ritual terms. This does not mean that they were wholly opposed to ritual, or that they were wholly innovatory or alone in emphasizing moral responsibility. Indeed, we have seen that they could appeal to ancient tradition. What is significant is that by placing the emphasis where they did, on morality rather than on cultic performance as such, they gave grounds for calling in question in their day the adequacy of the people's and certainly the kings' response to God, which no one merely watching the conduct of ritual could have perceived. At the same time, they spelt out the implications of a wrong relationship with God in terms of inevitable disaster.

The claim of the prophets to have represented God rightly seemed to be all too clearly vindicated by the disasters that occurred: first, the destruction of the Northern Kingdom of Samaria by the Assyrians in 721 BC; and then the destruction of Jerusalem by the Babylonians. But if the prophets were vindicated, then so also was the God of whom they spoke. In other words, it remained possible to believe in God as God despite the greatest plausibility crisis in Jewish history till that moment.

[37] 2 Kgs. 25. See Herrmann, 289 ff.; Hayes and Miller, 469 ff.

If these disasters were, as the prophets declared, the result of Israel's and Judah's obstinate refusal to maintain a right relationship with God, it followed that restoration and the avoidance of further tragedy would depend on achieving a right relationship. For this to be possible, the terms of a right relationship would have to be carefully defined.

The keyword in the Old Testament to express God's relatedness is 'covenant'. The word itself does not seem to have been much used by the earlier prophets, but they witness forcefully to a sense of special relationship to God and the obligations this placed on his people (e.g. Amos 3: 2; Hos. 11). Whatever the background of the word, its full meaning could only emerge gradually from the experiences of the covenanted people and the interpretations they placed upon them. It appears that a new approach towards defining the terms of covenant developed in the last years of independence before the exile. Deuteronomy bears witness to an attempt to codify traditional laws and to encourage a moral response. Josiah's reform (2 Kgs. 22-3) activated Deuteronomy's potential in possibly an even more significant way than is commonly recognized, even though his motives may have been political as much as religious. Herrmann suggests that Josiah's aim may have been to generate the idea of one united Israel under one God centred in Jerusalem, with Jerusalem and the house of David binding themselves without qualification to God's law, and so becoming the protector of the traditions of the former Northern State. According to this view, devotion to the one God, Yahweh, legitimated both the exclusion of all foreign cults and the unrestricted circulation of all traditions of Yahweh. At the same time, the idea of a united Israel acting as a totality from the beginning of history would support Josiah's claim to the territory of the Northern State:

In short, there is a move back through David to Moses. Only now, with Deuteronomy and the law of Israel, does Moses achieve the status of the great law-giver. The traditions of the north only seem to have gained unqualified significance for Judah also in full measure after the time of Josiah. The significance of this fact can hardly be overestimated, for both the outward and inner course of the later history of Judah and Israel from Isaiah on.[38]

[38] Herrmann, 267 f., following the thesis put forward by A. Alt.

Whether this thesis is fully accepted or not, the pooling of the traditions of the Northern and Southern Kingdoms did take place within an attitude of commitment to Yahweh and rejection of foreign cults. This happened only just in time, in the sense that the opportunity to consolidate the combined traditions in Jerusalem could hardly have arisen after the destruction of the city and its Temple. As it was, the loss of the holy place might almost seem to have been compensated for by the creation of a holy tradition under priestly influence, and of a sense of God's continuing transcendent holiness under prophetic influence.

The movement to determine the terms of God's relatedness which thus began before the exile was given further impetus by it. With the loss of the Temple and its institutional structures, the written tradition became the most significant, accessible, and tangible form in which God could be represented. Commitment to the traditions defined those who stood in the covenantal relationship with God even in a foreign land, and even though full observance would be possible only if the people could return to the holy land. The gathering together of a wide range of traditions from both north and south concerning God's relatedness thus served to show what God had done for his people in creating the covenant relationship, and what he required of them in response, both in acts of worship and in everyday life, if it was to be preserved. Also, and by no means least, these traditions disclosed what means God had appointed for mending the relationship where his people were guilty of infringement but not wholly lacking in good intention. It has been maintained that after the exile it was participation in the cult, rather than obedience to the Law as such, that secured Israel's continuing relationship with her God. Nevertheless, 'the Law alone determined who could come within the cult, and so be a member of the elect community'.[39] Thus, the Law remained supremely important.

Within this activity of attempting to discover and define the terms of right relationship with God—an activity which was to continue after the return from exile—the priestly

[39] A. C. J. Phillips, *Deuteronomy* (The Cambridge Bible Commentary; Cambridge, 1973), 10 f.

and prophetic motifs continued to interact. They can be associated respectively with two distinct emphases, namely ritual and ethical, though not with the implication that concern for one necessarily excluded the other.

The prophets had emphasized God's righteousness, and in the challenge of the hour required of the people a corresponding righteousness. Their ethical concern was loud and clear, but in the nature of the case did not issue in detailed practical requirements or universally binding regulations. The response of the heart could not be codified (Jer. 31: 31-4).

There is no need, on the other hand, to deny any moral concern on the part of priestly guardians of tradition. They were not necessarily closed to prophetic influence and, as observed above, could point to the ethical concern already expressed within the tradition. But their tradition also had much else to say about the ordering of the people's relationship to God, not least in the formal context of the cult. Thus it incorporated regulations concerning proper performance of the cult, and rules of purity which governed the persons and places involved. Whatever the origins of such rules, and however they were interpreted in later ages, they were handed down essentially in their traditional form as constitutive elements in the total ordering of humanity's relationship to God, and therefore as binding on all who wished to stand within that relationship. The significance of this will be explored below.

The traditions pertaining to the foundation and preservation of God's relatedness finally took shape many years after the return from exile in the form of the Pentateuch (the first five books of the Old Testament). The whole collection was subsumed under the name of the person who was believed to have played a key role in the history of God's relatedness with Israel, and to have first articulated God's will for his people in specific terms, namely Moses. The word 'Law', while appropriate to much that the books contain, is somewhat misleading as a description of the composite whole. The Hebrew term *Torah*, meaning guidance or instruction,[40] may therefore be preferred, though it is

[40] de Vaux, 354.

ambiguous in a different way: its meaning is sometimes extended to cover every recognized interpretation of God's will, in the early books or later, in written or oral form. But, with very few exceptions, nothing could be admitted as Torah which was thought to conflict with the Pentateuch, the acknowledged foundation of the Torah. Our present concern is therefore primarily with the Pentateuch.

It will be argued below on the basis of the polarity model that the very success of the enterprise which created the Pentateuch was the source of the crisis which was to come to a head with Jesus. First, we must consider the dramatic events which led from the creation of the Torah to its elevation as the ultimate form of revelation.

The exact date of its appearance in history as a complete text remains uncertain, but the Torah could not have been long in existence before a serious challenge to its authority arose within the Jewish community itself. In the violent confrontation which followed, the opponents of the Torah, aided by the ruling foreign power of the day, seemed for a time to be sure of success in their attempt to abolish it completely. Against all expectations, the tables were turned, the enemies of the Torah were defeated, and in the outcome it came instead to be acknowledged as the supreme revelation of God to which total commitment was due.

The anticipations here of another story of triumph out of disaster may not be entirely coincidental, but before proceeding we must consider the implications of these developments and their historical consequences in the light of the polarity model.

2. JUDAISM TILL THE MACCABEAN REBELLION
THE SUPREMACY OF FORMAL REVELATION

(a) The Persian period

In 538 BC the Persian king, Cyrus, defeated the Babylonians. In accordance with his general policy, he allowed those Jews who wished to do so to return to their native land (Ezra 1).

The hope of a glorious and triumphant home-coming, so powerfully expressed a few years earlier by the poet-prophet commonly known as second Isaiah (Isa. 40–55), was scarcely fulfilled. Only a relatively small contingent chose to return, and when it arrived it faced poverty and hostility from jealous neighbours.

These conditions delayed the rebuilding of the Temple for about twenty years. It was finally undertaken with the encouragement of the two prophets Haggai and Zechariah.

In this period we find a strengthening of the status and authority of the priesthood. Interest in the restoration of the monarchy appears to have been limited and short-lived. Quite apart from the likelihood of Persian opposition, there seems in fact to have been a positive desire in Judah to abandon the monarchy, which had failed so badly in the past, and to return to the direct rule of God. Whatever the reasons, the disappearance of the monarchy meant that an important check on the consolidation of divine authority was lost. The High Priest became, in effect, God's prime minister. The office was by sacred custom held for life, and restricted to members of the family supposedly descended from Aaron through the chief priest of Solomon's reign, Zadok. His lineage was accorded highest recognition by the priest-prophet of the exile, Ezekiel (Ezek. 40: 46).

It might be argued that the priests had earned their promotion. It seems clear that they took a lead during the exile in defining and defending the identity of the Jewish community in relation to its God; and a large proportion of the returning exiles were priests. However, it is important not to over-simplify or idealize their role, or to suppose that these developments went unchallenged. When nearly a hundred years later Nehemiah returned from the Persian court, with permission to secure Jerusalem's defences and serve as governor, he found much to provoke his anger: for example, failure to preserve the purity of the Temple; profanation of the sabbath; and mixed marriages with foreigners involving even the High Priest's grandson (Neh. 13).

Conditions were little different when Ezra arrived from Persia, probably about a generation later. He brought with him a 'Book of the Law' which had strong affinities with Deuteronomy, but his reading of it caused grief and amazement (Neh. 8: 9). This stemmed, it seems, not merely from the disclosure of widespread failures to keep the Law, but from apparent ignorance of what it required.

The authority Ezra exercised in reasserting the Law was reinforced by Persian support. It may even be the case that the comprehensive codification of laws for the Jewish community was officially encouraged by the Persians.[41] In that case, Persia can be credited not only with making it possible for the Jews to return from exile, but with enhancing the status of priests in Jerusalem, and even with adding a major impulse towards the creation of the Pentateuch and securing its recognition.

The date when the Pentateuch was completed remains a much-debated issue. The question is linked with another development during the Persian period, the widening of the breach between Samaritans and Jews. This seems to have been a lengthy and uneven process of drifting apart, rather than a sudden event.[42] Coggins argues that the Samaritans originated as a religious community of conservative Yahweh worshippers centred on the ancient town of Shechem; they should not be confused with the surrounding mixed population inhabiting the region of the old Northern Kingdom (called Samaria after its former capital);[43] nor should polemical references to the latter be misconstrued as evidence of early conflict with the Samaritans of Shechem.

The Shechem community was not alone in supposing that Yahweh could be served and worshipped outside Jerusalem. Documents from about this time, discovered at Elephantine in Southern Egypt, reveal not only the existence of a temple of Yahweh there, but that the Jews serving it did not know they were doing anything wrong.[44]

The Old Testament, by contrast, witnesses strongly to the belief that only Jerusalem, its Temple, and priests possessed the ritual purity—the holiness—necessary for the true worship of Yahweh. This view is associated with the returned exiles and particularly with Ezra. When we realize that the Old Testament was their book, or at least the book of those

[41] Hayes and Miller, 515.
[42] R. J. Coggins, *Samaritans and Jews* (Oxford, 1975), 63.
[43] Ibid. 9 ff.
[44] Ibid. 101 f.

who stood in that tradition, its emphasis on the claims of Jerusalem is not surprising, though still misleading.

The building of a Samaritan temple on Mount Gerizim, probably towards the end of the Persian period,[45] may not have been the direct cause of schism, as used to be supposed, but its existence could not help but be an affront to the Jerusalemite priesthood, the more they pressed their exclusive claims. The subsequent failure of the Samaritans to take sides with the Jews in the Maccabean crisis may help to explain the deep bitterness which persisted between them in later years, as witnessed to in the New Testament (cf. Luke 9: 51-5).

Despite this enmity, the Samaritans acknowledged (and still acknowledge) the Pentateuch as their only Bible. It must, then, almost certainly have been completed before the breach became irreconcilable. This means that at the time when the Pentateuch was being brought to completion the Jerusalem priesthood had not yet achieved a complete monopoly of the cult of Yahweh. Interestingly, there is surprisingly little support in the Pentateuch itself for the centralization of the cult in Jerusalem specifically. The recurrent references in Deuteronomy to 'the place which the Lord will chose as a dwelling for his Name' (Deut. 12: 11, 14: 24, etc.) are clearly open to more than one interpretation. This may help to explain why the Samaritan position could not easily be refuted; but in Jerusalem there could be no question about the allusion.

To appreciate the significance of the Pentateuch in Jewish history, we must recognize the importance not only of its content, but of its context. It was revered not only in Jerusalem, but in the context of other writings which explicitly exalted the status of Jerusalem. These other writings were in due course recognized by most Jews as part of the Torah, alongside the Pentateuch. They were never accepted in the Samaritan Torah.

That much of this material was being prepared when the status of Jerusalem was still being challenged may be significant. If one accepts that conflict tends to harden opposing positions, one would expect to find in the Jewish Torah an

[45] Ibid. 94 ff.

emphasis on, if not an exaggeration of, the claims of Jerusalem. We do, in the later writings especially, such as Chronicles. The implications would be far-reaching when the Torah came to be regarded as divine revelation valid for all time.

The immediate effect of the publication of the Pentateuch would be to enhance the status and authority of the priests, even if the exclusive rights of those in Jerusalem had yet to be established. Priests and Pentateuch reinforced each other. The former found their legitimation in the latter. It served the priests' interests to emphasize the Torah's sacred authority to secure their own. Yet their monopoly was still at risk. Others might look to the Torah directly for guidance, without relying on its priestly interpreters. This was already happening and, as we shall see, led to further divisions within Judaism. Ironically, they sprang up just when it seemed that the problem of the Samaritans had been successfully resolved by their exclusion.

(b) The Greek period

Jewish history entered a new and critical stage when Alexander the Great brought the Persian empire to an end with his victory at the battle of Issus in 333 BC. Alexander's triumph completely transformed the political order of the ancient world. His own reign was short; after his death his conquests were divided between his generals.

Egypt went to Ptolemy and Asia Minor to Seleucus. Palestine became a contested buffer region between the two kingdoms. After Ptolemy's initial seizure of it, it remained in the possession of the Ptolemaic kings for a hundred years, despite occasional Seleucid attempts to win possession. Finally, in 198 BC the Seleucid king, Antiochus III, succeeded in wresting the region from the Ptolemies, though the latter never abandoned their interest in it.

Recent research has made it clear that Judaea was not a stagnant backwater in this period, as used to be imagined. The Ptolemies managed their kingdom as a commercial enterprise and were as keen to maximize their profits in the Judaean sector as in any other.[46] The rural population there,

[46] Hengel, *Judaism*, 35, 39 ff.

as elsewhere, was liable to suffer exploitation as a result, but the upper classes had tempting opportunities to share in the exploitation and the profits to be made through expanding commercial activity.

Thus, Judaea was not isolated from the Greek world or immune to the impact of the Hellenistic civilization which had so suddenly overwhelmed the oriental world.[47] Jewish literature of the period provides considerable evidence of minds stimulated by Greek thought and culture and reacting to it, positively or negatively, consciously and often unconsciously. The influence of Hellenism was greatest in the city of Jerusalem. Here competing political, financial, and religious interests helped to generate a wide variety of attitudes and groupings, but out of these two main factions began to polarize. One side reacted against the pervasive influence of Hellenism with a conservative defence of traditional Jewish custom and, above all, of the sacred and definitive authority of the Torah. The other side was drawn with increasing enthusiasm towards the Hellenistic way of life, adopting Greek practices and dress[48] and regarding the Law of Moses as more or less irrelevant, or worse, as a tiresome obstacle to progress.

The transfer of Judaea to Seleucid rule made little difference in principle, since both the Ptolemaic and the Seleucid kingdoms were equally Hellenistic. However, the change was to have serious repercussions. The Seleucids ruled on more traditional Persian lines, allowing their subjects a greater measure of internal autonomy in a loose federal relationship.[49] This could serve to encourage a greater sense of national or city identity, and by the same token stimulate greater political interest and activity within the ruling classes. However, Judaea's position as a buffer State created dangerous conditions. It seems likely that there had long been different factions favouring the Ptolemies and the Seleucids and looking to each respectively for support. In pursuit of their internal interests, such factions risked becoming embroiled in great power politics, with the prospect

---

[47] Ibid. chaps. 2 and 3.
[48] 1 Macc. 1: 11–15; 2 Macc. 4: 12–15. See Hengel, *Judaism*, 72 ff.
[49] Ibid. 10.

of power and riches on the one hand, but equally with the danger of bringing dire punishment on themselves and their people if they backed the losing side.

In such circumstances, Judaea moved swiftly towards its greatest crisis since the exile. The details of the drama are too complex to be unravelled here, and can be followed elsewhere,[50] but the main actors can be identified.

In Egypt, the Ptolemaic kings were eager to recover Palestine and happy to encourage disaffection within its borders. In Syria, the Seleucid kings were anxious to discourage disaffection by force or persuasion, and to encourage their own supporters. However, the defeat of Antiochus III at Magnesia in 190 BC by the Romans, and the heavy burden of reparations which they imposed on him, left the Seleucids in serious financial straits. This led them to impose heavy taxation on their subjects, to welcome financial aid from any source, and even to try to secure it by robbing temples. (Antiochus III lost his life in such an attempt.)

The rural population of Judaea, therefore, soon had good economic grounds for hating their Seleucid rulers and those of their leaders who were siding with the oppressors. Though not subject to religious interference, let alone persecution, they could see that the aristocracy in Jerusalem, including many priests, were being drawn into the Hellenistic way of life and behaviour at the expense of strict observance of the Torah. In reaction to this, a group came into being whose origins are obscure, but which was to play a crucial role in the years to follow, namely the *Hasidim*. This Hebrew word means 'pious ones', and was applied to those who maintained the strictest observance of the Law. In due course some of them would even let themselves be massacred rather than fight on the sabbath (1 Macc. 2: 29–38).

In Jerusalem, by contrast, the majority of the people, it seems, were responding positively to the attractions of Hellenistic civilization, despite appeals in defence of the Torah by such learned conservatives as Ben Sira (the author of Ecclesiasticus in the Apocrypha, otherwise known as the

---

[50] Hayes and Miller, chap. x; D. S. Russell, *The Jews from Alexander to Herod* (The New Clarendon Bible, 5; Oxford, 1967).

Wisdom of Ben Sira), and even he reflects the influence of Hellenistic thought in his writings.[51] Against him were ranged the powerful lay family of Tobiah, and even members of the high-priestly family of Onias.

The Hellenists seemed sure of success soon after the accession of Antiochus IV in 175 BC. The king was short of funds and anxious for support. He readily accepted a bribe from Jason, a member of the high-priestly family, and appointed him High Priest in place of his brother, Onias III (thus flouting the law which ordained that the office should be held for life). Led by Jason, the Hellenists then embarked on their plans to transform Jerusalem into a Greek city.[52] But after three years Jason was outbid by Menelaus, who replaced him as High Priest. This set the stage for disaster. Not only was Menelaus appointed while his predecessor was still alive, but he was not even of high-priestly lineage. In consequence, the pro-Hellenist party was split down the middle.[53] On one side were moderates, who had been ready to welcome reform but who still remained loyal to the Torah in principle. On the other side were the extremists, who were indifferent to the Torah and happy to abandon it altogether if they could.

The failure of the broad pro-Hellenist consensus led the extremists to recognize that the Torah was the main obstacle to their success, and that, now that there was opposition in the city as well as in the country, they could not hope to remove it without force. The force they needed could only be provided by King Antiochus, and he might well be persuaded to give it to his committed supporters.

Traditional accounts of the events which followed have generally portrayed Antiochus IV Epiphanes as the blasphemous tyrant, intent on destroying Jewish religion and setting himself up as God. However, Hengel has persuasively argued that the initiative came from the Jewish Hellenists, led by the High Priest Menelaus himself,[54] and

[51] Hengel, *Judaism*, 147.
[52] Ibid. 278.
[53] Ibid. 280.
[54] Ibid. 288. (For a brief assessment of the debate, see Hayes and Miller, 562. Cf. 2 Macc. 13: 7–8.)

that Antiochus did little more than provide royal legitimation and military backing for the party in Jerusalem which was most obviously on his side. This is borne out among other things by the fact that the Samaritans escaped persecution, despite continuing to follow the religion of the Torah and observing customs, such as keeping the sabbath, which in Judaea were punishable by death.[55] Having lent his support, however, Antiochus was bound to treat opposition as rebellion.

Tension increased after the appointment of Menelaus. The Temple sanctuary was entered and robbed by Antiochus, perhaps to make up the payment Menelaus owed. Not long afterwards, the city was subjected to severe retribution in the wake of an unsuccessful attempt by Jason to recover control. Finally, a royal edict was issued in 167 BC (1 Macc. 1: 41), with the explicit aim of abolishing the religion of the Torah in Judaea. It required all Jews to sacrifice to Zeus Olympios, to give up circumcision and other sacred customs, and to eat prohibited meat, namely pork, on pain of death. Such demands struck at the heart of Jewish religion and betray remarkably detailed knowledge of it. Towards the end of 167 BC (15 Chislev, i.e. 6 December) the Temple was renamed after 'Zeus Olympios' (2 Macc. 6: 2), and the 'abomination of desolation' was erected in it[56] (probably an altar-stone set on the great altar).[57]

The royal edict triggered off rebellion. Mattathias, a country priest of Modein in the north-west of Judaea, refused to sacrifice and killed the royal officials.

The rebellion was led by his son Judas, nicknamed Maccabaeus, 'the Hammer', and was soon joined by the Hasidim. It met with unexpected success. Historically, it is possible to attribute this in part to Judas' military skills and his followers' dedication, but even more to the power-vacuum existing in the Middle East at the time. The Maccabeans (or Hasmonaeans, as they are also called after their family name) ultimately succeeded in recovering Jewish political independence at a time when Rome had already helped to

---

[55] Hengel, *Judaism*, 294.
[56] Dan. 12: 1; cf. Mark 13: 14.
[57] Hengel, *Judaism*, 295.

break the power of the Ptolemaic and Seleucid kingdoms but had not yet laid claim to their territories. It was not till the arrival of Pompey in 63 BC that the power vacuum was filled and Jewish independence ended.

For the Jews, however, their unexpected deliverance was a miracle and proof of God's rule. The cause for which they had fought, suffered torture and death, was the Torah. Its claim upon them was infinitely strengthened in consequence.

This conclusion holds good whether we agree with Hengel that the Maccabean rebellion was in effect a civil war,[58] or with the traditional view that it was provoked by an over-weening foreign tyrant. Either way, the threat in Judaea was directed explicitly and with extreme zeal against the Torah. The failure of the assault could only strengthen zeal for the Torah and elevate its authority beyond all question. Its claim upon the people of the covenant was binding and un-conditional, even unto death.

Thus, the polarization in Jerusalem between those anxious to preserve and those wishing to abolish the Torah was ended by the defeat of the latter party. The consequences were twofold. First, the possibility of further creative interaction between the ancient tradition of Israel and the new spirit of Hellenistic civilization was radically restricted, (in Judaea; the writings of Philo of Alexandria show that this interaction was not snuffed out completely in the Graeco-Roman world). Secondly, the supreme authority of the Torah was now established over all who counted themselves members of the Jewish community.[59] The only differences, and they could indeed be bitter differences, would arise on questions of interpreting and applying the Torah. Before turning to these, we shall digress from the historical survey and consider some of the theoretical implications of the elevation of the Torah in the aftermath of the Maccabean rebellion, when it became the absolute norm of revelation in the formal mode.

---

[58] Ibid. 290, 300.
[59] Ibid. 252.

3. THE LOGIC OF REVELATION IN THE FORM
OF THE TORAH

(a) Loss of the polar dialectic

The elevation of the Torah as the supreme revelatory authority, binding the whole Jewish community, was the most significant outcome of the Maccabean rebellion. But, as we have seen, the creation of the Torah did not lie in that period but in the years of exile and slow recovery after the return. Something more needs to be said about what it was that became absolute as revelation in the formal mode, and about the implications of this development.

The final formulation of the Pentateuch could be described as the product of the creative spirit of the prophets flowing through priestly channels. It bears witness to a stream of creative activity within the constraints of an acknowledged tradition. An adequate evaluation of it requires recognition of these two facets, the creative interaction of vitality and form.

Creative vitality is manifested in and through the Pentateuch in different ways. It was the prophets especially, as we have seen, who provided the underlying rationale for the enterprise which produced it. Further, it may be supposed that the ethical interest of the prophets and their profound insights concerning God strongly influenced the shaping of the final product.[60] Ancient traditions were not merely strung together; their presentation in the written texts shows evidence of creative minds at work. They imparted new interpretations to ancient sources in the light of later experience and of a new awareness of the character of the God who, the writers were still convinced, remained in relationship with his people despite everything. One has also to recognize that the sources thus employed were themselves originally the product of a living awareness of God's relatedness interacting with earlier tradition.

On the other hand, the very desire to bring together the

[60] See Clements, esp. chap. 4, where a close connection between the prophets and the Deuteronomic movement is claimed. Also Hayes and Miller, 485.

ancient traditions concerning the terms of God's relatedness, and the belief that these should still define Israel's relationship with God, reflect a priestly interest. The scope of creative freedom was thus severely constricted by the nature of the enterprise itself. Opinions may differ over the relative age of component parts of the Pentateuch[61] and the extent to which ancient traditions have been reshaped in transmission. What seems undeniable is that many of the traditions and cultic regulations incorporated in it long antedated the age of the great prophets. Whatever their creative insight when first formulated, they expressed interpretations of God's relatedness to the world which had taken shape in a world now long since vanished and which, it might be supposed, often fell far short of later insight. Yet, as part of the ancient and sacred corpus, they were included in the Pentateuch in their own right, whether subjected to reinterpretation or not.

More than this must be said. The very latest material, reflecting perhaps the creative genius of the final editor, became in the completed Pentateuch part of the formulated tradition[62]—a fixed component of revelation in the formal mode. There it would stand as a representation of God's relatedness conditioned not only by its own past, but by a present which itself immediately began to recede into the past.

Thus, while the Pentateuch witnesses to the polar dialectic of form and vitality, it represents at the same time the consolidation of tradition and the upgrading of revelation in the formal mode. Its completion, and the acknowledgement of it as the definitive statement of the terms of God's relatedness, created a radically new situation within the polar dialectic in two fundamental respects: first, there was a loss of balance through the overweighting of formal revelation; secondly, and as a consequence, the positive interplay of the polar dialectic itself was lost. This needs clarification.

For the sake of simplicity, we have associated the polarities of form and vitality within Judaism with the priestly and prophetic motifs (without denying that both could be, and

---

[61] See Jagersma, 2–8, for a useful summary of biblical and extra-biblical sources and their probable dates.

[62] Cf. Clements, 40, 57.

to some extent must be, the concern of any individual interpreter of revelation, whether called priest or prophet). Following that distinction, we find the priestly motif outweighing the prophetic both in the constitution of the Pentateuch and in the situation created by its constitution.

The priestly emphasis in the constitution of the Pentateuch results from the fact that it was put together out of ancient traditions, or material purporting to be ancient. Even if in fact it incorporates later material and some measure of prophetic interpretation, it remains on its own account orientated to the past. The acknowledged writings of the prophets and other later writings are excluded from it. This is perfectly understandable, in that the explicit concern of the creators of the Pentateuch was to establish the right terms of relationship with God. This led them to concentrate on the inauguration and content of the original covenant in which the community of Israel was constituted, and within which the prophets emerged at a later date. But the attempt to establish first principles in temporal terms resulted in a paradoxical reversal of emphasis. Historically, it was the later interpretation of tradition by the prophets—their reformulation of the terms of God's relationship springing from the depths of their own experience of God and offered to their generation—which had played such a crucial role in the development and indeed survival of Israel's religious life. But once the Pentateuch was composed—and what could be presented as earliest in time was considered as first in importance—then the prophets themselves and all other later interpreters of God's relationship to humankind were subordinated to the earlier tradition, or at least had to be accommodated to it.[63] Later creative insights were not allowed to displace earlier tradition, whatever its worth. Even if much in that tradition had been reshaped in the light of later insight, much had not; and once the Pentateuch came into being as the definitive formal expression of the terms of God's relatedness, binding for all time in the world, Jeremiah's hope for a new mode of relationship with God had

---

[63] Hengel, *Judaism*, 173, 'The canonical books of the "prophets" and the "writings" which were not part of the Pentateuch, and the "oral Torah", were in the last resort only indirectly authoritative as interpretation of the law given by Moses.'

to be relegated to all intents and purposes out of this world
(Jer. 31: 31–4).

Thus, the Pentateuch, incorporating ancient traditions
and orientated on the past, comes to be acknowledged as the
supreme source of revelatory authority. In some circles it
would be acknowledged as the exclusive source and hence
as synonymous with Torah. In others it would be acknowledged as the foundation of revelatory authority, the
basis of Torah, even if the writings of the prophets and other
later writings could be set alongside and incorporated in
Torah in a wider sense. The difference between the narrower
and wider definitions of Torah is important, and will be
examined below, but it does not fundamentally affect the
issue, namely, that once creative insights are recorded in
writing they become part of a fixed tradition receding into
the past. The greater the revelatory authority attributed to
the total tradition, the more dominant revelation in the formal mode becomes.

The living dialectic of form and vitality, which might have
been preserved in the conjunction of the Law (tradition) and
prophecy (continuing revelatory activity), is only witnessed
to as a past fact in the conjunction of the Law and the
prophets in a written revelatory deposit. That deposit itself
becomes a composite representation of revelation in the formal mode. Because it contains the priestly and the prophetic,
the ancient and the more recent, it becomes an immensely
rich interpretative resource, but at the same time it has a
negative effect on the continuing dialectic. This second effect
of the formulation of the Torah (which we may now regard
as comprising the Pentateuch and the prophets) must now
be examined.

It must be acknowledged, first, that the emphasis on formal revelation in Judaism, seen in the revelatory authority
attributed to the Torah, was not at the expense of subjective
revelation in the sense of a continuing deep awareness of
God's presence. Jews have often protested against the Christian representation, or rather misrepresentation, of Judaism
as 'dry and arid legalism', or as a religion of works-
righteousness. Happily, that protest has lately been reinforced by Christian scholars, among them in recent times

E. P. Sanders.[64] Although he deals with a later period than
the one with which we are immediately concerned, what
he has to say about the religion of the Torah establishes
possibilities which in principle hold good for both early and
late periods. In respect of Rabbinic Judaism, he has argued
persuasively and with a mass of evidence that the grace of
election[65] was fundamental in Jewish understanding; that
the covenant relationship required observance of God's laws
on man's part, not as a means of entering into relationship
with God but as a sign of belonging within such a relationship and of being willing to remain within it;[66] and that
self-righteousness was not therefore the inevitable con-
comitant of the belief that men should and could keep God's
laws. The motive for observing the Torah was love rather
than fear,[67] and gave rise to a sense of living in God's presence[68] far removed from ideas of God as remote and inaccessible. The Jews knew a personal God, and so within
Judaism knowledge about God stood side by side with a
knowing and being known in the immediacy of personal
experience.

All this can be acknowledged without reserve. The critique proposed here on the basis of the polarity model makes
a different point, which, it will be argued (Part V), is equally
applicable to Christianity in many of its manifestations and
to other formal religions as well as Judaism. The case is not
that the dimension of subjective revelation is totally lost, but
that the polar dialectic is broken. The loss of dialectical
interaction would at one and the same time result from overemphasizing revelation in the formal mode and also reinforce
that overemphasis. Once the terms of God's relatedness were
formulated in the Torah, they could not in principle be
reformulated under the continuing impact of God or the
world or both on experience. It remains true that there were
other later formal representations of God's relatedness that

[64] See above, p. 37 n. 1.
[65] Sanders, 85.
[66] Ibid. 93, 141, 420.
[67] Ibid. 120-2.
[68] Ibid. 221.

influenced the course of events in Judaism, but they were
subordinate to the dominating form of the Torah.[69]

It will be argued in due course that the dominance of form
over experience, and of the form of the Torah over other
representations of God's relatedness, was not reversed in the
later history of Judaism before or after the time of Jesus; and
that the recovery of the polar dialectic and the corresponding
shift in the balance of the poles of revelation are one of the
two distinguishing characteristics of the interpretation of
God's relatedness that emerged with and derives from Jesus.
(The other was the shift from the form of the Torah to the
form of Jesus as the content of knowledge about God.) Before we pursue these issues, it is necessary first to examine
more specifically the implications of the dominance of the
Torah in relation to the experience and account of God in
Judaism.

(b) *Limitations of formal revelation*

The questions before us now are both theoretical and practical; they concern the effects which the shift of emphasis
towards formal revelation had upon the experience and
understanding of God in the context of Judaism. Again,
many points to be made will have wider application, and
some repetition of general theoretical considerations may
be unavoidable, but the aim will be to keep to the specific
historical circumstances of Judaism before and at the time
of Jesus.

If a genuine sense of God's presence in the experience of
Jews faithful to the Torah is acknowledged,[70] as it is here, it
might appear that nothing more could or should be said. It
might be argued that there is in principle no way in which
the adequacy of such an inner experience can be tested and
no ground for doubting its validity.[71] If that were true, however, it would seem that a right relationship with God in the

[69] See above, n. 63. The same could be said of the Mishnah and Talmud (cf.
also Hengel, *Judaism*, 312).

[70] Sanders, 214.

[71] Cf. Macquarrie, 171, 'All I am saying is that one can commit oneself within
one's own community of faith and in terms of the symbols established in that
community, and yet believe that for a person in other circumstances, the same God
reveals himself in another community and under different symbols, and that there

spirit was possible regardless of any accompanying representation of it.

Grounds for questioning both this premise and the conclusion have been put forward in Part I. While one would have to approach the question of another person's inner experience with great respect and reserve, it is not necessarily completely private and incommunicable. The question raised previously was whether pure experience is ever possible, or whether experience must always come with interpretation. Certainly no significant experience can occur without a significance-imparting interpretation, even if the initial interpretation is open to question and may in due course be modified or replaced. Where the interpreted experience serves as a motive for action, the character of the interpretation becomes a matter of importance for more than the individual concerned. The interaction between experience, interpretation, and action is well illustrated by a friend who, experiencing certain inner tensions, wondered whether he had indigestion or was in love. Much depended on the answer he gave.[72]

On this argument, there cannot be an experience of God that does not call upon an already existing interpretation of God,[73] however much that interpretation may subsequently be revised under the impact of the experience. But that dynamic interaction and movement is precluded where an unquestionable authority is attributed to an existing interpretative resource. Thus, in the first place, an established and unchangeable interpretation gives any immediate experience of God that may occur a specific quality and character. In the second place, as was previously argued, it excludes the dynamic interaction of other interpretative possibilities which might be available in the immediate circumstances of a given community, or within some other community in another cultural setting, or even within the same community at different times or places in a changing world. In other words, the possibility of dialogue is excluded. Moreover, if an account of God is derived, as it must

may be *nothing defective or inadequate* about that person's commerce with God' (my emphasis).

[72] He is still happily married.

[73] See above, p. 48.

be, from conceptual resources of a given age and place, then the further removed it is from that age and place, the less it will correspond to the forms of actual life and experience. It will increasingly appear as an unrelated, alien phenomenon, with less and less capacity to relate meaningfully or impart meaning to the world that now is. Accordingly, the God revealed in this historically conditioned but unchangeable form will appear more and more to relate only to the world as it was, or might be, and not as it is; it will become harder and harder to relate an experience of God conditioned in such a way to the immediate experience of living in the changed and changing world of today.

A gulf opens up between God and the world. It may be bridged to some extent, and various ways in which this was attempted within Judaism will be considered below (chapter 4), but the paradox remains. The defence of a given revelatory form, which itself springs out of an encounter with God in the world, drives towards the exclusion of God from the world as it is, or at least to the restriction of his supposed presence to the narrowest confines of private experience in isolated groups.

If the influence of interpretation on experience and on practice is accepted, the adequacy of interpretation becomes an important issue, and here in particular the adequacy of the Torah as an interpretation of God and his relationship to humanity has to be considered.

The starting-point is the principle already enunciated, that any formal representation of God's relatedness is always the product of experience mediated through human consciousness and interpretative categories, and therefore a product of a given time and place.

This applies to all books acknowledged to be revelatory (i.e. to all sacred scriptures), and hence must apply to the Torah. Even if as a composite work its formulation was extended in time and its content derived from many places, nevertheless, in its totality it is still limited in this way. However adequate the interpretative categories and however well understood and well expressed God's relationship to humankind may be at a given moment, the terms in which it is expressed—that is, the total delineation of it and of all

its practical implications—cannot properly remain unchanged in a changing world.

To give some examples, the prevailing view of God might
certainly affect the way in which foreigners, slaves, or women
were to be treated; but it can hardly be disputed that patterns
of social behaviour in such instances are conditioned by very
many different factors. These in turn influence the understanding of what is right within a relationship with God.
Hence, much of what is found in the Torah represents to
the understanding of a later age not so much a completely
false, but often a very inadequate, understanding of God's
relationship and its practical implications. Such inadequacy
is not restricted to the earliest strata. The profound and the
appalling may be in closest proximity. To take an example
from the Psalms, religious poetry of the highest order is
combined in Psalm 137 with the terrible sentiment in the
last lines, 'Happy is he who shall seize your children, and
dash them against the rock.' Much of the richness of the Old
Testament lies in the diversity of human interpreting minds
represented there; but in its totality in written form it remains a human product, incorporating both insight and distorted vision. Its practical demands might have given
positive expression to the understanding of God at a particular time, but at other times and places might seem arbitrary, or to be in conflict with new understanding of God's
relatedness and the implications of such a new insight.[74]

Nothing that has been said need detract from the value of
the Torah as a witness to God's relatedness and as a resource
of lasting value for interpreting it. But where contingent
human understanding is written into a revelatory deposit
and treated as binding for all time, the effect, as we have
already seen, is to absolutize it by attributing to God what
is necessarily an imperfect, and may be a very imperfect,
understanding of the right ordering of the relationship between human beings and God, and with each other. What is
denied here is not that the Torah points to the real possibility
of entering into a relationship with God, but the claim that
it provides the binding and enduring terms for constituting

---

[74] For example, the treatment of a stubborn and rebellious son: Deut. 21: 18–
21; cf. Luke 15: 20.

and remaining in this relationship. The effect of making such a claim on behalf of a witness to God which is in itself necessarily limited and imperfect must now be considered.

(c) Penalties of overemphasis

When the Torah or any holy book is treated as final and 'perfect', as sharing eternity with God unconditioned by evolutionary existence, the effect is to affirm the equal and supreme value of the whole of its content, without the possibility of discrimination, let alone correction. In other words, in the extreme case, the good and the bad, the positive and the negative, the shallow and the deep, are accorded equally binding authority. In this section we shall critically examine the logical implications of the extreme case, leaving the various ways in which it was qualified in practice within Judaism, not least by the development of oral Torah, for consideration in chapter 4 below.

The implications of attributing absolute revelatory authority to the Torah will be explored here in terms of the fourfold effect: upon the person submitting to that claim—the human actor; upon his actions; upon those affected by them—both God and other people.

First we may consider the effect on the actor, which means the person, not in the immediacy of experience as already discussed, but as confronted by the challenge to act. Here we are close to the motivation that lay behind the production and recognition of the Torah—the desire to discover and to conform to God's will, and so to be in right relationship with him. The whole enterprise hinges on the question of holiness. God is holy, and it is therefore necessary to be holy and to eschew what is unholy in order to approach and be with God.[75] Thus, the holiness of God required a corresponding holiness in his people. Even if the possibility of a relationship with God was due to God's initiative, it was incumbent on his people to be holy if they were to remain within that relationship. The fundamental question was what constituted holiness. The Torah offered the answer and became the measure of holiness in theory and practice. It defined the conditions of holiness. It was by the same

[75] Lev. 11: 44, 'Be ye holy; for I am holy' (RV); cf. 1 Pet. 1: 16.

token the yardstick by which the professed desire to be in right relationship with God could be tested.[76] Willing acceptance of the Torah signified that desire, to which God would respond even if intentions were not fully realized in practice.[77] But where they were, holiness would be actualized, and it was incumbent on those who willed it to actualize it. In this role the Torah became not only the exclusive interpretative resource of experience, but also of right actions. Whether what was commanded was understood or not, or had recognizably beneficial effects or not, was in the last resort immaterial. Obedience was what mattered.

Despite the very positive religious motivation behind such an attitude, it can be seen to have negative consequences. Just as an exclusive interpretative resource limits the possibilities of illuminating any immediate experience of God from other sources, in the same way the possibilities of conduct and action are equally constricted. It is the interplay of interpretation and experience, with interpretation both shaping and being reshaped by experience, that confers on a person the freedom to respond to the unique configurations of each particular historical situation. Without this freedom, responsibility is diminished. Instead, every practical response will be subject to the givenness of an existing, regulative interpretation and directive. The individual's responsibility will be reduced to the simple choice of whether to act or not to act in accordance with the given forms, i.e. the given rule; and if the sanctions, religious or social, which are applied to this decision are heavy, there may be little choice left.

The narrowing down of the actor's responsibility has further implications (to repeat, I am here exploring the logical implications of the extreme case, and not describing Judaism as it was in practice at any time). The disquiet evoked by the defence 'I was acting under orders' illustrates the point to be made, even if it is supposedly God's orders with which we are concerned. When a person acts in order to conform to a particular rule because conformity to it signifies

[76] See above, nn. 66 and 67.
[77] Sanders, 125, 147.

acknowledgement of God's sovereignty, and not in response to the ethical imperative of a specific situation, then the dignity of both human beings and the world is jeopardized. This is so because in this case the creative freedom of persons as truly responsible beings living within the dynamic conditions of an evolutionary world is denied, and consequently the true value and purpose of life in that world is put in question. To say this is not to make light of human responsibility before God; nor is it to imply that human responsibility is wholly lacking in the position criticized. It is there in so far as human freedom to acknowledge or not to acknowledge God is recognized, but it is affirmed in this way at the expense of a person's responsibility to his fellow human beings and his world. That God's sovereignty should be acknowledged in every action is not in question; what is at issue is *how* it is most truly to be acknowledged.

Consideration of the negative effect on the actor of a dominating formal representation of God's relatedness brings us immediately to the closely related question of its effect on the actions. Not only is full human responsibility repressed, but actions take on a new meaning, or in a sense lose all meaning but one. The meaning is reduced to the acknowledgement of God's Lordship. But while that is supremely important, it is not enough—if the God acknowledged is to be thought of not merely as a sovereign king, but as intimately concerned for the world and for human beings in all the complexity of life and relationships. It would make no sense for such a God to impose conditions on human beings which in themselves made no sense to them or had destructive consequences, not just for individuals but within the total setting of human relationships. A general account of how this can happen in relation to a dominant formal revelation has already been presented, but two specific effects must be identified here.

In the first place, it has been shown that when the practical implications of God's relatedness are spelt out in history, they are unavoidably historically conditioned. Any 'rules' will therefore reflect and relate to patterns of social behaviour at a given time, and quite possibly serve a useful purpose at that time. From the moment they are reckoned to have binding authority, they will continue to exercise as great or even greater constraint as time passes and in very different worlds, whether they have been illuminated by later insight or not, and whatever the practical consequences of conforming to such rules might be in very different circumstances. The greatest danger perhaps is the imposition of primitive patterns of social behaviour and an undeveloped understanding of human relationships on later generations. Such attitudes, and the actions springing from them, would inhibit the emergence of a deeper awareness of the possibilities of human nature, or of human relationships. Worse still, they would come into conflict with such developments when they occurred, when those in relationship with God should rather be leading the way. The example of attitudes to foreigners, slavery, and women may be mentioned again here.

Secondly, if an action is performed to signify allegiance to God, and to preserve a relationship with him, then, whatever its apparently beneficial consequences, its moral character is, to say the least, transformed. An act of charity motivated by the actor's concern for his own salvation, or even by piety towards God, demeans the humanity of the person supposedly benefited by the act, by making him or her a means to another end (it is this that gives 'do-gooders' a bad name). Such an act cannot serve to build up a mutual human relationship, which an act performed out of immediate concern for another person is able to do.

We have been considering the situation in which a definition of holiness is proposed which is at best approximate and at worst misleading, but acceptance of which is put forward as the necessary condition for entry into and for remaining within a right relationship with God. There need be no doubt that those who accepted these conditions were able to experience and enjoy a sense of God's presence. But it need not be supposed that observance of such conditions alone secured this, or that only observance of such conditions could secure this, or that what was secured, or rather given— the sense of God's presence—was or is a fixed quantity, either present or absent, and not open to being deepened or diminished, or even transformed.

Thus far we have considered the negative effects of a binding formal revelation on the actor, his actions, and those affected by them. The fourth negative effect, then, concerns the loss caused to God, and the further consequential loss to human beings.

It can be seen in theory that if the terms for entering into a relationship with God are misrepresented, those who enter into such a relationship will in their devotion be committed to things that may be inessential to or even positively in conflict with such a relationship. Alternatively, if the conditions seem unacceptable or impossible, the desire for such a relationship will be frustrated and the pursuit of it will seem pointless. Ironically, those who love God, by accepting or imposing conditions that are not his, may deprive God of those whom he loves. Further, if the lines defining the possibility of relationship between humankind and God are wrongly drawn, and have implications for human relationships, then the desire for a right relationship with God will result in a wrong relationship with one's fellow human beings. If the condition for inclusion within and enjoyment of God's presence was exclusion from the presence of other human beings, it might have to be accepted for the sake of a higher good; but if such a condition was not necessary, and even contrary to God's will, observance of it would not serve God or man.

The final question here is whether these theoretical grounds for criticism do in fact apply to the Torah. A prima-facie case is already established, in so far as the claim that it represents God's will perfectly cannot, on the premisses assumed here, be accepted. More specifically, the issue may be brought into focus by examining the particular idea of holiness that the Torah represents. We have argued that holiness relates both to what God is and what he requires, and that if that which constitutes holiness is wrongly conceived, then the conditions for achieving it will be wrongly conceived. The general grounds for suggesting that an inadequate conception of holiness is to be found in the Torah have already been presented, namely, that it is derived from understandings of God's relatedness drawn from different ages and of different worth.

We may identify here once again the priestly and prophetic motifs. Together, they create a concept of holiness embracing both ritual and moral elements, though the logic of the former is not the same as that of the latter. The physical character of ritual purity requires a physical correlate, in practice, physical separation, the avoidance of the polluting source, whether it be blood or dead bodies, sexual activity, foreigners, or whatever. On the other hand, moral judgement implies moral discrimination, the avoidance of immoral attitudes or acts, rather than physical separation from persons acting immorally. Where the two logical strands of these models of holiness are intertwined, and the logic of one is applied to the other, a new model of holiness emerges.

It is often remarked that the Old Testament witnesses to the spiritualization of ceremonial rites;[78] so that, for example, sacrifice is reinterpreted in terms of righteous living, and impurity or defilement is interpreted in terms of moral failure. This is commonly and rightly seen as evidence of spiritual advance. Yet there is a risk of a reverse flow, resulting in the transposition of moral into ritual terms, so that immoral persons are conceived of as ritually unclean.[79] It then follows that they must be physically avoided by the 'holy' to avoid contamination, while those who are 'contaminated' are reckoned to be excluded from the realm of the holy, which is the community of the holy.[80]

Where emphasis on ritual holiness is greatest, a sense of moral holiness may be least, though this need not be so. The moral seriousness of those who for the sake of holiness

[78] F. M. Young, *Sacrifice and the Death of Christ* (London, 1975), 32–7.

[79] E. Schürer, *The History of the Jewish People in the Age of Jesus Christ*, vol. ii, rev. and ed. G. Vermes, F. Millar, and M. Black (Edinburgh, 1979), 396, '. . . a separation from uncleanness is always a simultaneous separation from unclean persons. The first without the second—in the Levitical concept of purity—is not possible, since impurity adheres to persons.'

[80] G. Theissen, *The First Followers of Jesus* (London, 1978), 92, 'The identity of Israel was grounded in the law; the more seriously it took the law, the greater had to be its concern over its own failure and the loss of identity which followed from that. It turned into anxiety about defilement, which was conceived of in materialistic terms.' He quotes Josephus (*Jewish War*, ii. 488) concerning Jews living in their own districts in Alexandria 'the better to be able to preserve the purity of their way of life, uncontaminated with aliens'. Theissen's analysis of the intensification of norms (pp. 80–7) is highly relevant to the issues under discussion here, setting them within a sociological perspective.

separate themselves from uncleanness need not be in doubt. But in such circumstances their moral earnestness, however wide-reaching in theory, is circumscribed in practice by being restricted to those within the circle of holiness.[81] Holiness expressed in moral concern and compassion,[82] even for all humankind, cannot be exercised outside the circle, lest it be contaminated by unholiness, conceived in quasi-physical terms. The question is whether holiness is here rightly conceived.

The logic of ritual holiness is physical exclusiveness. Thus, in the first place, foreigners who stand outside the covenant relationship and its constituting symbol, the Torah, are *ipso facto* outside the circle of holiness. In the second place, native-born Jews who do not fulfil the Law are in grave risk of exclusion. Though good intention to keep the Law could to a large extent compensate for failure to do so, opinion varied as to what the limiting point might be.[83] All agreed that the Torah determined what constituted holiness, and that holiness was constituted in terms that entailed exclusiveness. It also defined the consequences for those who fell outside the circle of holiness. These consequences were also derived from the more or less ancient understanding of God's relatedness found in the Torah. As such they too are open to reconsideration as to their adequacy and appropriateness, but this very large subject (i.e. ideas about hell) cannot be pursued here.

Whether the account of holiness derived from the Torah is true or not—that is, whether it corresponds as closely as possible to the requirements of God in his relatedness to humankind or not—is ultimately incapable of proof one way or the other. The argument presented here attempts to show why the assumption that it does so correspond cannot easily be accepted without question, and to demonstrate that the

---

[81] Ibid. 81, with reference to the Essenes, '. . . these intensifications [of norms] were related primarily to fellow members of the community. Aggression against other members was strictly forbidden . . . However, there was an injunction to hate all men outside the community (1 QS 1. 10; 9. 21 ff.).'

[82] Hengel, *Judaism*, 161, quotes the motto ascribed to Simon the Just (Mishnah Aboth, 1. 2), 'The world stands on three things: on the Torah and on the (temple) cult and on works of love.'

[83] See Sanders for an account of the different answers to this question within Judaism.

interpretation of holiness represented by the Torah is not the only possible interpretation; and further, that in its isolation from the polar dialetic, and in its exclusive binding character, it conflicts with the concept of God as the personal ground of the totality of evolutionary existence.

4. Judaism under the Torah
Formal Revelation Qualified

INTRODUCTION

THE last section of chapter 3 explored some of the theoretical and general implications of placing such great emphasis on formal revelation, specifically the Torah, as to disrupt the polar dialectic. In theory, according to this argument it might seem that a creative dialectical interaction between the Torah as given, and the experience of God in the world, was no longer possible. But, as argued in Part I, continuing change in an evolutionary world compels adaptation even of that which is supposed to be the perfect and immutable revelation and representation of God. Formal revelation cannot stand immune from the conditions imposed by the polar dialectic. It must be received for its authority to be perpetuated, and, in being received, it must yield in some measure at least to the operation of the subjective polarity.

Appropriation involves interpretation, whether admitted or not, and interpretation is conditioned by various factors. A given sentence or single word in the original may be firmly upheld, without the realization that its meaning has shifted within the dynamic of language development. Ambiguities and obscurities of expression will also call for interpretation, and the subtle influence of personality or of changed cultural conditions will bear on the result, with regard to both meanings preferred and where the emphasis is placed. Such factors as these alone can give rise to wide divergences of understanding and expression between different groups that acknowledge a single revelatory form, and between such groups and their forebears in time.

Only to a limited extent can uniformity of interpretation be maintained by entrusting the authority to interpret to one or a few privileged individuals. They cannot ever completely override the act of personal appropriation by members of their community. Historically, communities acknowledging a given formal revelation have rarely seemed able to expand or to establish themselves in different places without at some point diverging over the rights of interpretative responsibility, and in consequence dividing into subgroups.

On these grounds alone, the emergence of diversity within the overall community constituted by recognition of the revelatory authority of the Torah, should occasion no surprise, especially since this community from very early days was not only differentiated internally, economically, and socially, but was scattered geographically and lived through cultural and political changes of worldwide significance.

Despite the hidden operation of the polar dialectic, the attempt may nevertheless be made to keep the subjective qualification of formal revelation to a minimum. Alternatively, its claim to absolute revelatory authority may be qualified by intention. However, the mere fact of qualification in some way or other by no means necessarily serves to restore the true creative balance of the central polar dialectic of form and vitality. It may only demonstrate an awareness of its continuing operation, without its distortions being overcome.

Qualification by adaptation may occur in a variety of ways. It happens when holy scripture is reinterpreted in changed circumstances. However, there is an important distinction to be made. On the one hand, there may be adaptations of formal revelation which remain effectively under the constraint of the original form (the controlling authority of holy scripture is upheld in this case). On the other hand, there may be adaptations or reinterpretations which, in reality and whatever protestations are made, become alternatives to the original and compete with it. Thus, a new formal revelation may more or less openly supersede an old one, but in neither case is the central polar dialectic recovered. In the former case, the dominance of the original formal revelation remains and may even be reinforced; in the latter case, while its authority may still be acknowledged theoretically, in practice a distinct formal revelation is accepted alongside it, which effectively stands over against it.[1]

[1] For example, the Bible used by Jehovah's Witnesses.

Where two formal revelations emerge in competition, dialectical interaction between them cannot be admitted, without their exclusive claims to validity being undermined. In consequence, the tension between the two forms generates conflict which will only be resolved when one or other is deprived of its revelatory status, that is, when one is accepted as corresponding to the truth and the other is dismissed as erroneous or at best incomplete. The true dialectic can return only when formal revelation as such, that is, any revelation in the mode of form, is seen as the complement of the immediacy of God's relatedness in experience—shaping experience and being reshaped by it. When the validity of creative experience is acknowledged as standing between two distinct forms, the apparent conflict between them may be open to resolution. The two apparently fixed and logically mutually exclusive representations of truth may be seen to relate within the larger totality of the revelatory dynamic.

Within this simplified theoretical construct, variations and permutations of every kind are possible. Many such are to be found within Judaism before Jesus.[2] These range from the narrow restriction of revelatory authority to the form of the Pentateuch alone to a speculative freedom in apocalyptic that verges on the anarchic. There are also to be found, though almost unnoticed in many commentaries and history-books, cases of undisguised reliance on the immediacy of God's presence, which, in conjunction with the Torah, might seem to have offered a basis for the recovery of the polar dialectic, and perhaps did.

Throughout this inquiry, a crucial underlying issue will continue to be the question of holiness. How a right relationship with God is to be defined, what the community related to God is meant to become, and of whom it consists, are all questions whose answers hinge on the understanding of holiness. Different solutions will emerge in the various movements to be considered. The final critical questions will therefore be: first, whether the ways in which formal revelation was qualified within Judaism, or in any of the movements within it, were such as to demonstrate the recovery and continuity of the polar dialectic of God-relatedness; and secondly, whether the account of God's

[2] See J. Bowker, *The Targums and Rabbinic Literature* (Cambridge, 1969), 8.

relatedness, and the conditions for human beings to relate
to him (that is, the interpretation of holiness, as defined by
or through the Torah), does justice to the God to whose
relatedness the Torah and the movements governed by it
constantly bear witness.

The survey offered here of the various attitudes towards,
and ways of using, the Torah will be far from complete; but
some account of the main differences is necessary to complete the investigation into Judaism in terms of the polarity
model as the context for interpreting the significance of Jesus
and the distinctiveness of Christianity.

In the following sections, we shall examine some of the
most significant ways in which the binding revelatory authority of the Torah was qualified in practice in the various
movements within Palestinian Judaism. The even greater
diversity to be found among the Jews dispersed over the
world outside Palestine would further illustrate the scope for
diversity in relation to formal revelation, but apart from
being too large an issue to pursue, this would be less directly
relevant to the background of Jesus' own life. In the final
section of this chapter, mention will be made of some few
but significant examples of resistance to the Torah's binding
authority, which was made possible by attaching greater
weight to subjective revelation.

1. THE SADDUCEES AND THE QUMRAN COMMUNITY

(a) Sadducees

We begin with those who tried to keep qualification of the
Torah's revelatory authority to a minimum.

'Sadducee' was the name given to the party of the priestly
aristocracy and the rich which was centred on the Temple
in Jerusalem. In Jesus' day it still exercised considerable
political power within the limits set by the Roman authorities, through the Jewish council or Sanhedrin.[3]

The origin of the term 'Sadducee' is uncertain; it may well

---

[3] See Schürer, 200–26.

have been derived from Zadok (see above, p. 63).[4] However, the Sadducees emerged as a distinct group combining priestly and non-priestly functions only after the Maccabean rebellion. They probably stemmed from the moderate Hellenists who had opposed Menelaus and supported the Maccabees, in the cause of political independence as much as for religious reasons. Certainly they tied their fortunes to the Hasmonaean dynasty. Their involvement in power politics opened them again to Hellenistic cultural influences and impeded rigorous obedience to the Law, to the disgust of its more passionate advocates. At the same time, in contrast to their critics, the Sadducees maintained a more conservative attitude towards the Torah. Like the Samaritans, they attributed canonical authority to the Pentateuch alone, and rejected the developing tradition of interpretation, or 'oral Torah'. It is unlikely that they also rejected the prophets and other writings, though they probably regarded these as less authoritative. Yet even they had to settle points of dispute and appear to have recorded and deposited in the Temple a book of decisions.[5] Their conservatism is not perhaps very surprising, if they are identified as heirs to the group within Judaism that produced the Pentateuch. Their religious and social status and economic rights were specifically guaranteed by it,[6] and they thus had little cause for questioning its authority or for looking with favour on the claims of others to represent God's rule.

Still less would the Sadducees welcome the idea that God's rule could be established only after the destruction of the present world order. In rejecting any ideas which could not be substantiated in the Pentateuch, they rejected belief in resurrection. Hence they could see that they had everything to lose and nothing to gain in a clash with a major foreign power, especially Rome (cf. John 11: 48–50). So it transpired. Their disappearance from history after the fall of Jerusalem may not be open to a single explanation,[7] but the fall of the city itself was fatal to their political existence.

---

[4] G. R. Driver, *The Judaean Scrolls* (Oxford, 1965), 76–8; Schürer, 404–14. But cf. Russell, 155–9.

[5] Bowker, *Targums*, 42 n. 1.

[6] Theissen, 44.

[7] W. D. Davies, *The Setting of the Sermon on the Mount* (Cambridge, 1964), 259.

Their failure to survive as a religious body may be attributed largely to the fact that their conservative and literalistic attitude had prevented them from developing the kind of religion that could be viable outside the localized Temple structure and the fixed sacrificial system. In terms of the polarity model, they had no place for creativity or the polar dialectic. Change could only mean destruction.

Before disaster struck, the fact that the Sadducees included in their ranks the High Priests, who were in charge of the Temple and who alone had access to its sanctuary, might seem to have guaranteed their position as guardians of the nation's holiness; but this was by no means the case. Such a claim could be disputed, either because the priesthood in Jerusalem was judged to have forfeited its holiness in practice, or because an alternative principle of holiness was discovered, quite apart from the priesthood.

The first occasion for questioning the legitimacy of the High Priest arose, as we have seen, with the appointments of Jason and Menelaus. The success of the Maccabees in restoring the Temple and the Torah might seem to have remedied the situation; but this was not so. The office of High Priest remained too important politically to be ignored by the politically active. Antiochus IV had conferred it on his nominees; a descendant of Judas Maccabaeus, Jonathan, though not of Zadokite lineage, claimed it for himself in 152 BC. It may well have been in protest against this that some of the Hasidim abandoned Jerusalem, its Temple, priesthood, and cult, and withdrew to Qumran by the shores of the Dead Sea to establish a holy priesthood and holy community there, until the propitious time when they could be restored in Jerusalem.

(b) Qumran

The origin of the community at Qumran has been the subject of considerable controversy since the discovery of the Dead Sea scrolls in 1947. However, it is now widely agreed that it was associated with the Essenes,[8] a Jewish sect already

[8] G. Vermes, *The Dead Sea Scrolls* (London, 1977), 116-30; Schürer, 555-90. For a contrary view, see Driver.

known from other sources[9] and certainly not restricted to
Qumran. (The question of the connection between Qumran
and other Essenes need not detain us.) The name probably
comes from the Greek plural form *Essenoi*, which corresponds to the Aramaic plural *hasen*[10], which in turn corresponds to the Hebrew plural *Hasidim* (the 'pious ones'; see
above, p. 79). That the Qumran community was established
by one branch of the Hasidim after Jonathan's assumption
of the High Priesthood seems highly probable.[11]

However, between the pious Hasidim, who rallied to Judas
Maccabaeus, and the pious Essenes of Qumran stands the
enigmatic figure of the Teacher of Righteousness, who set
his own individual and remarkable stamp on the community
he led into the desert.

It is likely that he had been in Jerusalem in 175 BC and
witnessed the attempt to create a Greek city and overthrow
the Torah.[12] This would have been seen by the faithful not
merely as a challenge to tradition, but as defiance of God.
For those who saw themselves as heirs of the great prophets,
such apostasy on the part of fellow Jews was unprecedented
wickedness, and would inevitably incur the wrathful ven-
geance of God.

A sense of standing on the threshold of final judgement—
the end-time—is witnessed to in the literature that arose
during and after the Maccabean rebellion. The most notable
example of this kind of literature in the Old Testament is
the book of Daniel, which can be plausibly associated with
the early Hasidim. It seems unlikely, in the earlier period at
least, that a complete end of history or of the physical universe as such was envisaged. Rather, the worldly rule of
God's enemies would be ended by God's final intervention;
his righteous rule would be established on earth, and the
faithful would be vindicated and share in God's rule. In

[9] Philo, *Quod omnis probus*, 12 (75)-13 (91), *Hypothetica*, 11; Josephus, *Ant.*
xviii. 18-22, *Wars*, 11. ii. 119-61 (see n. 69 below); Pliny the Elder, *Natural History*,
v. 15/73. For further references and analysis, see Schürer 562-74; also Vermes,
Scrolls, 125-30.
[10] So Hengel, *Judaism*, 175. In Schürer it is suggested that the word is derived
from an Aramaic root meaning 'healers' (p. 559).
[11] Hengel, *Judaism*, 175.
[12] Ibid. 224.

either case, an end of things as they are is anticipated. (The term eschatology is commonly used where attention is turned to the end-time (Gk. *eschaton*) or last things, however portrayed.)

Another distinctive feature of much of the literature of this period is its claim to reveal the hidden purpose of God. Hence the term *apocalyptic* is used, which means 'uncovering' or 'revelation'. Apocalyptic writers resorted to cryptic and highly symbolic language to point to the working of God in the events which seemed, on the surface, to prove his absence or failure. Their message of hope was that the time of suffering would soon end with God's final triumphant intervention—to the dismay of his enemies and the joy of the faithful. Thus, the latter are called to repentance for their own sin, and to unconditional obedience to the laws of God (like the hero, Daniel), come what may.

What came to the faithful was cruel repression, the desecration of the holy Temple, bitter fighting, and then the miraculous deliverance and the rededication of the Temple in 164 BC by Judas Maccabaeus (see above, pp. 80 ff.). At this point the Hasidim, their religious objectives achieved, withdrew from the fighting. It had begun to take on a more political character as a war for national independence.

Thereafter, for the Hasidim, the early triumph of the Maccabees began to turn sour. The people as a whole, and their leaders especially, had failed to repent and submit themselves to the Torah wholeheartedly. The age of national apostasy was, after all, not yet over.

Jonathan's usurpation of the High Priesthood can then be seen as the last straw, which provoked the exodus[13] from Jerusalem into the desert to create a holy community until the expected time of fulfilment finally arrived. Although the community's literature speaks of returning to the covenant of Moses,[14] it speaks also of God making a new covenant.[15] This sense of new identity was reinforced by the adoption of a different calendar, so that the great feasts were not even celebrated on the same days as in Jerusalem.

[13] Davies, 115 f.
[14] Community Rule I, V; see G. Vermes, *The Dead Sea Scrolls in English* (Harmondsworth, 1975), 72.
[15] Damascus Rule, VI (ibid. 103); see Schürer, 579 f.; Vermes, *Scrolls*, 165.

Within the community we find, then, a great emphasis on
the Torah. Far from seeking to accommodate the commandments to the exigencies of everyday life or practical
politics, strict observance was rigorously maintained. It
would seem that the strictest rules of purity could be kept
only in a desert monastery far away from the ordinary world,
(though evidence of Essenes living away from Qumran must
be noted).[16]

A distinctive characteristic of the community was its emphasis on both ritual and moral (spiritual) purity. The problem posed by the covenanters' self-exclusion from the
Temple and its cleansing sacrificial rites was met, on the one
hand, by the introduction of numerous rites of purification
by water, and, on the other, by the teaching that a holy and
righteous way of life atoned for sin.[17]

Recognition of the importance of the priesthood in principle was in no way diminished. Priests of impeccable pedi-
gree were given first place in the community.[18] This may
suggest that the Teacher of Righteousness himself belonged
to the Zadokite priestly nobility.

However, it is clear that the priestly tradition was no more
than one strand in the make-up of the Qumran community.
Another basic strand was, it seems, the tradition of popular
piety in direct descent, perhaps, from the classical prophets;
this may have been more typical of the Hasidim before the
Teacher of Righteousness emerged as leader.

Three characteristics of Qumran may be related to the
prophetic tradition. First, there is the emphasis on the individuals and their responsibility before God. This we may
suppose played a part in the extension of the laws of holiness
in the Torah from the priests in the cult to the laity in
general. Secondly, we can note the admission, even within
the context of total commitment to the Torah, of inspiration
and possibilities of new revelation (within limits to be considered below). Thirdly, the sense of heightened eschatological expectation can be linked with the prophetic
tradition, even if it takes a new form in apocalyptic.

[16] See above, n. 9.
[17] Comm. Rule III; Vermes, *Scrolls in English*, 75.
[18] Ibid. 78.

Despite the disappointment with the aftermath of the
Maccabean rebellion, the eschatological hopes of the Hasidim clearly did not fade away at Qumran. Combined with
their practice of the Torah was a continuing sense of the
imminence of God's decisive intervention, to which they
devoted much thought and writing. In their vivid descriptions of the conflicts which would precede it (as in the
War Rule),[19] ideas appear which cannot be found in the
Torah. They seem rather to betray the influence of Persian
religion, particularly its dualistic representation of warfare
between light and darkness.[20]

The covenanters looked forward to a holy war in which
the archangel Michael would supply heavenly aid to the sons
of men against the adversaries of God led by Belial (Satan).
The Last Judgement would follow the victory of the righteous. After the godless had been punished and the world
destroyed by fire, the Qumran community, finally cleansed,
would take its place in the new creation. In that new age even
the Law would be redeemed,[21] at least by being interpreted
aright. This implies that for the sect, despite their commitment to it, the Torah as given was not completely adequate.[22]

Of interest to us is not so much the detailed content or
possible sources of new ideas and beliefs, but how they
gained acceptance in 'the present age' within a community
totally committed to the Torah. In short, how was such
seemingly free speculation and innovation possible under the
constraint of an acknowledged, dominant formal revelation?
The answer lay in shifting the focus of revelatory authority in
such a way as to make it possible to introduce new revelation
alongside, or even under the guise of, the old. This was made
possible without apparent contradiction by the application
of a new method of exegesis, called today the *pesher* method.

The Hebrew word *pesher* means 'interpretation'. It occurs
regularly in the commentary on Habakkuk found at Qumran
in the form which introduces verse-by-verse comments, e.g.
'*its interpretation* bears on . . .'. Thirteen principles implied

[19] Ibid. 122.
[20] Hengel, *Judaism*, 230.
[21] Davies, 155.
[22] Ibid. 149.

in the *pesher* manner of interpretation at Qumran have been identified,[23] which together permit almost any verse in the prophetic text to be applied to contemporary events, and to the Teacher of Righteousness in particular.[24] Not only were forced constructions and allegorical interpretation permitted, but possibly even the text itself was subject to alteration to allow the desired interpretation to emerge.

Such treatment of the text would be justified, it would appear, by the assumption that the end-time was near, to which all true prophecy must point; and, more especially, by the conviction that the Teacher of Righteousness was inspired to interpret hidden mysteries and reveal divine truth. This claim may have originated with the Teacher of Righteousness himself. The Habbakuk commentary 7: 1 reads:

And God told Habbakuk to write that which would happen to the final generation; but He did not make known to him when time would come to an end. And as for that which He said, *That he who reads may read it speedily*, interpreted this concerns the Teacher of Righteousness, to whom God made known all the mysteries of the words of His servants the prophets.[25]

The freedom to interpret God's relationship to the world and to humanity in the light of present experience is thus demonstrated at Qumran. Such freedom had been exercised by the prophets; yet here it is prophecy with a difference, compared with the past. What is undertaken is prophetic interpretation in which the normative revelatory authority of the Torah (Pentateuch and prophets) remains unchallenged, but new truth is found in, or rather read into, the ancient sources.[26] The prophetic voice 'Thus saith the Lord' yields to a new voice—'Thus saith the Torah, rightly interpreted'.

[23] K. Stendahl, *The School of St. Matthew* (Philadelphia, 1968), 191 f. See also Schürer, 58 n. 3.

[24] Stendahl, 183, 190. See also W. H. Brownlee, *The Midrash Pesher of Habbakuk* (Missoula, 1979), 23-6, '[Its purpose was] to sustain the Community in their present hour of suffering and perplexity.'

[25] Vermes, *Scrolls in English*, 239.

[26] Hengel, *Judaism*, 206, 'The free working of the spirit, without reference to extant tradition which had already been fixed in writing and had in effect acquired "canonical" validity, was now impossible. From now on the "prophetic" self-awareness was at work not least in the *inspired interpretation of prophetic writings which had already been composed*' (emphasis original).

The community committed to the Torah was thus bound
to the rigorous observance of its commands, but at the same
time was free to express new insights and to incorporate into
its religious understanding new ideas and concepts derived
from its immediate cultural, historical, and religious setting.
In terms of the polarity model, it stands poised between the
formal revelation of the Torah and the new subject-
dependent formal revelation derived from the Teacher of
Righteousness. Ostensibly, it is committed to the Torah; in
practice it is dependent on the interpretation of the Torah
by the Teacher. Almost certainly the latter would have lost
his following if he had overtly contradicted the Pentateuch.
Thus, it continued to exercise its constraint. But virtually
no constraint could be exercised over his interpretation of
prophecy, beyond the limiting factor of faith in God's ultimate triumph.

The ambivalence of the community's standing between
Torah and Teacher is reflected in the language of returning
to the covenant of Moses and of entering a new covenant.[27]
On the one hand, the unacceptable implication that the
Mosaic covenant has been superseded is avoided, and at the
same time its powerful legitimating value is preserved for the
community. On the other hand, the danger of contradiction
between ancient text and new Teacher is avoided by attributing to the Teacher of Righteousness the God-given
powers of right interpretation and knowledge of truth. On
this basis ultimate revelatory authority is vested in him, on
the existing foundation of the Torah.

That the Teacher was the end-point of revelation may be
seen as a corollary of the community's conviction that it
stood at the end-point in history. That it drew to itself the
language of end-time and ultimate commitment is hardly
surprising. However, in attributing ultimacy (in the present
at least) not merely to the Torah, but to the Torah as interpreted by the Teacher of Righteousness, the community
created a barrier between itself and all other movements
within Judaism, which acknowledged the supremacy of the
Torah but not that of the Teacher of Righteousness. Total
dedication to revelation in the form of the Torah, combined

[27] Sanders (240 f.) seems anxious to play down this ambivalence.

with the inescapable necessity of interpretation, led paradoxically to the anarchic radicalism of which Hengel speaks.[28]
The Torah was fixed, but the basis for interpreting it could
not be fixed. The claim to be able to provide true interpretation could only appear arbitrary in the face of competing claims. In so far as the truth of God was at stake, the
competition, not surprisingly, was fierce and often irreconcilable between those who were genuinely committed
to the same form of revelation, the Torah.

In our terms, we see here the consequence of a breakdown
of the polar dialectic. Over-reliance on formal revelation
cannot prevent the polar dialectic functioning, but causes it
to function in a disordered way. A situation is created in
which extreme rigidity requiring total conformity can lead
within the same overall community to conditions verging on
anarchy. Under the dominance of formal revelation in the
Torah, the vitality of the prophetic spirit was not lost in
Qumran, but neither could it escape the constraints of the
polar imbalance, or avoid generating new tensions within the
wider community committed to the Torah. No resolution of
the problem was possible as long as the polar imbalance
remained.

In conclusion, at Qumran we find first, that there developed within the community a means of relating new ideas
and expectations of God to Torah-based religion. Secondly,
in its commitment to the Torah it took to a new extreme the
command to separate a holy people apart for God, excluding
from the circle of holiness not merely foreigners or apostate
Jews, but any Jew who remained impure by failing to con-
tract into the new covenant of Qumran.[29] Thirdly, the sect
also emphasized ritual purity—the physical aspect of holiness—to a new extreme, which necessitated withdrawal to a
geographical location where any contamination could as far
as possible be avoided. This perhaps sealed their fate when
the contaminating Roman armies finally reached their retreat
and destroyed it, without God's intervening to purify his
creation, as they had so ardently hoped. The covenanters
had developed the means to accommodate to the world of

[28] Hengel, *Judaism*, 306.
[29] Sanders, 243.

ideas and to the end-time, but not to the everyday social, political, physical world, with all its changes and stresses, within which, despite their attempts to isolate and purify themselves, their own lives were set. The polar dialectic was not recovered. The creative possibilities of new interpretation were introduced in such a way as to verge on the anarchy of uncontrolled speculation, while the dominance of formal revelation was not overtly challenged. Thus, paradoxically, the community that lived under the most rigorous formal constraints in daily life was at the same time on the verge of conceptual chaos, and may have contributed to that state of affairs which flourished in Gnosticism.[30]

2. SCRIBES, PHARISEES, AND RABBIS

The Qumran community struggled to achieve holiness by isolating itself from the world, and failed—at least in so far as it disappeared from history. But while the covenanters were still secure on the shores of the Dead Sea, another movement stemming from the Hasidim was pursuing the ideal of holiness in a very different way and very much more in the world. In more or less direct continuity it survives to this day, in the form of orthodox Judaism. In New Testament times this movement was represented by the Scribes and Pharisees, and subsequently at the end of the first century AD by the Rabbis. The Scribes, however, though at a later date closely associated with the Pharisees, could claim a much more ancient professional history, extending beyond the exile into the period of the Monarchy.

In order to understand the later developments in this alternative Hasidic movement, we must identify one more strand in the web of post-Maccabean Judaism and trace it briefly from its source, namely the Wisdom movement or tradition.[31]

The first Israelite king to have wide international cultural

---

[30] See below, p. 185 n. 14; Hengel, *Judaism*, 228.

[31] See E. W. Heaton, *The Hebrew Kingdoms* (New Clarendon Bible, Old Testament, 3; Oxford, 1968), 165-96; J. L. Crenshaw, *Old Testament Wisdom* (London, 1982); W. McKane, *Prophets and Wise Men* (London, 1965); R. N. Whybray, *The Intellectual Tradition in the Old Testament* (Berlin and New York, 1974).

and economic relations was Solomon, and he may well have
established in Jerusalem a 'school of Wisdom' modelled on
the very ancient Egyptian lines.[32] Scribes would have been
involved in it, writing down and copying ancient wisdom,
proverbs, and rules of etiquette.

The Wisdom literature of the ancient Near East shows
remarkable similarities of style and content. A distinctive
characteristic of it is its man-centred perspective and lack of
interest in the cult. We see this in the Old Testament Wisdom books such as Proverbs and Ecclesiastes. Particularly
striking in these books is the absence of a concern which
pervades the rest of the Old Testament, namely God's dealings with his people in history.

However, Israelite Wisdom writers were by no means indifferent to 'true religion and the fear of the Lord'; and the
ideal of Wisdom was much more than a humanist ethic. It
was closely integrated with Israel's monotheistic faith. This
came about above all through the assimilation of the concept
of Wisdom with the divine ordering of creation. A literary
device which was to have profound theological significance
for later Judaism and Christianity was the poetic representation of Wisdom as a personal being beside God.
Proverbs 8: 22 represents her (the word for Wisdom is feminine in Hebrew, as is *sophia* in Greek) as a lively little girl
playing before God and delighting in his creation. Elsewhere
she is mature and virtuous, inviting the godly to seek her
out, or looking for some place where she will be welcome.[33]
Such imagery in the context of Jewish monotheism does not
imply belief in some goddess alongside Yahweh. It is rather
a vividly symbolic way of speaking of God's wisdom, which
serves at the same time to put the Wisdom tradition and its
ideals to the service of God.

It remains true that this tradition, in its earlier phase especially, was practical rather than speculative in character.
The concern shown in Wisdom literature for the correct
behaviour of those in high office reinforces the likelihood
that kings drew on the educated circles of scribes, Wisdom

<hr>

[32] Cf. Heaton, 171. Whybray is less sure (pp. 33 ff.).
[33] Prov. 8 and 9; Ecclus. 24.

teachers, and their pupils to serve as counsellors and civil
servants. For their part, wisdom writers show great respect
for constituted authority.

In so far as the Scribes were a professional class, they were
not at any time necessarily to be associated with any one
particular faction. Thus, even before the exile there were
scribal schools responsible for instructing priests and Levites
and interpreting ancient law.[34] Besides these probably conservative practitioners, there would have been others sharing
the more cosmopolitan outlook characteristic of the Wisdom
tradition, and so likely to be more open to foreign influence.

During and after the exile it was no doubt the more conservative scribes who played a key role in collating and transmitting the Torah, and who re-established schools devoted
to the study of it after the return. Ezra the scribe stands out
as a key figure in this tradition. At the same time, the more
open attitude did not disappear. At a later date both the
Hasidim and the Hellenists would have had their scribes,
with each side claiming to represent true wisdom.

Against the tendency of the Hellenists to depreciate the
Torah and traditional Jewish wisdom in favour of Greek
wisdom, the conservative scribe Ben Sira launched a powerful counter-attack in the early years of the third century BC.
He not only castigated opponents of the Torah, but took
the radical step of identifying it with Wisdom. Thus, after
reciting a hymn in praise of Wisdom, Ben Sira concludes:
'All this is the covenant-book of God Most High, the law
which Moses enacted to be the heritage of the assemblies of
Jacob' (Ecclus. 24: 23). To identify the Torah with Wisdom
was to identify the Torah with the divine plan for creation,
and to place it with God before creation.[35]

Wisdom was a symbol rich with meaning not only for Jews,
but for Greeks as well. This was so in so far as the later
Jewish idea of Wisdom as the divine plan of creation could
be merged with the Greek, particularly the Stoic, idea of the
Logos as the rational principle of reality.[36] Hengel remarks

---

[34] Hengel, *Judaism*, 78; Schürer, 415–22.
[35] Hengel, *Judaism*, 159 f.
[36] For the further development of these ideas in the Church, see below, chap. 7,
sect. 2.

that Wisdom in Ben Sira could be understood analogously to the Stoic Logos. He adds a quotation attributed to Zeno, the founder of Stoicism: 'The universal law (*nomos*), which is the true wisdom (*Logos*) permeating everything, is identical with Zeus, the director of the pervading of all things.'[37] This assimilation of ideas would in itself reinforce the traditional, universalistic connotations of the idea of Wisdom.

However, Ben Sira's identification of Wisdom with the Torah had radical implications for both Wisdom and Torah. On the one hand, the concept of Wisdom was shorn of its universality. It was now the exclusive possession of the Jews. The Wisdom claimed by others, above all by the Greeks, was regarded as false wisdom. Thus, Ben Sira contributed to the spiritual segregation of Judaism in its later development.

On the other hand, by this identification the Torah acquired absolute authority and eternal validity in thought, which would soon be sealed by the blood of martyrs in action. Indeed, Ben Sira undoubtedly strengthened the resolution of the Torah's defenders in the approaching crisis.

It was not till after the Maccabean crisis that the chief defenders, the Hasidim, diverged into two streams. One flowed to Qumran, as we have seen, and would have taken its own scribes and experts in the law. The course of the other must now be traced. It gave rise to the Pharisees,[38] with whom the Scribes have traditionally been most closely associated. As long as it is recalled that not all scribes were necessarily Pharisees, the former do not need to be considered further independently.

The origin of the name 'Pharisee' remains uncertain,[39] but it probably means 'separated' (from what is unclear).[40]

As a movement, the Pharisees had four distinctive characteristics. First, they were a lay movement, often opposed to the Sadducean priestly aristocracy. Secondly, they not only

[37] Hengel, *Judaism*, 159 f.
[38] Schürer, 388–403. J. Neusner, *From Politics to Piety: The emergence of Pharisaic Judaism* (Englewood Cliffs, NJ, 1973), is very cautious over what can be known of the Pharisees before AD 70 (cf. p. 143). See also J. Bowker, *Jesus and the Pharisees* (Cambridge, 1973).
[39] Bowker, *Pharisees*, 1–15.
[40] Sanders, 154, 'from what God demanded one be separate from . . .' (cf. Lev. 11: 44). See above, p. 97 nn. 79, 80.

acknowledged the sacred authority of the Torah, including
the prophets and the other writings, but were, like the Qumran covenanters, willing to associate new ideas and later customs with it and to ascribe to this continuing tradition or
'oral Torah' the same authority as the written Torah.
Thirdly, in marked contrast to the Qumran covenanters,
they endeavoured to extend the Torah and its demand for
holiness to all Jews, and not merely to priests or élitist minorities, and to all spheres of life—domestic, social, and
political, as well as the explicitly religious. Fourthly, despite
the admission of oral tradition, they exercised much stricter
control than the covenanters on the interpretation of the
Torah, and did not concede definitive authority to any single
individual.

The Pharisees faded from view as a party in the century
following the fall of Jerusalem in AD 70, but their tradition
was carried on by the Rabbis. The word simply means 'teacher' and was already used in earlier times, but the Rabbinate
was institutionalized after AD 70 (see below, p. 181). The
Rabbis understood themselves to be passing on and developing the tradition of the Hasidim and Pharisees, and
succeeded in imposing the stamp of this tradition on the
subsequent history of Judaism. One problem in the evaluation of early Jewish sources is the difficulty of dating material as belonging to the Pharisaic or later Rabbinic
tradition.[41] To some extent this difficulty will be glossed over
here, since our concern is mainly with underlying principles
whose exact dating is not all-important. It is as well, however, to note that early Pharisaic Judaism was probably not
as uniform or stable as later tradition might suggest. The
picture presented in later tradition may in fact owe much
to Hillel, a contemporary of Jesus. His main significance,
Neusner suggests, was his disengagement from political activity and concentration on piety under the Torah. He thus
provided his followers with a way of coping with the disaster
of AD 70, and thereby secured the survival of his brand of
Pharisaism.[42]

[41] Neusner repeatedly emphasizes this problem. See his chapter on 'The Use of
Rabbinic Sources for the Study of Ancient Judaism' in W. Scott Green, ed.,
Approaches to Ancient Judaism, iii (Chico, Calif., 1981).
[42] Neusner, *Politics*, 92, 146

Our main concern is with attitudes to the Torah and to the question of holiness. With the Pharisees, and later the Rabbis, we find a very different answer to the question of where and how holiness could be achieved, compared to what was to be seen at Qumran or among the Sadducees. Instead of concentrating on the holiness of the Temple and cult, or withdrawing from all uncleanness to the purity of monastic life by the Dead Sea, this tradition explored a possibility of holiness that could transcend all geographical limitations and be open to all, not just to priestly or religious minorities.[43] The route to holiness lay through the Torah, through an understanding of it and obedience to it in everyday life.

To succeed in rendering the Torah intelligible and applicable would involve a considerable degree of creative interpretation. This was necessary since what was to be rendered applicable to all Jews, wherever they were and whatever they did, included a large body of regulations which originally concerned an exclusive minority (the priests), in an exclusive place (the Temple). But this creativity would not necessarily impair the authority of the Torah. On the contrary, it could reinforce it. If the underlying conviction that the Torah was the binding revelation of God for all time was the motive for attempting to demonstrate its intelligibility and applicability, success in the enterprise would serve to strengthen the conviction.[44] We have already seen how this might seem to be achieved through allegory, but that way ultimately threatened to undermine the original revelatory source completely. In the Pharisaic Rabbinic tradition we shall discover an alternative methodology that avoided this danger to a much greater extent. It served to reinforce the binding revelatory authority of the Torah, which accordingly continued to constrain the exercise of creativity throughout the long process of interpretation.

It is therefore important to recognize the element of creativity within this tradition, but equally important to recognize its limits. One word in particular may help us to

---

[43] Bowker, *Pharisees*, 1–15.
[44] Bowker, *Targums*, 40.

appreciate the relationship of creativity to constraint in this
particular instance, namely 'translation'. The dynamic of
form and vitality is implicit in translation, where a given
form has to be re-presented in a new way. But the polarities
are not equally balanced. A given text remains unchanged
and authoritative in itself and strictly determines the scope of
re-presentation. The possibilities of translation may extend
from transliteration to paraphrase, and the variations may
seem considerable, but a limiting point exists beyond which
a text ceases to be a translation at all and can only be assessed
as an independent entity that cannot claim the authority of
the original. The object of all translation is to communicate
meaning, but the danger of trying to bring out meaning is
losing it; especially if different words and images are used to
bring out the supposed underlying meaning of a text.[45]

Translation was a major preoccupation of those heirs of
the Hasidim who did not wish to withdraw from the world,
but rather to extend religion and holiness into the world.
The Pentateuch was written in Hebrew, and in the past. In
the Persian period, Aramaic was becoming the language of
the people. After the conquests of Alexander the Great,
Greek became increasingly widespread, even in Palestine.
If the Torah was to be made intelligible and applicable,
translation was necessary in terms of both language and
meaning. Perhaps the necessity for the former increased the
scope for the latter.

One of the most important undertakings of this kind was
the translation of the Old Testament into Greek (commonly
known as the Septuagint, or 'LXX', because of the legend[46]
that it was undertaken by seventy-two Jewish elders, at the
behest of Ptolemy I of Egypt). This work played a very
important role in enabling Greek-speaking Jews, not least

---

[45] E. Earle Ellis, *Prophecy and Hermeneutic in Early Christianity* (Tübingen,
1978), 179, quoting T. W. Manson, 'We tend to think of the text as objective fact
and interpretation as subjective opinion. It may be doubted whether the early
Jewish and Christian expositors of Scripture made any such sharp distinction. For
them the meaning of the text was of primary importance; and they seem to have
had greater confidence than we moderns in their ability to find it. Once found it
became a clear duty to express it.'
[46] In the *Letter of Aristeas*; see Charles, 94–122. Cf. Russell, 19; Hengel, 102.

those in Alexandria, to remain within the covenant relationship and to order their lives according to the Torah.[47]

In the Aramaic-speaking world translation was even more
widespread, and was combined with interpretation to a much
greater extent. The Aramaic works came to be known col-
lectively as *Targums*[48] (literally 'translations'). Their origin
is associated with the synagogue. This place of assembly
was one of the most significant innovations in post-exilic
Judaism, and was intended primarily, it seems, to promote
study of the Torah.[49] To quote Bowker: 'By constantly confronting the believer with the Torah, the synagogue was in
a sense confronting him with God, but that could scarcely
be so if he understood little of what he heard. The practice
therefore began of accompanying the recitation of the text
with a translation, or *targum*, of it.' Thus, the original Hebrew text was read publicly and remained normative. 'The
purpose of the Targum was to make the text meaningful and
bring home its significance to the congregation.'[50]

The Targums were not only the form in which past revelation was translated into changed situations, nor was
translation restricted to any one section of the Jewish community; but those associated with the synagogues and scribal
schools, and with the Pharisaic Rabbinic tradition, developed it with the greatest thoroughness, com-
prehensiveness, and strictness. The members of this
tradition did not consider that their task was merely to translate sacred texts into other languages, but, as we have already
noted, to translate the pastness of the Pentateuch into the
practicalities of the present, whether in Hebrew, as was still
often the case, or in other languages. For this purpose they
developed their own methodology. They believed that the

[47] Bowker, *Targums*, 5. But see G. W. Anderson, 'Canonical and Non-
Canonical', in *The Cambridge History of the Bible*, i (Cambridge, 1970), 146, 'The
Septuagint rendering of the five books of Moses is characterized by a faithfulness
and consistency which are not found in the other books.'

[48] For a concise introduction to the writings of Judaism, see R. C. Musaph-
Andriesse, *From Torah to Kabbalah*, (London, 1981).

[49] Originally, the synagogue does not seem to have been a house of prayer. 'A
house of prayer was unnecessary for the Jew living in Judaea: within certain limits
of purification he could pray anywhere' (Bowker, *Targums*, 10). Cf. Schürer, 423–
63.

[50] Bowker, *Targums*, 12, 13.

solution to any problem, actual or theoretical, lay within the text of Torah itself,[51] and would be discovered if the rules of interpretation were properly applied. Gradually a tradition of scholarly opinion built up, which became the oral Torah.

Two important components of oral Torah were *Haggadah* and *Halakah*,[52] which might briefly be said to correspond to the two sides of interpretation: illustration and practical implication.*Haggadah*, derived from a verb meaning 'tell', denotes 'what is related'—the stories told which expanded upon the material of scripture. Under this heading come the interpretations and illustrations of scripture designed to instruct or encourage the seeker after God.[53] *Halakah*, derived from a verb meaning 'walk', denotes the legal norms which are arrived at on the basis of the study of Torah and the desire to conform to it. '*Halakah* defines the implications of Torah and how it should be applied; *haggadah* illustrates Torah, and encourages people to accept it as binding on themselves.'[54] The aim, then, was not just to inform understanding, but to inform practice, to bring every aspect of life and activity under God's law. It is perhaps the practical implications that concern us most, precisely because it is here that belief in God bears on his world and other people, and not just on the believer.

The objective of translating the rules which governed priestly functions in the Temple into regulations to be observed by ordinary people in everyday life meant stretching the possibilities of translation almost to breaking-point. Nevertheless, the connection between original and authoritative source and later teaching was not broken, or at least was not considered to be broken. This was avoided, one might say, by the enlargement of the authoritiative source. *Halakah* could be established not only on the basis of direct proof from scripture, according to the accepted rules of exegesis or as mediated through earlier scholars, but on the basis of life lived under the Torah, so that custom, whatever

[51] Ibid. 40.
[52] Schürer, 337–55.
[53] Bowker, *Targums*, 48.
[54] Ibid. 43.

its provenance, could acquire a derivative sanctity. Thus, *halakoth* (the Hebrew plural form) in oral tradition could become as authoritative as the original written Torah without the necessity of scriptural reference.[55] In a sense, therefore, there was a two-way traffic. Rules were read out of the Torah, but rules could also be read into Torah. By the same token, Torah, in the broader sense of 'sacred tradition', could be extended to cover every aspect of life and practice, including that which could not be directly connected with the Pentateuch. Nothing, however, could be incorporated in this way which was in direct conflict with the original Torah or with firmly established tradition.[56]

In the second century AD—outside the period we are considering—the *halakoth* were gathered together in the Mishnah,[57] and significantly this body of post-Pentateuchal tradition, having acquired a sacred authority equal to that of the Pentateuch, became the object of further study and commentary. This was eventually gathered together to form the Talmud.[58] The Pentateuch—the basic Torah—thus appears as the trunk of a great tree, whose spreading branches and twigs reach into every age, place, and detail of life, and with very little scope for pruning. Veneration for the Torah was in no way relaxed, but was rather extended to embrace the continuing accumulation of Torah-governed tradition. This tradition is unlikely to have reached very full expression by the time of Jesus, but it was already taking shape in his day.

The continuity of the creative process within commitment to the Torah has been clearly demonstrated, as also its limitations. Attention still needs to be drawn to one particularly important innovation, and to what was perhaps the most significant constraint, before conclusions in terms of the polarity model are drawn.

As has already been said, it was possible for customs to

[55] Schürer, 343.

[56] Ibid. 343, 'However far halakhah departed from the written Torah, the fiction was nevertheless maintained that in essence it was an exposition and restatement of the Torah itself. Formally, the latter was still regarded as the supreme norm from which every legal precept must stem.'

[57] Translated into English by H. Danby, *The Mishnah* (London, 1933).

[58] See above, n. 48.

become accepted in sacred tradition, although they did not derive directly from the Torah but from those who lived under it. Ideas could be incorporated in this way as well as customs. Such ideas may have reflected the influence of surrounding cultures, but it can be argued that they were shaped as much by the creative response of those who lived under the Torah to the challenges of their day. Suffering and persecution posed the greatest challenge to faith in God's relatedness and holiness. In this connection, the most important new ideas were belief in resurrection and in God's ultimate triumph, which would transcend the conditions and limitations of physical existence. The Sadducees are said not to have accepted these ideas. Significantly, those who did sought to establish their presence in the Pentateuch,[59] disclosing once again their fundamental reliance on and commitment to it.

The point at which the greatest constraint was exercised was over the individual, and over the possibilities of personal insight, originality, and creativity. The creative process, we have discovered, was largely a social process. The interpreter of the Torah had to be familiar with the primary sources, and the whole history of previous interpretation and rules of exegesis, before he could venture a judgement on any outstanding issue, and even then majority opinion had to be respected.[60] Differences of opinion could arise, on conclusions and even on the rules by which they were reached,[61] and these could be tolerated as long as they were arrived at by careful argument and won scholarly support. But such differences of opinion as there were, though perhaps occupying much space in learned debate and giving rise to divisions and different schools of thought, were very minor compared with the vast area of consensus concerning the Torah. Outside Qumran, no one could claim the kind of individual revelatory authority that was exercised there by the Teacher of Righteousness.

The situation is forcefully illustrated in the famous story

---

[59] Mishnah Tractate *Sanhedrin*, x. i, 'He who says that the resurrection of the dead is not to be inferred from the Law has no part in the world to come' (as quoted in Driver, 86; cf. Danby, 397).

[60] Schürer, 342.

[61] Bowker, *Targums*, 54.

of Rabbi Eliezer in the Babylonian Talmud (Baba Meziʿa), summarized conveniently by Bowker:[62]

R. Eliezer tried to establish a *halakah* on a disputed matter of cleanness or uncleanness, but the other rabbis refused to accept his arguments. He then brought various miracles to his support, but they remained unimpressed. 'He said, "If the *halakah* agrees with me, let this stream prove it." At once the stream began to flow backwards. They said "A stream of water is no proof at all." . . . . At last (after other miracles) he said to them: "If the *halakah* agrees with me let it be proved from heaven." At once a *bath qol** proclaimed: "Why do you argue with R. Eliezer? In all matters the *halakah* agrees with him." But R. Joshua stood up and said, *It is not in heaven.* . . . What did he mean? R. Jeremiah said, "He meant that the Torah had already been given on Mount Sinai, therefore we take no notice of a *bath qol*, since it was long ago written in Torah, *Follow after the majority* [Exod. 23: 2]." ' R. Eliezer was in a minority of one, and therefore his *halakah* or ruling could not be accepted.

    * Lit. 'daughter of a voice', the divine voice from heaven.

The incident is set at around the end of the first century AD. Whatever the date of its actual composition, it demonstrates the ultimate dominance of Torah and tradition as the formal definition of God and the terms of his relatedness; over against it no other mode of inspiration or insight derived from interpreted experience can be admitted, not even the voice of God from heaven. The Torah, viewed in this way, could tolerate no prophet[63] and scarcely even prophetic interpretation, except under the strictest exegetical controls. The possibility of relationship with God and of living in the awareness of his presence is not denied; the object of the whole movement was to achieve this. But the interpretative resources governing this experience, and more importantly its practical implications, were fixed, external, and binding. There was no place for any radical reinterpretation of the traditional understanding of God and his requirements for men and women, under the impact of new experience.

   [62] Ibid. 44 f.
   [63] G. Vermes, *Jesus the Jew* (London, 1973), 81. Cf. J. D. G. Dunn, *Christology in the Making* (London, 1980), 135, 'In rabbinic writings the Spirit is pre-eminently the Spirit of prophecy. But this is a role which belongs almost entirely to the past.' (Note Dunn's further comment, 'Only in the Dead Sea Scrolls does Spirit come back into prominence as a force in present experience.')

The strength and religious vitality of the Pharisaic Rabbinic tradition were demonstrated by its capacity to survive the disasters of the destruction of the Holy City and Temple, and finally even expulsion from the Holy Land, and by its continuing development. A measure of hypocrisy or 'arid legalism' no doubt manifested itself at times within this tradition, but the failure within any great movement cannot justify its wholesale condemnation. If criticism is to be made, it must be at a deeper level which does not call in question the sincerity, or the truly religious motives, or the personal sanctity of those who sought relationship with God in this manner.

The two critical questions posed at the beginning of this chapter concerned the recovery of the polar dialectic and the concept of holiness. On the first count, we conclude that the true polar dialectic of form and vitality in revelation was not achieved in the Pharisaic Rabbinic tradition.[64] We see instead a theoretically immutable formal revelation, qualified by the admission of strictly controlled methods of adaptation and enlargement.

These methods, and the practical concern for holiness in everyday life, helped to generate distinctive attitudes and concerns. Unlike the Qumran covenanters, the Pharisaic branch of the Hasidim grew less and less concerned with speculations about a future world,[65] speculations which could do little to help render the Torah applicable to this world. Behind this shift of emphasis there would seem to have been a fundamental shift of attitude towards the Torah. Though totally committed to it, the early Hasidim and the Qumran covenanters preserved the prophetic belief in God's control of history. Their eschatological hopes, though seemingly bizarre, represented at heart their faith in God's ultimate triumph in the world at a time when he seemed to have been overwhelmed by the forces of history. Obedience to the Torah in the course of history was the condition for

[64] Neusner interestingly alludes to a 'third force . . . opposed to the two primary elements of charisma and traditional routine', and also to 'an alternative focus for religious life to either cultic ritual or charismatic action', but this is set under the dominance of the Torah (*A Life of Rabban Yohanan ben Zakkai* (Leiden, 1962), 38, 64).

[65] Driver, 83.

participation in God's kingdom at the end, but the status and role of the Torah at the end remained somewhat unclear.[66]

Any uncertainty about the eternal validity and absolute status of the Torah would soon cease to have any place among the Pharisees and Rabbis. This conclusion can be seen to stem from the ideas of Ben Sira. The assimilation of Wisdom to Logos and the identification of Wisdom with the Torah resulted, in Hengel's words, in an ' *"ontological" understanding of the Torah*'. To quote further:

The consequences . . . were manifold and far reaching: from the time of Ben Sira, the Torah could be understood as a spiritual light that lightened men; it lasted for ever and was immeasurable; in its absolute significance it was regarded simply as the 'the good'. Thus it became the *mediator of creation and revelation between God and the world*. Here the development of a crude doctrine of inspiration or better 'mediation' was a matter of course: 'The whole Torah is from heaven', no verse may be excluded.

In this way, however, its six hundred and thirteen individual commandments and prohibitions received a 'cosmic' significance going beyond the realm of the individual; they were 'materialized forms of expression' of the divine ordinance of creation and salvation. Each individual commandment, indeed each individual consonant possessed absolute importance; . . .

From this there followed with logical consistency both the casuistic securing of the commandments by the oral Torah, the hedge round the law, and the scrupulous fixation of the text. A further necessary development was the unique valuation of the study of the Torah . . . This fact also explains the growing intellectual power of the scribes: they were the only authoritative exponents of the Torah, and as the 'wise men' had the key to the right understanding of it and thus to the mysteries of the present and the future world.[67]

This extended quotation bears on many issues with which we have been dealing, not least on the way in which the Torah came to be seen as the concrete ('material') form of the divine. The main point here, however, is that, with this 'Platonic' ontologizing of the Torah, a sense of God's active dealing in history, to which the Torah witnesses, gave way

[66] Davies, 147–50. See below, pp. 147–50.
[67] Hengel, *Judaism*, 171 f.

to a desire to conform to the suprahistorical pattern of divine truth, of which the Torah was the perfect representation.[68] It is significant that the great Israelite and Jewish tradition of history-writing finally ended with Josephus, if not earlier,[69] and was replaced by commentaries and expositions on the Torah. The object of eliciting rules for the present, rather than secrets about the future, called for interpretative skills of a different order from those which might serve to reveal the meaning of history. However, one may still judge that the Pharisees, in their intention to guide the lives of the whole community of Israel according to the Torah, conformed quite as closely to its original purpose as did the Qumran covenanters, who applied its commands more literally perhaps, but only to an exclusive minority. Certainly the Pharisees and later the Rabbis were successful in extending the authority of the Torah to the Jewish community as a whole, without weakening the ideal of total commitment, to an extent that was impossible at Qumran. The creativity of interpretation was present in both these expressions of Judaism, but the one which interpreted it rationally, more or less at its face value, with some attempt at exegetical control, and above all under the criteria of existing tradition and majority opinion, may be reckoned to have safeguarded its original intention in a way that treating it as a secret code was in danger of losing.

In the Pharisaic Rabbinic tradition we discern a flow in two directions. On the one hand, authoritative revelation is adapted to new circumstances. On the other hand, new circumstances are made to conform to the ancient authoritative revelation: that is, patterns of behaviour in a changed world are made to conform to those prevalent in

[68] Ibid. 173, 'Any understanding of history as the sphere of the revelation of the divine salvation was thus excluded'; and p. 175, '[The Jewish people] lost the sense of the free action of God in history . . . The Torah became an "essentially unhistorical entity." . . . the almost thousand-year-old tradition of Israelite and Jewish history writing came to an end.' This did not happen overnight. See Crenshaw, 151, 'The fervent prayer in [Ecclus.] chapter 36: 1–17 implies that Sirach also nourished strong eschatological hopes that God would manifest his power once again in political events, restoring the chosen race to its former glory.'

[69] Josephus' purpose was propagandist (to defend Judaism against Roman hostility), rather than theological (to discern the hand of God in history, as in the old tradition of Jewish history-writing). His four books, the *Antiquities*, the *Jewish Wars*, the *Life*, and the treatise *Against Apion*, still serve as major sources for the history of this period, despite their bias. References are made to the Loeb editions.

the world whence the revelation came. In this exchange, the position of the authoritative revelation remains dominant. Within this tradition it developed the capacity to survive change, but not to inspire it. It is not unfair to say that only that which is taken away is given up: Holy City, holy Temple, sacrificial rites; what can be conserved is conserved. This proves to be, above all, the things pertaining to human conduct and relationships, and, more especially, the things which pertained originally to a select class in the elect community, namely the rules concerning ritual purity and the avoidance of impurity,[70] as once laid down and applied to priests in the very distant past.

This brings us directly to the question of holiness. By vesting holiness in the Torah, that is, in the tradition borne by persons in history, and in the persons who bore it, this movement could survive the loss of holy places and preserve its understanding of holiness—its understanding of the terms for being in relationship with God—in new worlds and foreign lands. Nevertheless, the understanding of holiness preserved in the Torah and perpetuated in this way had its origin in an ancient world, and lies open to the criticisms raised in chap. 3, sect. 3. Ethical insight was not lacking, but the priestly or ritualistic motif, with its own logic, exercised as great if not greater constraint. The issue is clearly defined by a Jewish scholar, G. Allon, quoted by Bowker,[71] in a passage concerning the two fundamental aims or principles governing this approach: 'One was to make *halakah* accord with the needs of the living, and the other was to extend holiness (*qedusha*) to every man (not only to the priests), and to every place (not only to the Temple), and to every moment of time. The second principle made it necessary for the Hakamim [the Wise] to teach ritual purity to Israel and to demand complete separation.'

The final sentence raises the key issue of this discussion, whether holiness understood in these terms truly corresponds to the holiness of God and the holiness he requires of humankind. If that is questioned, the foundation of this view of holiness, the Torah, is put in question.

[70] Schürer, 345; Neusner, *Politics*, 83, 91.
[71] Bowker, *Pharisees*, 17.

3. ZEALOTS AND CHARISMATICS

The movements we have been considering within Judaism developed out of or were reactions against the religious situation in Jerusalem. Our attention now turns northward to two groups, the Zealots and the Charismatics. The latter were few in number and left scarcely a mark on the history of the period, and yet their experience and understanding of God's relatedness may have a significance for us as great as and even greater than that of the Zealots, whose militancy provoked the Jewish revolt of 66 AD.

(a) The Zealots

The first century BC saw the decline of the Seleucid empire. In Judaea, there followed a period of independence coupled with internal strife, until Pompey finally marched into Jerusalem in 63 BC and established Roman power in the region.[72] Thereafter, local political authority passed from the Hasmonaeans to a family that was not even properly Jewish. An officer from Edom (south of Judaea) called Antipater secured advantageous terms for himself, and the Jews in general, as a result of his well-timed decision to go to the aid of Julius Caesar during a crisis in Alexandria in 48 BC.[73] Antipater's son Herod became governor of Galilee, a region on the northern boundary of the old Northern Kingdom and which had been annexed by the Maccabeans in about 100 BC. In due course Herod, with Roman help, after a period of fighting and intrigue, secured the death of the last Hasmonaean, Antigonus, and became king of Judaea.

As Governor in Galilee, Herod ruthlessly suppressed a group of rebels and killed their leader, Hezekiah,[74] but the rebellious spirit was not crushed. Hezekiah's own descendants continued to inspire the cause of resistance against foreign or illegitimate rule till one of them, Eleazer, led the last defiant resistance against Rome at the fortress of Masada, and preferred suicide with all his surviving followers to falling into Roman hands.[75] How far these later resistance movements could claim direct descent from the Hasidim cannot

[72] Russell, 79 ff.
[73] Hayes and Miller, 614.
[74] Ibid. 615; Driver, 239.
[75] Hayes and Miller, 662.

be determined, but they certainly shared with them, to a greater degree than did the Pharisees, the conviction that God's active involvement in history was not yet over.

Various groups under various *ad hoc* leaders resisted Roman authority in the period before the revolt; and the contemporary Jewish historian Josephus was ready to attribute to them the basest motives of brigandage and self-interest. However, it is clear that there was a powerful religious motive. Josephus describes Judas, probably the son of the Hezekiah murdered by Herod, as author of the 'fourth philosophy' in Judaism (after Pharisees, Sadducees, and Essenes).[76] He describes Judas' outlook as conforming closely to Pharisaism, and associates with him a Pharisee called Zaddok. The members of this movement were distinguished by their 'invincible passion for liberty and would tolerate no ruler but God; they preferred any kind of death for themselves and even for their families to paying taxes and so admitting any human being as lord and master.'[77] Judas himself perished after leading a rebellion against paying taxes in AD 6-7.

The spirit of resistance seems to have been strongest in Galilee,[78] but spread south and finally, despite opposition from many Jews, swept the nation into revolt. The name 'Zealot' was specifically applied to the followers of John of Gischala at the time of the revolt.[79] It may have had the particular connotation of resistance-fighter long before, or have been used more widely of any who were zealous for God's law (2 Macc. 4: 2; cf. John 2: 17). The dating of the term matters less than the fact of continuing resistance out of zeal for God and in the face of overwhelming odds, resulting in the end in a challenge to the might of the Roman empire.

Whether the Zealots or the followers of the 'fourth philosophy' were closely associated with Qumran or not,[80] there

[76] Josephus, *Ant.* xviii. 23.

[77] Driver, 99 f.

[78] Vermes, *Jesus*, 46.

[79] Schürer, 601 f., where the question of whether or not the Zealots are identical with the *Sicarii* ('dagger-men') is also discussed. (Josephus, *War*, iv. 161, vii. 268, is scathing about their zeal for wickedness.)

[80] Driver, 232-4.

was common ground in their understanding of holiness. The covenanters withdrew from the established holy places to preserve holiness in the wilderness, either until God should act to put things right in his own time, or until the moment seemed propitious for his zealous followers to embark on the purification of the land themselves. The dividing-line between these views was narrow. The quietist might be persuaded to become an activist if he was convinced that the moment for God's intervention had arrived, and that his people must rally to the colours.

Whatever the views of the Qumran sectarians, the Zealots were impatient in their desire to restore holiness where it belonged—in the holy land, the Holy City, and the holy Temple—and were prepared to take the initiative in attempting to bring this about. The obstacle in their path was the power of Rome, which they could not hope to remove by their own unaided efforts. Yet only with its removal could the direct rule of God and true holiness be restored. Political intervention by God was therefore necessary, and could be expected on behalf of those totally dedicated to his cause.[81] Many looked to God to send as his special representative, a worthy successor to David, the Messiah (Heb. 'anointed one'; cf. 1 Sam. 24: 6) to complete the work of purification which the small Jewish forces would initiate.

The objectives of the Zealots were therefore political in practice, however religious in inspiration, and pursuit of them would in the event have disastrous political consequences. These can be explained either in terms of failure on God's part, or as failure on the Zealots' part to construe correctly the true terms for God's relatedness. The latter is perhaps more likely, especially as we see once again an underlying view of holiness conceived of in quasi-physical ritualistic terms, which localized its realization within geographical limits. In addition, though it need not be thought that ethical concern was completely absent from the Zealots' religous outlook, they became notorious for their murderous brutality not only against foreigners, but against fellow Jews of good reputation who did not happen to share their views.[82]

[81] Hayes and Miller, 662.
[82] Ibid. 655 (Josephus, *War*, vii. 268).

Whatever ethical concern they had was subordinated to an understanding and pursuit of holiness which it would be hard to defend as God's holiness, and which few of their fellow Jews could accept as such, though the latter had to suffer the consequences as grievously as those who provoked them. Thus, the practical course of action dictated by the Zealots' presuppositions tragically obstructed the realization of the great potential of Judaism's ethical insight and understanding of God.

It is of interest to note that as the crisis approached the Qumran covenanters joined the rebellion[83] and suffered the same fate as the Zealots in the destruction of their holy place[84] and community.

Among the Zealots, a view of God's universal sovereignty was coupled with a concept of holiness in which the notion of ritual purity was still potent. Taken to the extreme, this would require not only the exclusion of all that was morally impure, but the elimination of all that was ritually contaminating and of all that was lawless—in the strict sense of not possessing or not conforming to the Torah—not only from the land of Israel, but from the whole world. The Qumran community derived similar ideas from the Torah concerning the nature of God's holiness, and hence of the conditions which must be fulfilled if this holy God were to rule on earth. Such ideas led naturally to the imagery, so characteristic of apocalyptic writings, of the total destruction of the impure world—that is, the physical universe—and its replacement by a purified or completely new and pure physical world. Again, the moral dimension was not lacking but was inadequately differentiated from the ritual and physical, and this is the main point at issue.

In effect, a concept of holiness—an understanding of the terms of God's relatedness—which was derived from the distant past and long antedated the time when the Torah achieved its final form, was coupled with an understanding of God's universal and transcendent sovereignty that was

---

[83] So Hayes and Miller, 662; queried by J. Barr (personal communication).

[84] Ibid. 666. For reasons which I shall develop in Part III, I would judge the comment here, that Qumranians and Christians met these issues 'in a manner essentially similar', to be fundamentally wrong.

the product of much later insight. The terms governing the relationship between one God among many to one people among many may appear appropriate and reasonable. The same terms applied to the relationship between the one sole God and all the peoples of the world, who by definition have not been governed by the same traditions concerning God, may seem far less appropriate.[85]

The combination of early and later insight in the understanding of God had its own logical outworking in apocalyptic literature. The enlargement of God's sovereignty, matched by the restriction of his relatedness and the relative enlargement of the sphere to which he could not be related, tended towards a dualism which would paradoxically undermine the doctrine of God as sovereign creator. Here again the realization of the ethical potential of Judaism in the world was almost completely lost, because unattainable conditions were imagined to be the necessary prerequisite of holiness. In consequence, the world with most of its inhabitants was barred from entering into relationship with God, and so was denied the possibility of becoming holy. Holiness, it seemed, would only be possible at the expense of the world which God had created, and could not embrace it.

(b) The Charismatics

With Charismatic Judaism we encounter a phenomenon very unlike anything we have considered so far in the period following the composition of the Torah. The term 'Charismatic' comes from a Greek word signifying 'spiritual gift', and, since Weber,[86] it has been commonly used of individuals who appear to possess extraordinary spiritual gifts and hence to enjoy a special and immediate relationship with the divine. This would be further manifested in a spirit of independence, which set relatively little store by external and institutional forms of authority. Surprisingly little reference to this phenomenon as it appeared within Judaism at the time of Jesus is found in New Testament scholarship,

[85] See Sanders, 206-12, for an examination of Rabbinic views on the destiny of Gentiles. Some Rabbis hoped that godly Gentiles would not be condemned, but their generosity was not easily accommodated within their basic presuppositions.

[86] M. Weber, *The Sociology of Religion* (London, 1963).

but a useful account is provided by Geza Vermes in 'Jesus the Jew'.[87] It will be necessary here to summarize only the more significant characteristics which he mentions.

In the first place, it is of particular interest to discover that the Charismatics are associated with Galilee.[88] This region, as we have seen, could claim ancient association with the people of Israel, but its history was very different from that of Jerusalem and the southern State. Though recovered by the Hasmonaeans from the Seleucids and placed under the authority of Jerusalem, its remoteness rendered it hard to control and it continued to be known for its bandits and religious eccentrics.[89] By the time of Jesus, it was still only 'a little island in the midst of unfriendly seas',[90] separated from Judaea geographically by the hostile province of Samaria, and politically by a different administrative system under the Romans. Such factors no doubt helped to preserve a strong independent identity, to the discomfiture of the Roman political authorities and the Jerusalemite religious authorities. Not only did the Charismatics incur disapproval for their lack of conformity to the Torah, but Galileans in general seem to have been regarded by the southern élite as a boorish and undisciplined mob, readily distinguished by their northern accents (Matt. 26: 73). The word 'Galilean' was an insult 'synonymous with a cursed, lawless rabble'.[91] According to tradition, the great Rabbi Yohanan ben Zakkai, after eighteen years in Galilee, exclaimed in exasperation, 'Galilee, Galilee, you hate the Torah!'[92]

Yet it was in this region that the Charismatics exemplified a remarkable awareness of God's living presence, and in their 'lawless' holiness won grudging admiration even from their opponents. The Gospels witness to a similar contemporary ambivalence towards Jesus until the forces of opposition finally combined against him.

Various roles of the Charismatics, such as rain-maker, healer, or exorcist, witnessed to a power believed to derive

[87] See above, n. 63.
[88] Vermes, *Jesus*, 72.
[89] Hayes and Miller, 610.
[90] Vermes, *Jesus*, 44.
[91] Ibid. 55. See John 1: 46; 7: 52.
[92] Vermes, *Jesus*, 57. See also Neusner, *Life of ben Zakkai*, 29.

directly from God, and could be linked with the prophets in
ancient Israel, especially Elijah (1 Kgs. 17; 18: 41-6).

Vermes mentions two Charismatic figures in particular,
whose significance may emerge from the quotations given
below. One was called Honi the Circle-Drawer by the Rabbis, and Onias the Righteous by Josephus. He lived in the
first century BC.[93] The other, Hanina ben Dosa, was active
before AD 70.[94] The former was a famous rain-maker. The
familiarity of his address towards God evoked disapproval
in his own day and subsequently. 'Nevertheless, in the last
resort, even his rabbinic critics likened the relationship between the saint and God to that of a tiresome and spoilt
child with his loving and long suffering father.'[95] Josephus
describes how in a contemporary political crisis partisans
who believed Onias' curse would be as effective as his prayer
for rain appealed to him for support. When in spite of his
refusals and excuses he was forced to speak by the mob, he
stood up in their midst and said: 'O God, king of the universe, since these men standing beside me are thy people,
and those who are besieged are thy priests, I beseech thee
not to hearken to them against these men nor to bring to
pass what these men ask thee to do to those others.'[96] His
desire to bring both the disputants into the embrace of relationship to God resulted in his being stoned to death by
the disappointed partisans.

Hanina ben Dosa was credited with miraculous cures even
at a distance, also with power over natural phenomena,[97]
and with detachment from possessions. Vermes draws the
natural comparisons with Jesus and adds, 'Again, both Jesus
and Hanina, and no doubt the Hasidim (Charismatics) in
general, showed a complete lack of interest in legal and ritual
affairs and a corresponding exclusive concentration on moral
questions. Hanina is never quoted as an authority on Jewish
law in either Mishnah or the Talmud.'[98]

[93] Vermes, *Jesus*, 69.
[94] Ibid. 73. Cf. Neusner, *Life of ben Zakkai*, 29 ff., for the tradition that Hanina
was a disciple of ben Zakkai, but that there was tension between them.
[95] Vermes, *Jesus*, 70.
[96] Josephus, *Ant.* xiv. 22-4 (quoted by Vermes, *Jesus*, 71).
[97] Vermes, *Jesus*, 76 f.
[98] Ibid. 77.

In such figures as Honi and Hanina we are confronted
with the continuation of the prophetic spirit—a sense not
only of living in God's presence but of deriving from the
immediacy of that experience the right to speak and act
without direct reference to external authority. Since he was
not concerned to ground his opinions firmly in established
tradition, Hanina, as we have seen, would not have had the
credentials to be quoted as an authority on law. Individual
interpretation could carry no weight. His authority was of a
different kind. To quote Vermes, 'These holy men were
treated as the willing or unsuspecting heirs to an ancient
prophetic tradition. Their supernatural powers were attributed to their immediate relation to God. They were ven-
erated as a link between heaven and earth independent of
any institutional mediator'.[99]

Not surprisingly, the representatives of established tradition and institutional authority were highly suspicious of
these independent spirits. It is true that words of approval
are not wholly absent from this direction. Vermes quotes an
anonymous saying from the Midrash Rabbah, 'No man has
existed comparable to Elijah and Honi the Circle-Drawer,
causing mankind to serve God';[100] but the weight of Rabbinic opinion was against them, because of their refusal to
conform in matters of behaviour and religious observance,
and because of 'the threat posed by the unrestrained authority of the Charismatic to the upholders of the established
religious order'.[101]

It is unlikely that these holy men were unduly disturbed
by such disapproval. Honi's courage has already been displayed. Beyond that, the kind of relationship they enjoyed
with God would seem to have counted for more than the
approval of men. Tradition speaks of the time they spent in
prayer and of the familiarity of their address to God as
'Abba' (Father), in contrast to the customary post-biblical
style of 'Lord of the Universe'. The idea of sonship was also
employed explicitly to characterize their relationship with
God, without any implication of a claim to divine status.[102]

[99] Ibid. 79.
[100] Ibid. 72.
[101] Ibid. 80.
[102] Ibid. 210 f.

Here, in a far more positive way than elsewhere in Judaism, we discover the reality of God's relatedness in the immediacy of experience, conveying a degree of freedom in word and action in sharp contrast to the movements we have considered previously. It would be wrong to imagine that the boundary-lines were rigidly fixed in Jesus' day. Traces of a tradition of God's immediacy and inspiration are found elsewhere, particularly in the concepts of the *bath qol, Shekinah*, and Holy Spirit.[103] But these were increasingly reduced to symbols of the divine presence with, or of divine approval for, certain holy persons, who nevertheless spoke and acted not out of the immediacy of experienced relationship with God, but under the authority of the generally accepted external revelatory sources.[104] The case of John the Baptist is the exception that proves the rule. He appeared after a long period in which no generally accepted prophet had emerged. He encountered suspicion and hostility, from the religious as well as the political authorities, and had no successor in the later history of Judaism.

(c) Conclusion

The sincerity, courage, and total dedication to God on the part of many Jews who accepted the revelatory authority of the Torah in the period preceding and during Jesus' lifetime is not to be doubted; nor is their profound awareness of living in God's presence to be discounted. The point at issue here, however, is not their sincerity, or virtue, or whether their experience of God was genuine or not; the question is rather: In what way was the experience of or encounter with God apprehended and interpreted? And what implications were drawn from it concerning human beings and their obligations towards God and each other?

We have found all the movements and groups which we have considered, except for the Charismatics, to have accepted the Torah as the definitive and binding representation of God's relatedness towards, and of his will for, humankind. It remains to sum up the effects and implications of this

[103] Bowker, *Targums*, 44 n. 3; cf. Sanders, 214 f.
[104] Vermes, *Jesus*, 91 f. See above, n. 63.

recognition. First, the act of recognition constituted the unity of Judaism despite all the diversity.[105] Secondly, that which was recognized as divinely authoritative imparted its distinctive character to those who accorded it this recognition, despite the variations of interpretation of the Torah and qualifications of its demands. In particular, the Torah exercised the strongest influence over the most important question of all, namely the terms governing the relationship between God and humanity, which came to focus in the concept of holiness. The present argument maintains that the understanding of holiness found in the Torah was historically conditioned—the product of a given time and place—combining profound insight with imperfect vision. For that reason, the claim that it is eternally binding must be seriously questioned by any who in the light of scientific investigation accept the evolutionary conditions and limitations of human existence. In particular, the understanding derived from the Torah of what it is that separates humanity from God, though incorporating profound moral insight, incorporates also ideas which have contradictory implications. The logic of ritual purity, tending towards the separation of the holy God from the unclean world (see above, p. 90), runs counter to the doctrine of a good creation. Again, as extended to human beings, ritual purity gives rise to a kind of practical exclusiveness that runs counter to the doctrine of God's universal love and fatherhood.

Such developments in the understanding of holiness had their natural place in the history of humankind's discovery of God.[106] The negative consequences of an imperfect account of God only become serious when a stage on the path of discovery is treated as the goal, so that reappraisal and further development are precluded.[107] Thus, the third effect of holding the Torah to be divinely authoritative and eter-

[105] Schürer, 314 f.

[106] This is not to imply a Pelagian viewpoint (man by his own efforts able to find God). The discovery of God presupposes a God who lets himself be discovered—who meets humankind—and is revealed in the dynamic interaction of giving and receiving.

[107] Hengel, *Judaism*, 308, 'The failure of the attempt of the Hellenistic reformers to abolish the Torah by force in effect *fixed* intellectual development *on the Torah*' (emphasis original).

nally binding is the breaking of the polar dialectic. Human insight, even at its best, can never correspond perfectly to the divine truth; projecting it on to God isolates it from critical reflection under the impact of new experience. This leads to the loss of the creative role of human beings in interpreting experience, and hence denies them the possibility of arriving at a profounder awareness of God and of what God desires of them.

Historical movements rarely conform tidily to summary representations of them, and are rarely as internally coherent or logically consistent as the desire to categorize them is likely to suggest. Nevertheless, their continued existence in history is usually dependent on certain underlying principles by which they define what they are, what they are not, and who is entitled to belong. In this chapter an attempt has been made to discover, on the basis of the polarity model, what such principles were in the overall tradition of Judaism which Jesus inherited, and how they were interpreted within the diverse expressions of this tradition which were active in his time in Palestine. The Torah has emerged as the foundation document and norm of the community, conceived of not only as a gift of God himself but as expressing his eternal will and plan for creation. There certainly remained scope for creative interpretation, but once the premiss of the divine and binding authority of the Torah was accepted, the possibility of a basic reassessment of its terms by any individual in the light of any immediate experience or intuitive awareness of God was ruled out.[108] Any person claiming to speak or act for God, except within its terms, was by implication claiming an authority equal with or superior to the Torah's, and in effect claiming divine status in opposition to it, or at least independently of it. Hence we see the mixture of admiration and suspicion aroused by the Jewish Charismatics. They would seem to have been willing to live out their independence, drawing on tradition but not subjecting themselves to it totally, without pressing the conflict inherent in their position *vis-à-vis* most of their contemporaries to its logical conclusion.

[108] Ibid. 309, 'This fixation meant that any fundamental theological criticism of the world and the law could no longer develop freely within Judaism.'

If, as Vermes suggests, Charismatic Judaism illuminates the background from which Jesus the Galilean emerged, two questions arise. First, why did Jesus pursue a course which brought the issue to a head in the way it did? Secondly, what distinguishes him and his position not only from his fellow Jews in general, but from those whom we might call his fellow Charismatics? A brief answer to the first question could simply be this. A person who shared with perhaps some few Charismatic fellow Jews an immediate sense of filial relationship and personal intimacy with God, could well have been open to the possibilities of a special vocation, which might well have seemed illegitimate to those governed more strongly by public authority or majority opinion. Why, in the interpretation and pursuit of his vocation, Jesus took the precise course he did, is a question which perhaps can never be adequately answered in human terms; but an examination of the implications and effects of his course of action may take us some way towards an answer.

Our object, then, will be to discover, as far as the evidence permits, what understanding of God's relatedness came to expression through Jesus' words and actions. It is assumed here that Jesus' whole life was set within and organically related to the total structure of evolutionary existence and human history. The understanding of God's relatedness which he expressed must therefore be examined in the same terms as were applied to the other interpretations which we have considered, and which provided the context for Jesus' own activity. In short, the same critical questions concerning the polar dialectic and its preservation, and the concept of holiness and its implications, which have been applied to the other movements of Jesus' day, must be applied to the interpretation of God's relatedness that emerges with and from the figure of Jesus.

III

GOD'S RELATEDNESS
IN JESUS

INTRODUCTION

WE have been exploring the context into which Jesus came
and within which he lived. Without such an inquiry, it would
be impossible to appreciate the significance of any historical
figure. But in the case of Jesus more is at stake than with
figures of history in general. The question to be raised in
due course is, 'What are we to make of the claim that this
man was and is of universal and ultimate significance, and
accordingly, the one to whom the language of universal and
ultimate significance—the language of God—belongs as it
does to no other?'

Such a question pushes the contextual boundaries for the
understanding and evaluation of Jesus beyond any natural
limit in time or space. It can, indeed, only be raised where
the transcendent notions of universality and ultimacy have
already emerged in human thought. Part of the purpose of
this study so far has been to show how such notions took
shape in the Palestine of Jesus' day. Without this development, he could not have been acclaimed as of universal
and ultimate significance.

However, the conditions to be met if such claims are still to
be made today are not all identical with those which applied
in Jesus' day. Some of them were not and could not have been
in the mind of Jesus' contemporaries, or in his own mind, if
he shared their human condition (see below, p. 186). Yet they
must be met now if the claims made for Jesus are not to appear
arbitrary and unintelligible to our generation.

These new conditions are primarily those created by a

scientific evolutionary understanding of existence, as out-lined in Part I. How they bear upon the claim that Jesus is of universal and ultimate significance, and how those terms should be understood, may be briefly considered before we proceed with the story of Jesus himself.

In the first place, it must be emphasized that 'universality' is used here in the widest sense of embracing all that is, and not merely all who are. We are faced with the question of how Jesus relates not just to human beings, but to the totality of which we see ourselves to be a part—the universe as such.

Ideas of the universe are in fact very varied and have changed dramatically in the course of history. This points to their incompleteness and imperfection. Yet the claim that Jesus is of universal significance can be made sensibly today (and that means it can be accepted responsibly by rational beings) only if he can be seen to relate to the universe as we now actually conceive it to be, and not merely to the concept 'universe'. Whatever the limits of our understanding, for Jesus to be significant for us now he must in some way relate at least to those ideas about our world which have in fact compelled our assent, and which have in practice helped to determine our own self-understanding. The way he relates may be disturbing and even shattering, but that he can be seen to relate to the totality of ourselves in the total context of our existence is a precondition for the claim to his universal significance. If he cannot relate or be related to what we are, he cannot be a source of significant meaning for us. If he only relates to a part of what is, even the whole human part, he is not of universal significance in the fullest sense.

For many, if not most, people today evolution and the conditions pertaining to it are factors in their understanding of the universe and themselves which cannot be re-linquished. It is this as much as anything that distinguishes our thinking from that of Jesus and his contemporaries. If he was not only ignorant of the conditions of evolutionary existence (as a man of his age), but was actually exempt from them, it would be very hard to see how his mode of existence, if conceivable at all, could be related to our mode of exist-ence, or be reckoned to offer any clue to its meaning or any way of overcoming its disorders. It would be a different

matter if he were simply *portrayed* in this way. The problems
posed would then provoke a critical reconsideration of such
a portrayal,[1] and not leave us confounded by an underlying
'impossibility'. Our present aim is to show how Jesus might
be fully involved in the conditions of evolutionary existence,
as we are, and yet still be of universal and ultimate significance, without any whittling down of those concepts. The
response to him in that conviction would not then require
him to have been exempt from evolutionary conditions, nor
would it require us to surrender our scientific understanding
of the universe and of evolutionary existence within it.

The theory of evolution is not, of course, the only significant component in our modern world-view, but the need
here is not so much to identify other factors as to clarify the
second precondition of our question—ultimacy. No account
of the context of Jesus' life and ours would be complete if
it excluded the historical fact of humanity's pursuit of the
ultimate—the ground and goal of existence, the source of
meaning (who is sometimes called God)—and search for a
right relationship with him and for the symbols to express
it. The question of the ultimacy of Jesus could not have been
raised in his own day if the question of ultimacy had not
already been raised. It cannot be raised today where the
question of ultimacy makes no sense (if that is possible). If
it is to be raised, it is necessary to have some understanding
of the terms in which is was originally raised about Jesus,
and of the terms in which it is raised in the very different
world within which we live.

Our survey of the Israelite and Jewish tradition has been
necessary to answer the first question. The way in which the
question of ultimacy was raised, and answered, in Jesus' day
and age could not help but shape the way in which it was
raised and, as some believed, answered in Jesus. More than
this, it could not help but shape the way in which Jesus
experienced and reflected upon this question himself.

The second question, of ultimacy in present-day terms,
has already been engaging our attention; but before we can
consider further how Jesus may be seen to bear on it, we
must turn our attention to the way in which Jesus himself

[1] See above, p. 45.

confronted the question of ultimacy in the terms of his world. We will then have to look at the movement which gained its identity by acknowledging Jesus to be of universal and ultimate significance, and at how it developed the language to express this conviction, not only in the world Jesus shared, but in different worlds of thought and experience where the question had been asked in different terms. Despite its many failures, it has been the responsibility of that Jesus-centred movement to go on raising the question of ultimacy and pointing to Jesus as the source of the answer, in every world of thought and life down to the present day.[2] Only by doing so could that movement remain true to itself.

Before we proceed, the limitations imposed by the historico-critical method must be acknowledged.[3] We do not have direct access to information about Jesus, and must rely on accounts which critical investigations have shown to be subject to various influences, at greater or lesser remove from the situations they purport to describe. I accept that no absolute certainty attaches to any specific word or action concerning Jesus as recorded in the New Testament. Nevertheless, though careful discrimination is necessary in attributing greater or lesser reliability to different sections of the texts, in the writings as a whole a more or less coherent picture emerges of a figure who made a striking impact on his contemporaries. The reasons why Jesus made such an impact emerge with considerable force in the available records. The uncertainties and apparent discrepancies, so far from undermining the underlying validity of the story of Jesus, reflect in part the inescapable limitations of any human product (including all historical records), and in part also the genuinely varied, creative impact of this figure on different individuals. These brought to their encounter with him various presuppositions, preoccupations, and ways of thinking and talking; hence they would be bound to differ in their account of the experience of meeting him at first hand, or of encountering him indirectly through the original witnesses. In a similar way, the impact of an important new play on theatre-goers may be very varied, and the reviews

[2] J. A. T. Robinson, *The Human Face of God* (London, 1973), 16.
[3] See above, chap. 2, sect. 3.

of it may be strikingly different; yet, taken together, they will provide more illumination than can be found in any single report. To conclude from their differences that no play occurred would be absurd; to conclude that, if it occurred, nothing can be known of the central character would be almost equally absurd. If the point at issue were not the central character in some sort of hypothetical isolation, but his impact on others and in particular on the reviewers themselves, their own reports would have the value of direct evidence.

Such an analogy does admittedly over-simplify the matter. In contrast to a play and its review, the New Testament writings and the original event of Jesus are separated by a period of many years. The precise length of the interval is disputed, but probably at least thirty years separate Jesus' crucifixion from what is believed by most scholars to be the earliest Gospel, St Mark.

As a result, biblical critics must distinguish between what may be the authentic words of Jesus, eye-witness reports, and the record of the earliest responses to him on the one hand, and the later reaction of the Church to the earliest tradition on the other. Finally, the evangelist's own creative role in organizing the complex material available to him must be evaluated.[4]

The task is difficult and leaves plenty of scope for disagreement. Nevertheless, it can still be argued that there is indirect evidence available concerning Jesus, and particularly concerning his interpretation of God's relatedness, which need not be treated with exaggerated scepticism. Beyond this, the New Testament writings do provide us with direct evidence from a large though uncertain number of near contemporaries of Jesus. Whether we know the authors' names or not makes little difference here. In their writings they convey their own interpretations of God's relatedness, and unanimously acknowledge that their convictions derive from the impact of Jesus on their lives, whether directly or

---

[4] This has been the main interest of much recent New Testament study (redaction criticism). See J. Rohde, *Rediscovering the Teaching of the Evangelists* (London, 1968). See also P. Henry, *New Directions in New Testament Study* (London, 1980), 138 ff.

through the tradition they have received. The fact that the historical Jesus is not objectively available to us does not mean, therefore, that he was not there, or is totally inaccessible. Our question now is, 'What was there? What sort of relationship with God and what understanding of holiness were expressed by that man at that moment in the course of evolution and human history?' We approach him in the setting of a community living by the Torah, but at the same time longing for the new age in which God would reign supreme.

5. The Originality of Jesus

1. THE TORAH AND JESUS' WAY

(a) The Torah and the new age

How the conviction came to Jesus that he had a mission to speak for God, even to the point of challenging the Torah, is a question that can never be fully answered, but certain factors and evidences may show that what happened was not wholly arbitrary or unintelligible.

One important factor was the continuing eschatological excitement. It flared up, as we have seen, in the Maccabean rebellion, and was not extinguished by the disappointment that followed. Indeed, it may well have been heightened by the plausibility crisis[1] evoked by the Roman occupation of Palestine. The point here is its bearing on the revelatory supremacy of the Torah. Pharisees and others could claim that the Torah was eternally valid as the revelation of God, but historically this conviction only arose after the exile, as evidenced by Ben Sira's identification of the Torah with Wisdom about two hundred years before Jesus' day. This view of the Torah did not entirely displace the earlier and, it could be said, more characteristically Israelite view that God disclosed himself not so much in words as in mighty acts in history. In times of oppression there was likely to be a resurgence of the hope that God would finally vindicate himself and his people by intervening on their behalf and thus revealing his Lordship over history. For this act of revelation to be complete and final, it must mark the end of history and inaugurate a new age of God's rule.

Closely associated with this hope was the highly charged symbol of the Messiah. The prophets, who judged the kings to have failed in their service to God, encouraged the hope that God would send a faithful king in David's line. This anointed one or Messiah would rule God's chosen people

[1] See Berger, *Social Reality*, 17, 154.

righteously and overthrow their enemies. Early expectations were for a human righteous king, who would act in history.[2] Later, the coming of the Messiah was associated with the final act with which God would bring history to an end. The Messiah would be God's agent in the inauguration of the new age. How well defined or widely accepted the idea of the Messiah was in Jesus' day is a subject of continuing debate,[3] but it seems likely that it already had an important place in the complex imagery of eschatological expectation.

Where such hopes were alive within Judaism, the question would arise of the Torah's standing in the age to come. The problem is created by the clash between two divergent concepts of revelation.[4] According to one, it is an already given suprahistorical disclosure of the way things are. What is revealed is the divine plan of creation and God's immutable will. This was the characteristic Pharisaic view of the Torah. On the other view, revelation is not a disclosure of truth about God or his creation, but a saving act of God. In times of trouble this could be eagerly anticipated, but could not by definition be thought of as an already present reality. Equally, from this point of view, what was already present could not logically be the final revelation and so, one would suppose, would be superseded in the final act of revelation.

The tension between these two points of view may help to account for the ambiguities surrounding the status of the Torah in the Messianic age. The question of whether some Jews believed it would actually be superseded, perhaps by a new Messianic Torah, has been considered by Davies and others. The evidence on the whole is against this,[5] though the filtering process to which early Jewish sources have been subjected by later orthodoxy prevents absolute certainty. It is at least interesting to find that Ben Sira's identification of Wisdom and the given Torah is apparently rejected in the

[2] See Schürer, 488-554.
[3] Cf. A. E. Harvey, *Jesus and the Constraints of History* (London, 1982).
[4] Cf. J. Neusner, 'The Use of Later Rabbinic Evidence for the Study of First Century Pharisaism', in W. Scott Green, ed., *Approaches to Ancient Judaism*, i (Missoula, Mont., 1978), 225.
[5] See R. Banks, *Jesus and the Law in the Synoptic Tradition* (Cambridge, 1975), 65 ff.

apocalyptic book of 1 Enoch, the earliest parts of which were probably written in the second century BC.[6] 1 Enoch 42: 1 reads 'Wisdom went forth to make her dwelling among the children of men and found no dwelling-place.'[7]

After quoting this verse, Davies refers to a number of other passages where it is claimed that Wisdom in its fullness is the mark of Messianic expectation (1 Enoch 48: 1; 49: 1 ff.; cf. 5: 8; 91: 10; and 2 Baruch 44: 14). He goes on to say 'and with Wisdom, we may confidently repeat, goes the Torah in its fullness'. However, once the identification of written Torah and Wisdom has been set aside, it is hard to see what the phrase 'Torah in its fullness' can mean, unless it serves simply as a symbolic expression of God's eternal righteous will. The problem is precisely how far the written Torah conforms to that.

The weight of available evidence, however, points to a different resolution of the tension between eschatological hope and confidence in the Torah as revelation. The belief was widespread that the Messiah would settle all points of dispute over the interpretation of the Torah and create conditions in which at last it could be perfectly understood and observed.[8] The eternal and immutable value of the given Torah would thus, it seems, be firmly upheld. Yet the expectation of new understanding implied that the Torah as currently received and interpreted might, at least in part or in some sense, be superseded; ultimate authority would shift from the book to be interpreted to the Messiah, its interpreter. Perhaps the difference between these two solutions is not so very great after all.

Whatever the status of the Torah in the age to come, most Jews would have agreed that strict observance of the Torah in the present age at least was the fundamental condition for participation in that age. Those less committed to the Pharisaic view of the Torah might have been even more willing to accept the possibility of its abrogation in the new age, and have been less committed to it in the present age.

Perhaps it was the survival of the prophetic tradition and

[6] Hengel, *Judaism*, 176.
[7] Quoted in Davies, 142, where the striking contrast with Ecclus. 24 is noted.
[8] Ibid. 142; Banks, 80; M. Hengel, *The Son of God* (London, 1976), 64.

apocalyptic hope in Galilee that stood in the way of the Torah's absolute claims there (to Rabbi Yohanan ben Zakkai's distress), and left room for the Charismatics. Perhaps it was this which left open the possibility of relinquishing the Torah's claims even among those deeply attached to it and committed to it in the present age.

It would not be unreasonable to see this as the milieu in which Jesus' own understanding and expectations took shape. A new wave of eschatological excitement was aroused by the appearance of John the Baptist. It certainly seems that he provided the immediate stimulus for Jesus to embark on his own ministry (Mark 1: 9).

However, the importance of apocalyptic expectation should not be exaggerated to the point of supposing that we cannot understand Jesus at all, since we do not share his apocalyptic world-view.[9] As we shall shortly see, he was not enslaved to existing political or religious systems; nor, we may suppose, was he so enslaved to the symbol-systems of his day that we cannot begin to appreciate his position unless we enslave ourselves to them.

On the contrary, awareness of this milieu may help us to see how within the broader context of commitment to the Torah it was possible for one man both to acknowledge its God-given value, and at the same time, without being totally idiosyncratic, to conceive that the possibilities of a new relationship between God and humankind were about to be realized; that the new age was indeed dawning in which the written Torah's claim to ultimacy would be set aside.

It is against this general background that the question of Jesus' own attitude to the Torah may be approached.

(b) Jesus' attitude to the Torah

Whether Jesus came to annul or to fulfil the Torah has been a controversial issue since his own day. We must give some attention to this question and consider what is at stake.

It is indisputable that Jesus challenged current interpretations of the Torah—the oral Torah. The harder question is whether in fact he took issue with the written

---

[9] Cf. Davies, 429.

Torah or, more fundamentally, was opposed to the Torah in principle.[10]

Any attempt to answer such questions is beset by the ambiguities surrounding the word 'Torah' and the problem of evaluating the available evidence. The point at issue is Jesus' attitude to the written Torah, specifically the Pentateuch. One problem is that different terms are used—'Torah', 'Law', 'Law of Moses', and 'Law of God'—which are often, but not always, synonymous and interchangeable. Secondly, the tensions we have already noted between ideas of the Torah now and the Torah in the age to come make it harder to evaluate just what was and what was not eternal and immutable about the Torah as it stood in the ancient texts. Modern writers attempt to express this sense of continuity within discontinuity by employing such expressions as 'the Torah in principle', or 'the essence of the Torah', or 'the Torah in its fullness', but it is virtually impossible to know precisely what such language means.

Thirdly, the New Testament writers give different impressions of Jesus' attitude to the Torah. Matthew, for example, seems to have been anxious to depict Jesus not only as fulfilling the Torah 'in principle', but as upholding the written Torah itself. His Jesus in fact reminds us of Qumran's Teacher of Righteousness; the same tension persists between upholding and fulfilling the Torah, though Matthew goes much further in attaching Messianic authority to Jesus.[11] Mark, in contrast, portrays Jesus in conflict with the written Torah (Mark 7: 14-15; cf. Lev. 11) and implies a more radical discontinuity.

Fourthly, the question arises as to whether the Gospels are depicting the conflicts of Jesus' day or of a later period, particularly the clash between Church and synagogue towards the end of the first century AD (see below, p. 180).

Those engaged in this debate are thus faced with considerable problems in evaluating the evidence and defining meanings. This means that no certain answer can be given to the question of Jesus' attitude to the Torah; but three further observations may be made which bear on the issue.

[10] Ibid. 428. See Banks for a full examination of the issue.
[11] Davies, 215 f.

First, since the Torah in practice bore on many spheres of everyday life, domestic and civil as well as religious, it is only to be expected that Jesus conformed to it most of the time. Only a fanatical anarchist might have tried not to, and Jesus was not that. His usual willingness to abide by it therefore offers no proof that he attributed absolute revelatory significance to the Torah, even if he regarded it as of great worth and as a gift of God.

Secondly, the possibility that Jesus rejected the ultimate authority of the Torah should not be taken to imply that his relationship to God was anarchical. In Jesus' day the identification of the Torah with the eternal will of God, through the symbol of Wisdom, carried the implication that to rebel against the Torah was to rebel against God. Anyone brought up on that identification who responded to Jesus might find it very hard to represent Jesus as annulling the written Torah. Was this perhaps Matthew's predicament? A similar problem arises when the terms 'Torah' or (more usually) 'Law of God' are used as virtual synonyms of 'form' in the present study. But the possibility that Jesus rejected the Torah or the Law of God, where that stands for the written Torah, does not mean that he rebelled against God's eternal will or that his relationship with God was formless. If this is clear, at least judgement concerning Jesus' attitude to the written Torah will not be distorted by misplaced anxieties over the implications of a negative conclusion.

Finally, in relation to such conclusions, the dividing-line may be extremely narrow between the view that Jesus upheld the Torah, even the written Torah, but reinterpreted it or intensified its demands in a radically new way, and the view that he annulled the existing Torah and brought to humanity a radically new understanding of God's will (which might or might not be described by analogy as the 'true Torah' or as disclosing 'the Torah in its fullness').

At this point we may suppose that the question of Jesus' own attitude to the Torah is not after all so very important (which may be why the New Testament fails to provide any clear answer to it). Not even the written Torah could be received as revelatory without interpretation. So the issue lies inevitably between interpretations, and not between written Torah and interpreted Torah. Either Jesus believed himself to be giving the true interpretation which was not to be found elsewhere; or he was giving what in his eyes was the true interpretation of God and his will which was not fully expressed even in the written Torah, let alone anywhere else.[12] Either way, Jesus represented a radical challenge to the Torah as currently received and interpreted. Those whose understanding and behaviour were shaped by the Torah without reference to Jesus were confronted by an alternative representation of God and his will through Jesus, whatever his own attitude to the written Torah may have been. In representing God in a new way, Jesus demonstrated his freedom from the constraints of written book and existing interpretation. In this sense he may be said to have rejected the sovereignty of the Torah, and we can speak of a conflict between a Torah-centred and a Jesus-centred understanding of God.

(c) Jesus' way of life

Jesus came from Galilee, the land of bandits and religious eccentrics, Zealots and Charismatics. He was a man of the countryside, as his use of rural imagery and avoidance of the larger towns of Galilee suggest.[13] Only a compelling sense of obligation would drive him to the city of Jerusalem, not merely as a pilgrim in the crowd, but to challenge the religious and political leaders of his day.

It may be that the discovery of extraordinary powers at his command, believed to derive only from God, strengthened Jesus' own conviction that God was with him.[14] For his contemporaries, in Galilee especially, these powers to heal and exorcize would certainly have legitimated his claim to represent God.[15]

It can hardly be doubted that Jesus experienced an intensely intimate relationship with God, whom he freely addressed as 'Father' (Abba). Within this relationship, it seems, he became conscious of a special vocation to witness

[12] Ibid. 428, 'There is much in his activity in the Gospels which suggests an attitude of sovereign freedom towards the Law.'
[13] Theissen, 47.
[14] Vermes, *Jesus*, 79. Cf. Weber, 47.
[15] Vermes, *Jesus*, 74.

to God, and to the possibilities of a new relationship with God. Out of the interaction of this experience with the historical and conceptual milieu within which he lived, the conviction may well have emerged in him that he had a special role to play in heralding and even inaugurating the longed-for new age.

The heart of Jesus' message was the good news of the possibility of a new relationship with God, a relationship made possible by God's love, but calling for urgent decision in the face of threatening godlessness, if it was to be enjoyed. In proclaiming his message, Jesus drew on the interpretative resources of Jewish tradition, on the familiar imagery of everyday life, and on apocalyptic symbolism; but, on the evidence of the New Testament, he did not need others to tell him what God offered and required. We may suppose that the more he was aware of God's presence with him, the less he would have had to depend on outside authority. In other words, he did not need to look to others to discover the meaning of holiness.

One of the most striking features of the Gospel records is in fact Jesus' disavowal of external authority. Mark records that after Jesus' first visit to the synagogue at Capernaum, 'The people were astounded at his teaching, for unlike the doctors of the Law he taught with a note of authority' (Mark 1: 27). The recurrent formula found in Matthew 5 points in the same direction: 'You have learned that our forefathers were told . . . But what I tell you is this . . .'

The most distinctive feature of Jesus' way of life was his disregard of so many of the conventional rules of holiness. He was taken to task for his lack of asceticism (Matt. 11: 19), for his own or his followers' failure to observe the rules of ritual cleanliness before eating (Mark 7: 2), and for his disregard of the stricter rules governing sabbath observance (Matt. 12: 1–7). This alone was enough to disturb those who believed that such matters were not trivial in any way, but the touchstone by which loyalty and love towards God could be tested.

Even more serious and blatantly scandalous was Jesus' willingness to associate with unholy people, foreigners and

notorious sinners, such as prostitutes and officials who col-
luded with the hated Roman occupation forces (Mark 2: 15).
In view of the company he kept, it might seem that he was
as ready to disregard the claims of moral as of ritual purity.
To behave thus and still to claim to speak and act in God's
name posed a challenge to his contemporaries which would
have to be taken seriously. The issue might still have never
come to a head if Jesus had been willing to remain on the
fringe of Jewish life, in the remote and already suspect northern province, where perhaps nothing better would be expected. But when this Galilean holy man presented himself
in person in the Holy City and in the holy Temple, and
continued to express his own interpretation of God's holiness publicly in words and action, the challenge to the Torah
and the concepts of holiness grounded in it could not be
allowed to pass.

By his readiness to put into practice the implications of his
own understanding of holiness, despite the risks he incurred,
Jesus demonstrated the character and strength of his inner
convictions and his integrity in living in accordance with
them, but not *ipso facto* their truth. Judgement on that issue
would then and can now only proceed from personal response to the challenge of Jesus. He never offered proof, but
called for decision and made a decision inescapable, whether
for or against himself. This he did by embodying an alternative account of God in the place which already claimed
to have the true account of God, and which logically and
theologically could not tolerate two different accounts of the
one true God. One or the other would have to go.

We must now examine the alternative way of holiness
which Jesus presented and see how it stood over against the
prevailing idea of God within Judaism and, more specifically, how the understanding of holiness derived from
Jesus contrasted with holiness grounded in the Torah.

(d) Jesus' way of holiness

Jesus' refusal to let the Torah define his relationship to God
had radical and far-reaching implications. It meant that the
logic of moral holiness could be liberated from the exclusivist
constraints imposed by the logic of ritual holiness, and be

developed in a new, inclusive way. Secondly, the character
of moral holiness itself would appear in a new light when its
basic point of reference was no longer the Torah, but that
understanding of God into which Jesus entered. Morality
defined in terms of a visible and fixed form of reference
brooks no modification in the context of changing circumstances in the world; and the more it is isolated from the
dynamic of personal interaction, the greater is the risk of a
state of alienation arising, as defined in contemporary sociology of knowledge (see above, chap. 1, sect. 3). At the
extreme point, morality then manifests itself as moralism or
legalism (the two forms, internalized or externalized, of an
alienated ethical standpoint).

Where recognition of a real sense of relationship with a
personal God lies behind the acknowledgment of the binding
authority of a particular code of law, the alienating impetus
will be held in check. But the less the awareness of that
personal relationship, or the more a static form is held to be
the form of God himself, the greater the risk of a state of
alienation with its symptoms of moralism and legalism. On
this account, neither unqualified condemnation nor unqualified defence of the Judaism of Jesus' day is justified.
There is evidence to be found in the New Testament and
elsewhere of different positions within its confines, and the
sweeping charge of legalism must be withdrawn, as we have
noted.[16] The case presented here is that Jesus took the
dangerous course of standing against the strong current
which was already driving the Jewish community towards
identifying the Torah with the form of God. In so doing he
checked the impetus towards alienation, broke through the
net of moralism and legalism, and restored the possibility of
a dynamic relationship with a personal, righteous, and loving
God.

As we have seen, in the eyes of most of Jesus' contemporaries love of the Torah in its totality and of God
belonged together; anyone who rejected the binding authority of the Torah in any respect rejected God. No distinctions could be drawn between its ethical exhortations,

---

[16] Sanders, 212–33.

its liturgical regulations and moral rules, and its function as a witness to God's covenant.

But Jesus drew a distinction. He loved God as the Torah enjoined, but not on the terms which it or its later interpreters defined. When he was asked what was the most important commandment, he drew upon the Law in his answer—but only to establish from it a principle that transcended all laws and required a total orientation of life in terms of personal response. 'Love the Lord your God with all your heart, with all your soul, and all your strength, and with all your mind; and your neighbour as yourself' (Luke 10: 27); a portrayal of neighbourliness follows, in the story of the good Samaritan, which shatters the circles of holiness that ring Samaritans and Jews.

In the light of the evidence, we may draw these conclusions. Jesus accepted the Torah as a witness to God and his love for his people, as a record of their response, faithful or faithless, and as a source of inspiration. He denied that the rigorous observance of the Torah and all the regulations stemming from it was the touchstone by which human love for God should be tested, or the condition for God's love to be exercised on our behalf. In short, he rejected the codification of man's relationship with God or God's relationship with man. But if the Torah and the tradition which declared God's relatedness did not adequately portray it, it would have to be reportrayed in word and action; and the matter was too important to be left on the fringes of provincial life where no notice need be taken.

It was Jesus' refusal to accept the absolute sovereignty of the Torah, and at the same time his refusal to reject it outright, that posed the biggest problem for his contemporaries and subsequent generations. Even though he did not tie himself to Pharisaic regulations, he most probably took the written Torah very seriously. But where regulations appeared to stand in the way of the immediate response of love to human need, he was ready to disregard them (Mark 3: 1–6).

His willingness, already mentioned, to associate with outcasts of every kind was unprecedented, and marks him out

from the Charismatics and the prophets before them.[17]
When, according to Mark, the Pharisees expressed their hor-
ror to Jesus' disciples—'He eats with tax-gatherers and sinners!'—he replied: 'It is not the healthy that need a doctor,
but the sick; I did not come to invite virtuous people, but
sinners' (Mark 2: 16). There was no established tradition or
authority for this kind of behaviour, and hence the distinctiveness of Jesus' own position is disclosed by it. To be
an outcast was to be excluded from the circle of holiness,
from the fellowship of those with whom God would be expected to relate, as supposed within circles committed to the
Torah. To enter the house of a foreigner, to touch a leper
(Mark 1: 41), to accompany and to eat with prostitutes and
traitors, would render the clean unclean, the holy unholy
(Luke 7: 39). In doing these things, Jesus either proved
himself to be unholy, and to be acting in the freedom of
irresponsibility and anarchy in opposition to God, as his
opponents supposed; or, as his followers came to believe, he
witnessed to the creative freedom and true holiness of God.
Which conclusion is correct is a matter of dispute now as it
was then. The answers we can give to three questions will
bear strongly on the decision to be reached. Was the kind
of freedom and quality of holiness which Jesus expressed
coherent and consistent, and not anarchic? Was it after all
in keeping with God as already known in Israel's tradition,
and not alien or opposed? And finally, did it prove to be
creative in its effects?

2. THE COHERENCE OF JESUS

(a) The logic of freedom

In the strength of his inner conviction, Jesus could draw on
the rich interpretative resource of the Torah without being
committed to the premiss that it represented the eternally
binding terms of God's relationship to humankind. The
same would apply to the oral Torah. Jesus' position had
negative and positive implications in theory and practice. He
was free from the constraints of the Torah's account of God's

---

[17] Vermes, *Jesus*, 224.

relatedness (though not, of course, from the hostility of those who accepted that account). This meant that he was free, in the first place, to relate to God on different terms; secondly, to relate to the world and his fellow human beings on different terms; and thirdly, to speak of God's relationship to the world and human beings in different terms. In effect, not only was Jesus freed from the traditional conditions of relationship defined by the Torah, but he freed God from the same constraints, or at least from appearing to be governed by the same constraints.

In this freedom Jesus could put forward his own understanding of God on the basis of his relationship with him, without being self-contradictory and without incurring the sense of guilt which is produced in a person who fails to conform to what he in fact holds to be authoritative. This brings us to the point where his understanding of God's relatedness, that is, his understanding of holiness, can be contrasted with the views prevalent in his day.

(b) *The logic of ritual holiness*

In the interpretation of holiness represented by Jesus, we can recognize the positive reaffirmation of one strand of the great tradition within which he stood, namely the acknowledgement of God as the personal creative ground of all that exists (Matt. 10: 29–30), righteous and loving, caring for his people despite their failures, requiring of them only that they turn away from false paths and respond to him again in love. This strand we previously associated particularly with the prophetic tradition.

The other strand, which was associated above particularly with the priestly tradition and the sense of sacred presence, represented God's holiness in traditional terms of ritual purity. Logically, ritual holiness can be maintained regardless of the presence or absence of moral response, and moral response can be exercised regardless of ritual observance. Perhaps the Sadducees in Jesus' day could be charged with being concerned merely with the requirements of ritual holiness. Certainly their reputation for righteousness was not always good,[18] but that was not typical of Judaism as a whole,

[18] Josephus, *Ant.* xx. 179–81.

least of all of the Hasidim and the Pharisaic movement. Here
the lesson of the prophets was well learnt, that ritual purity
was useless without moral purity. But the former was not
discounted. Rather, as we have seen, the two strands ran
closely in parallel, and almost converged, so that the languages of ritual and moral purity overlapped and became
almost interchangeable. This need have posed no problem
at the level of metaphor and imagery, but did so, as argued
above (pp. 96 ff.), where the logics of the two models were
combined. In this case the scope and quality of moral holiness came under the constraint of the logic of ritual holiness.
One manifestation of it can be illustrated from the paradoxical conjunction among the Essenes of love for all mankind[19] as one of their three fundamental principles, and the
rule that a senior member of the sect must wash himself after
contact with a junior as though he had been defiled by a
foreigner.[20]

Jesus was not bound by this two-sided concept of holiness
derived from Torah and tradition. In his account of God's
relatedness, the quasi-physical concepts of ritual purity and
impurity were not merely allegorized, but swept away. He
did not simply introduce a spiritual interpretation with moral connotations to be set alongside the literal observance of
traditional regulations. The mass of regulations that would
often have no moral content or bearing on human needs he
rejected as unnecessary burdens (Matt. 23: 4).[21] He took
an even firmer stand where regulations existed whose force
derived from the logic of ritual holiness, but whose effect
was to divide human beings from each other or to impede
the expression of love. Then, so far from holding their observance to be essential as proof of love for God, Jesus demonstrated that the practical expression of God-like love
necessitated their disregard, whatever reaction this might
provoke from others (Mark 3: 1-6).[22]

In theoretical terms, then, the contradiction between the
inclusiveness of moral concern and the exclusiveness of ritual

---

[19] Driver, 104.

[20] Ibid. 102; Josephus, *War*, ii. 150.

[21] In contrast to the Pharisees and Qumran: see Driver, 88; Vermes, *Jesus*, 65.

[22] But see Danby, *Mishnah*, 172, 'Whenever there is doubt whether life is in
danger this overrides the Sabbath' (*Yoma*, 8. 6; cf. *Shabbath*, 18. 3).

observance was resolved in Jesus' outlook by his denial of
the binding authority of the Torah; hence he was free to
disregard the logic of ritual purity. On this understanding,
God could reach out to his creation and his people without
the logical, let alone the practical, possibility of incurring
pollution in a quasi-physical way. At the same time, it followed that any person giving expression to God's righteous
love under conditions of worldly existence could do so without any risk of ritual pollution and, ritual observance being
no longer regarded as expressing his eternal will, without
risk of offending God. Only those who thought otherwise
might be offended.

(c) The logic of moral holiness

The position reached so far is that, apart from the pre-
supposition of the Torah, it is logically possible to hold that
the morally pure can touch and associate with the supposedly
ritually impure without contracting pollution. But mention
has already been made of the interchangeability of the languages of moral and ritual purity. The unclean who were
held to be excluded from the circles of holiness were held to
be excluded quite as much on moral as ritual grounds. If the
latter were disregarded, the pressing question would still
remain: How could moral purity relate to moral impurity
without compromising itself? How could the holy and righteous God relate to the wicked without compromising his
righteousness? To express the issue in brief, even if Jesus'
right to touch a leper (Mark 1: 41) is granted, what right had
he to forgive sins (Mark 2: 5)?

The nature of sin and the conditions for reconciliation are
matters on which volumes have been written. Here it is only
possible to present the issue in the briefest way in terms of
the present approach, without exploring every conceivable
line of argument in detail.

We have seen that Jesus no less than the Torah witnessed
both to God's love and to his righteousness. He did not
represent God's love as sentimentality devoid of any moral
concern and indifferent to the response of human beings.
The question, then, is how these two strands, love and

righteousness, can be reconciled. How can the logic of divine justice be reconciled with the logic of divine love?[23]

To begin with a general principle: where the sovereign freedom of a personal agent—human or divine—is acknowledged, an action on his part, however arbitrary or capricious, is not open to question or complaint. But where a sense of morality prevails and, in particular, where moral righteousness is attributed to God, it is less easy to admit to arbitrary or capricious acts on his part, contrary to the prevailing view of morality. Theodicy develops—the justification of God when his ways seem hard to justify. The more clearly defined the character of moral righteousness attributed to God—that is, when his demands are spelt out explicitly and his consistency in upholding them and punishing infringement is held to be unequivocal—the more clear-cut are the limitations on what can be said of him and on what he can do. A moral God cannot disregard his own law.

Within Judaism, the belief that God in his free initiative created the covenant with his people established the primacy of both his love and his sovereign freedom in an important way. If the covenant was not the result of any logical or external necessity imposed upon God, then neither pride nor complacency but gratitude and answering love were the proper response. The foundation of this covenant and the terms of it were preserved in sacred traditions and received final written form in the Torah. It combined, as we have seen, both affirmation of God's love and the demand for a proper response from God's people. This was to be expressed not only in terms of attitude or even of moral behaviour, but in terms of the performance of extensive and detailed regulations concerning ritual practice and everyday life. Within this combination lay the seeds of acute tension.

With increasing reverence for the Torah as expressive in every detail of God's eternal will, the principle of Law rose alongside that of love in the definition of God. In effect, divine status came to be attributed to that which from a

---

[23] As suggested by the title of R. E. Weingart's book on Abelard, *The Logic of Divine Love* (Oxford, 1970).

critical historical perspective remained a historically conditioned human product. Whatever the source or sources
that inspired it, in its tangible form this body of material
was a collection of detailed regulations governing religion
and everyday life, in a particular society at a particular time
(see above, chap. 3, sect. 3). The more closely it was identified with God, the more it would acquire the binding authority and immutability of God himself, as the perfect
expression of his righteous will. Such identification would
mean not only that men and women were bound by it, but
that God was too, since for him to exercise freedom in respect of what was taken to be his express and eternal will
would entail intolerable contradiction within God. He could
not be held to will something eternally and at the same time
will not to will it. It is at this point that commitment to the
Law incorporated in the Torah becomes the equivalent to
commitment to God himself. The original human ante-
cedents and contingent factors, such as the influence of the
logic of ritual purity, will no longer be admitted if the human
creative activity in the promulgation of these laws is forgotten, discounted, or denied, and they are seen as coming
direct from God—as expressive of his will—irrespective of
whether their purpose is intelligible to human minds or not.

But the denial of any possibility of conflict between God
and what was understood to be the expression of his will
entails a conflict of a different kind, that between his
righteousness or justice and his love. As equal attributes of
God, neither can yield to the other. Yet God's justice, as
now defined in terms of immutable law, has an objective in
conflict with the objectives of love. The Law as explicitly
defined requires for its satisfaction obedience or the paying
of penalties. The penalties are equally clearly defined as
entailing exclusion from relationship with God. But the object of love is the restoration of that relationship, and hence
the avoidance of penalties. An impasse of this kind was to
recur in an even more acute form in the Christian Church
when it accepted the Old Testament, including the Torah,
as the revelatory word of God. But here we shall confine
ourselves to the shape of the problem and ways of resolution
proferred within Judaism.[24]

[24] I hope to pursue the later developments of the problem within Christianity in
a book in preparation, *The Originality of Jesus and Symbols of Reconciliation.*

One might say that here the two elements—love as witnessed to in the Torah, and justice as conceived in terms of the Torah—were both affirmed, but that their conflicting logic was not fully reconciled. Both the binding authority of all the detailed law in the Torah and the fact of human failure to keep it perfectly were generally acknowledged;[25] but it was held that God in his love had already provided the means of wiping out offences and effecting reconciliation through the sacrifical system (Lev. 17: 11). It is interesting that sacrifices for sin and guilt seem to have come into prominence in Jewish religion just when sacred tradition was being formalized in the Torah.[26] The requirements of God's own justice could thereby be met on the terms which he himself provided. This provision was in itself evidence of the primacy of love, but we see it matched with a concern to preserve the immutability of law and justice in a way that could lead to the loss of the freedom of love.

In the Jewish tradition, the concept of sacrifice was greatly enlarged metaphorically to embrace all acts of piety, prayer, fasting, charity, and keeping the Law in general. This development made possible the survival of the religion of the Torah despite the destruction of the Temple and the ending of the system of animal sacrifice. These extensions of sacrifice as the God-given means of reconciliation still recognized the binding authority of the Torah—its normativeness in defining what God required of human beings, and so also in defining the nature of sin. Awareness of the nature of sin, and hence of the possibility of avoiding it, was thus available in principle only to those who lived under the Torah. At the same time, only those who had the Torah had the means of avoiding the divine wrath which sin incurred.

Within this conceptual framework, two lines of thought could develop, emphasizing the authority of the Torah or God's free love respectively. In the first case, God's love in giving the Torah is not denied, but thereafter conformity to the Torah is seen as the means of avoiding or atoning for sin, and so securing God's favour. God's free love can scarcely

[25] Sanders, 203.
[26] de Vaux, 432.

be exercised apart from this observance, without making a nonsense of his own divine law.

On the other hand, a deeper religious sensitivity, widespread in Judaism, recognizes that a person's capacity to keep the Torah can never be adequate.[27] The gap can only be bridged by God's mercy. This implies that the freedom of divine love transcends the binding authority of divine law. It raises the question of whether there can be any limit to God's love and mercy. A limit might be found in terms of membership of the community whose relationship to God is determined by the Torah. Yet the troubling suspicion that God's mercy could extend beyond this limit[28] did not entirely disappear and posed an unresolved question concerning the Torah.

The structure outlined here hinges on the assumption that the regulations specified in the Torah and tradition were derived from God himself and were eternally binding. No worldly historical or practical consideration could justify their infringement. The Pharisees were well known for their efforts to make it possible for ordinary people to keep the Law; only extreme rigorists such as the Qumran covenanters[29] could accuse them of making it easy. No law could be lightly regarded or set aside on grounds of expediency or compassion. Rigorous observance was required. It remains true that, compared with the attitude that looked no further than the written form itself, a sense of living in the presence of God and in dependence on his mercy would lessen the harsher characteristics of legalism or moralism. Nevertheless, the outward effects might seem to be the same in either case from the point of view of the morally fallen or the supposedly ritually unclean person. The more commitment to God was identified with commitment to every detail of the formalized Law, the less room there was for the devotee to respond in spontaneous compassion to the needs of those who failed to conform for whatever reason, or for God to do likewise. The solution in the last resort of consigning a person to the mercy of God when mercy could not

[27] Sanders, 203.
[28] Ibid. 209.
[29] Driver, 94. See Theissen, 83.

be shown to him by God's servants, betrays an unresolved and, one might believe, an unacceptable contradiction.

3. HOLY LOVE AND THE POLAR DIALECTIC

(a) The logic of holy love

The argument presented here is that the conflict between God's justice and God's love, as traditionally represented in the Judaeo-Christian tradition, is incapable of logical resolution. Appeals to paradox are as unsatisfactory as inadequate attempts at resolution. Contemporary studies can help us now to recognize that the two parties to the conflict as portrayed, love and justice, are not of equal standing. The love perceived by Jews in the creation of the covenant is believed by Christians to have come to light in a new way in the life of Jesus. The concept of justice, or rather, the content attributed to traditional concepts of God's justice, emerges as a human product, whether shaped by Jewish or by Christian minds.

The solution begins with the denial of the definitive status of the Torah. Liberation from the logic of ritual holiness, which was presumed to correspond to God's holiness, is then matched by liberation from the logic of a theory of justice, which was presumed to correspond to divine justice. By drawing on his own understanding of God—an understanding shaped by the Torah and tradition but not wholly determined by it—Jesus was free in logic and practice to interpret God's will in a new way,[30] totally consistent with his experience and understanding of God's love, unconstrained by the conditions assumed by others in his day. The corollary was that he could reappraise the nature of offences against God. Instead of treating any failure to observe the Law as failure to love God, he could treat any failure to love in practice as the true offence against God. At the same time, he was open to a new interpretation of the attitude of God towards those who offended against him. By setting aside the sovereignty of the Torah and the concept of law and punishment expressed in it, he could reaffirm

[30] Cf. J. Riches, *Jesus and the Transformation of Judaism* (London, 1980), 130 ff.

God's sovereign freedom in love to reach out to the morally 'unclean' as much as to the ritually unclean, without requiring conditions to be met which Torah or tradition laid down, or assuming that somehow or other they must be met before God's love could be freely exercised.

Far from eliminating the moral basis of the relationship between God and humankind, Jesus affirmed it in the strongest possible terms, but according to the logic of divine love and sovereign personal freedom, not according to the dictates of humanly conceived justice. God's righteousness lay in his being in the right in the constancy of his love in his relationship to his people—that is, all people—whom he had not betrayed. In his sovereign freedom he had the right to forgo his rights on their behalf, if he chose, rather than to exert his rights at their expense—to forgive in love rather than to condemn in law. That he would so choose would follow from his love. The only constraint on God to be admitted is the constraint of his essential nature, which Jesus experienced as and declared to be love. But this constraint is real. Love has its own logic. To create a relationship by force is incompatible with the logic of love. Love freely offered must be freely accepted for a relationship of love to come into being. Equally, to punish the rejection of love is incompatible with the logic of love. The necessity for retributive punishment derives from the logic of abstract justice with which God has been burdened for too long in the Judaeo-Christian tradition, at the expense of his sovereign freedom and love. In the logic of divine love, where justice is interpreted as the rights of love, the facts of failure can be acknowledged and the burden of guilt removed without contradiction. Love is free to forgive without denying the past. This is the joyful note that sounds in the story of Zacchaeus (Luke 19: 1-10).

This does not mean that failure to conform to truth does not bear any penalty. Failure to conform to the order of our physical nature as human beings, such as touching a live electric wire, has immediate destructive consequences. In the same way, it may be supposed that failure to conform to the true order of our spiritual nature will have destructive consequences. The urgency in Jesus' preaching, and his warnings, may be understood in this light. Love, by its own logic, must intervene in the desire to save the beloved from such destructive consequences,[31] not to inflict further vengeful penalties for the sake of satisfying honour, justice, or law. Thus, love cannot keep silent, but neither can it compel. Hence Jesus had to appear at the focal centre of Jewish spiritual life in order to declare the way of salvation to be the way of love, and to warn of the consequences of denying this truth. Yet he could not impose his message, but had rather to risk the consequences for himself of its rejection. Love must not only bear the suffering of rejection, but also suffer alongside those who by rejecting love bring suffering on themselves. Added penalties for past offences would only be necessary to vindicate immutable abstract Law which, once formalized, cannot be changed without ceasing to be what it is. A response in love is sufficient to vindicate love, to turn its suffering to joy and to avert the consequences of lovelessness.

These conclusions are not explicit in the New Testament records, though they lie nearer to the surface than is often realized, having been buried for so long under the weight of later doctrinal theory. They emerge with logical force from the words and actions of Jesus, and above all from his reaction to the crisis which arose when all his opponents combined against him.

The price Jesus was prepared to pay for his convictions cannot fail to be a source of admiration and inspiration to anyone who takes him seriously as a human being. At the same time, it is not hard to see that his attitude and actions would give grievous offence to those who believed that the Torah was the visible expression and norm of God's holiness. It is not surprising that they saw Jesus as a fundamental threat to their own convictions, and, in the light of those convictions, to God himself. But however great their sincerity, the point is not that, but the truth about God.

Whether Jesus himself was right about God is a judgement of faith, not a matter open to empirical investigation. The

---

[31] See Tillich, *Systematic Theology*, ii. 174, 'But the justice of God is the act through which he lets the self-destructive consequences of existential estrangement go their way.'

recurring New Testament theme of Jesus' perfect obedience to God signifies this faith, and it was perhaps implicit in the original designation of him as Son of God.

The belief that Jesus was not only loyal to his convictions, but in fact right about God, is the basis for drawing on Jesus' words and actions for knowledge of God himself. It is on this basis that certain claims will be made in the pages that follow. Such claims will not be open to proof or disproof on the basis of historical inquiry; but to the extent that they appear compatible with the historical account that can be given, we may have greater confidence in their validity.

The two critical questions raised in this inquiry concerned the concept of holiness and the operation of the polar dialectic. We must now sum up what we find.

With Jesus we discover a radical reinterpretation. The logic of divine love displaces the logic of divine Torah and transforms the meaning of God's holiness. No longer is it an obstacle to his outreach; the constraints of ritual purity are broken. The physically apart, whether separated by geography, race, occupation, physiology, or sex, are no longer separated from God. At the same time, holy love, freed from the logic of humanly conceived justice, is free without self-contradiction (and hence without 'injustice') to reach out to the morally apart and to all human beings. It is free to embrace not only those who sincerely attempt to conform to God's law, but also those who blatantly flout it; not only those who interpret it differently, but also those who have never heard of it. The embrace of holy love is all-inclusive. It only excludes, logically, the claim to final truth on the part of any account or representation of God which fails to express the truth of his love.

This, we would hold, is the new content given by Jesus to the meaning of holiness. To claim that this is God's holiness has direct implications for the polar dialectic, to which we now turn.

Given the situation into which Jesus was born, and the widespread consensus over the normativeness and virtual divine status of the Torah in its totality as God's revelation, his non-conformity is evidence of the intensity of his inner experience and the conviction of God's presence with him, to which all else had to be subordinated. Conditions in Galilee generally, and the presence there of the Charismatics, make Jesus' non-conformity sociologically intelligible. But these factors in themselves are not sufficient to explain or determine the character of Jesus' own experience of God.

Whatever the explanation, in Jesus we see revelation in the subjective mode overcoming the dominance of revelation in the formal mode of Torah.

This shift of emphasis in the case of Jesus is the first thing to note. But the position of his followers was not identical. For them, in virtue of their recognition of him, Jesus became the new source of formal revelation, giving a new content to knowledge of God (subject-dependent formal revelation, in terms of the analysis in Part I). The implications of this for the Torah were more radical than any of the qualifications of it we found in other Jewish movements. What the implications were, and, above all, what this meant for Jesus, will be pursued in chapter 6. A final question is whether Jesus not only gave new content to formal revelation, but also restored the dynamic interplay of the polar dialectic. How far this was manifested in his own life is our next concern.

(b) Jesus and the polar dialectic

It took time for the radical implications of Jesus' understanding and experience of God to emerge. This can be readily conceded in the case of Jesus' followers. It will be argued that this was also the case with Jesus himself, and that it is in the light of this that we can see how the polar dialectic was restored in his life. Once again, it was the shift from sovereignty of the Torah which opened up this possibility.

We have argued that it was the attribution of definitive authority to revelation in the form of the Torah that distorted the polar balance within the tradition of Judaism. If so, then the withdrawal of that authority would be one necessary condition for the restoration of the polar dialectic. But re-evaluation of the Torah could only open the way to its recovery; it could not guarantee it. On the one hand, an alternative formal revelation might have been substituted for the Torah, as seems to have almost occurred in Qumran, and, as will be argued, did occur in the later Christian Church. In this case, nothing would have changed in principle in respect of the polar dialectic; only the particular terms of formal revelation would be changed—one law replacing another. On the other hand, there could have been a shift from the formal pole to the opposite subjective pole, from fixed revelatory authority to exclusive reliance on the immediacy of experience in every individual, leading to anarchy. The reality of this danger was also evidenced amongst Jesus' followers, despite the fact that the freedom he expressed and confirmed was not absolute and without constraint. It was the freedom of love bound by the logic of love.

However, Jesus did not discover God's love in a merely logical framework, but, as we have emphasized, in the living world of his day. His apprehension of God as love and his interpretation of the implications of that love were not formed *in vacuo* without reference to the world within which his own life was set, and with which it was fully integrated. On the contrary, the Torah and its accompanying tradition, which included the great prophets as well as the Pentateuch and more besides, were the key interpretative resource which helped to shape and articulate his experience and understanding of that mysterious personal relationship of which he was so intimately aware. But Jesus did not allow the Torah-based interpretations of the character and implications of God's love fully to determine his own understanding. Rather, within the immediacy of his own experience of God he accepted the personal responsibility of working out and pursuing single-mindedly and consistently, with amazing courage and originality, the implications of that love to which the Torah witnessed and which he experienced. Whatever in the complex whole of the written scriptures and descending tradition conflicted with the logic of divine love, Jesus rejected. In short, we may hold that the testimonies of men and women to the love of God informed Jesus' experience and understanding of God, but he did not accept their testimonies as the binding form of God. Thus, within this dynamic of interpretation and experience, Jesus was open to the reality of each new situation that confronted him and to its possibilities, without being adrift in the swirling eddies of random choice.

This interpretation of Jesus can be supported with evidence in the Gospel record, not least in those passages which have tended to cause the acutest embarrassment to exponents of a very different account of Jesus' revelatory role—namely the passages where a thoroughly human reaction is recorded. A few examples may illustrate the point. Their incorporation in the Gospel record is significant, even if we cannot be absolutely certain of their historicity. First, Jesus is described as responding to the plea of a Roman officer and being astonished at the faith the latter showed (Matt. 8: 10). But he was not slow to acknowledge the worth of this faith evoked from beyond the confines of the traditional covenant relationship. The implication of the story is clear. Jesus learnt something at that moment from that officer. We can accept that, despite his intense awareness of God's love, Jesus was a man of his day and was brought up under the influence of contemporary attitudes. It may well be supposed that, as he matured and embarked on his active life, he brought to new situations not only the language and thought-forms within which he had been brought up, but some of the common assumptions. But what is absolutely clear is that conventional attitudes did not govern his outlook. Confronted with the fact of faith from an unexpected quarter, he responded openly to it with the freedom that is characteristic of love, not law, the freedom of an unalienated person.

Another example of this openness may be found in the story of his encounter with a foreign woman who sought his help. According to Mark 7: 27, he replied, 'It is not right to take the children's bread and throw it to dogs.' The harshness of this reply has long been a source of embarrassment to New Testament commentators.[32] But whether he spoke in that way to test her faith, or out of what would have been a conventional attitude towards foreigners,[33] perhaps matters less than some Christians believe. The reality of her

[32] See D. E. Nineham, *Saint Mark* (The Pelican Gospel Commentaries; Harmondsworth, 1963), 198 ff.

[33] Vermes, *Jesus*, 49, 'It may have been Galilean chauvinism...'. But Vermes does not take note of Jesus' subsequent response.

faith, implicit in her persistence and humble reply, 'True, sir, and yet the dogs eat the scraps that fall from their master's table', was at once acknowledged by Jesus and drew from him a compassionate response to her need.

Even though Jesus did not leave detailed instructions to his followers for a mission to non-Jews (had he done so, the controversy between Peter and Paul would be unintelligible),[34] the seeds of it were sown in his recognition of the faith and humility of such as these two foreigners, and in his own response to human need, whoever the humans were, and whatever their physical, racial, sexual, or moral condition. One might add that in his brief ministry he did not have time to work out or pursue all the practical implications of his understanding of God's love, to the full extent of organizing a gentile mission, or campaigning for the abolition of slavery in the Roman world or for the emancipation of women in social life. That was left to his followers to pursue in the same spirit of responsible freedom as that with which Jesus lived and acted. The likelihood that they had no explicit written or verbal instruction for the gentile mission in particular, but had to discover the implications of God's love for themselves, is of the profoundest significance. Controversies were bound to arise, and did so from the very beginning.[35] The creative possibility of exercising responsible freedom in love, which Jesus left to his followers, carried this risk. It was and is a price worth paying. If they could only have done what they were specifically instructed to do, some painful arguments might have been avoided; but the imposition of time-bound constraints upon their freedom and responsibility would have been more destructive of the human spirit than the most bitter conflicts.

Examples can be found not only of the challenges to act which confronted Jesus, and of his response in particular situations, but of his openness to the demands of his own vocation. First, the reality of temptation in Jesus' life [36] can be approached in this light, not as an embarrassing anomaly

[34] Gal. 2: 11–14; see also Acts 15.
[35] Ibid.
[36] The point stands whether or not the temptation stories are historical, or theological constructions by the Gospel writers (Matth. 4: 1–11; Luke 4: 1–13).

in the life of a supposedly omnipotent supernatural figure, but as evidence of love towards God wrestling with its responsibilities when faced with fundamental decisions in a situation full of ambiguities, uncertainties, and conflicting desires. Secondly, a quiet moment may be mentioned when Jesus, according to Mark, after extending himself in the compassionate work of healing, retired to pray. The next day, despite earnest pleas from his companions, he insisted on moving on to other towns to proclaim his message (Mark 1: 35-9). We may see in this incident Jesus responding to the immediate demands of human need, but then reflecting within his awareness of his relationship to God on the wider responsibilities of his vocation to make known the God he already knew. The expression of love offered more than a single choice and required a responsible and, we may imagine, a difficult decision. Similarly, on the last night of his life on earth, as the supreme challenge to his vocation approached, we find him wrestling in prayer with God once again on the course he should pursue if he was to be true to his cause (Mark 14: 32-9). We can scarcely imagine the agony of that moment, but still less can the reality of it be denied. It witnesses to the reality of human freedom and responsibility within the closest possible relationship to God, in no way in conflict with it or eliminated by it. Later, perhaps, the depths were plumbed when even the certainty of love may have wavered and all further freedom of decision was lost (Mark 15: 34). It was then entirely up to God.

Whatever the influences of later piety, and indeed despite them, the New Testament witnesses clearly to Jesus' openness to the unique challenge of each situation that he encountered, to his willingness to respond in the spontaneity of love, and at the same time to accept the responsibility of interpreting the implications of God's love for the decisions he had to take. To conceive of him achieving an ever deeper understanding of these implications is in no way to imply inadequacy in his experience of God's love. On the contrary, the continuing reality of it would feed the process of deepening and enlarging. The process would continue in others who followed Jesus, and who came to share in his experience of God's love themselves. This led speedily and despite all the disagreements to the full-scale reality of the gentile mission. In other matters, such as those just mentioned, his followers took, and are taking, far too long to recognize the implications of God's love.

Yet what is all-important is that they are free to go further. The significance of this possibility, and the tragic failure of Jesus' followers to take advantage of it, are the subject of chapter 8. It remains here to sum up our conclusions concerning Jesus in relation to the polar dialectic. The historical life of Jesus witnessed clearly to the reality of subjective revelation—to the immediacy of God in relationship. Within this relationship, Jesus showed a remarkable freedom in word and action, and an openness to new situations within the historical contingencies of his day. Most of his contemporaries were shocked by his rejection of established formal authority. Yet there was nothing anarchic, arbitrary, or capricious in the freedom he exercised. It demonstrated an understanding of God as loving, sovereign, and consistent in the exercise of his freedom in love. The sacred tradition which Jesus inherited bore powerful witness to this God, and without doubt informed his understanding. Yet his understanding was not formed exclusively by these received traditions, but rather in the continuing interaction of interpretation and experience. This conforms to the polar dialectic of form and vitality, which, we have argued, is the fundamental condition of evolutionary existence. Within the polar relationship, both the tyranny of form and the anarchy of freedom are avoided, and the dynamic potential of creation is open to realization.

In conclusion, Jesus himself set his words and work in the context of the question of ultimacy in the very place in which that question had been raised with the greatest seriousness. To acknowledge that the question had its answer in him and nowhere else was to acknowledge Jesus to be of universal and ultimate significance, and hence to see the ground of meaning and existence—God—brought to light in a new way. To believe that in the unconditional love expressed in Jesus' life and work God was made visible to humankind was, in our terms, to acknowledge Jesus to be the form of God.

To affirm one representation of God rather than another to be true would not necessarily imply that the other was wholly false, evil, and alien to God, though that illogical conclusion might sometimes be drawn. Nevertheless, in the name of one, the highest claims of the other could not be acknowledged, and would have to be rejected if God was taken seriously. Many different ways of conceiving ultimacy or of representing God can have value and be sources of inspiration, but only one can function as a criterion and norm for God. It was the fact that Jesus posed a challenge at this level that made the issue so serious.

Our next step is to examine the implications from the perspective of Jesus' followers of acknowledging him rather than the Torah to be the form of God. We shall then consider how the recovery of the polar dialectic in Jesus' life would bear on those who saw that life as the form of God.

6. Responding to Jesus as the Form of God

INTRODUCTION

AFTER Jesus' death, most of his contemporaries remained within the mainstream of unquestioning reverence for the Torah. A tiny minority aligned themselves with Jesus and acknowledged him to be the truth of God. It might be imagined that Judaism, with its diversity, its sects and Charismatics, could conceivably have had room for this minority and developed in continuous interaction with it. But this was not possible for logical, theological, and historical reasons.

In the first place, whatever may have been Jesus' own interpretation of his mission and of his standing in God's revelatory activity, after his death his followers did not come to regard him as one option amongst others, to be resorted to as one point of reference in interaction on equal terms with others. This would have been to imply his subordination to a higher synthesis or later manifestation of truth, perhaps arising from such an interaction. The challenge he posed went deeper than that, and raised the ultimate question of whether the definitive truth of God was to be seen in him or not; but this did not involve a stark choice between himself and the faith and tradition of Judaism as a whole. The sovereignty of the Torah was at stake, but not Judaism as such. This was because, as we have already seen, there still existed within the broad stream of Judaism a pattern of thought and expectation in terms of which the displacement of the Torah as the final form of revelation could be contemplated without any idea of the Torah or Israel's past being totally repudiated.

This possibility lay open precisely where eschatological hopes were strongest; and where those hopes were strongest, they embraced the expectation that some personal agent or agents would be active in the inauguration of God's rule,

whether Elijah restored to life, a prophet like Moses, the
Messiah, or possibly a supernatural figure (perhaps the Son
of Man, if that title is rightly interpreted as signifying a
supernatural being).[1]

What matters here is not the origin, exact identity, or
precise roles of these symbolic figures, but the fact that the
moment at which the Torah might be superseded was associated with the appearance of a personal agent who would
play a definitive role in the final revelatory act of God.

The basis of such a belief could, as we have seen, be
discovered in the prophetic writings in the Torah itself, so
that it could still be revered as a true witness to the ultimate
revelation, but not as still being the absolute fixed and final
form of revelation. It would be subordinated to the agent
and act of revelation yet to come.

However, within this frame of reference the Torah could
hardly be expected to yield place to a so-called inaugurator
of the kingdom who was a manifest failure. Whatever expectations may conceivably have been entertained of Jesus
during his lifetime, as things turned out, the evidence
seemed to count conclusively against him. So far from leading the pious to glory and bringing about the triumphant
overthrow of their enemies, he was opposed by the former
and put to death by the latter. How could anyone believe he
was the chosen one of God (Luke 23: 35)?

Those who had looked to him as the Messiah who would
reveal God's saving power were bitterly disappointed (Luke
24: 21). Those who had opposed Jesus because they did not
believe him to be the deliverer to come, though still ex-
pecting one, were only partially vindicated. The claim for
Jesus had been exposed as false, it seemed, but any subsequent claim for anyone else, or for any other supposedly
revelatory event, would also have to be subjected to the test
of history. Only final victory could vindicate such claims;
failure would falsify them, and falsified they were with the
fall of Jerusalem in AD 70, and with the crushing of the later

---

[1] The matter has been long debated. For a fresh examination in the light of
recent research, see B. Lindars, *Jesus Son of Man* (London, 1983). See also A. J. B.
Higgins, *The Son of Man in the Teaching of Jesus* (Society for New Testament
Studies, Monograph Series, 39; Cambridge, 1980).

rebellion led by the Messianic claimant, Simon bar Kochba, in AD 135.[2]

In contrast, the Torah had *already* passed through the fiery ordeal of Antiochus IV's reign and emerged triumphant. Jesus' failure and the failure of any other Messianic claim could only serve to reinforce belief in its eternal revelatory authority. Those who had opposed Jesus in that belief could count themselves vindicated.

For a time Judaism could continue to embrace various competing claims to revelatory authority, whether made by the Sadducees, Pharisees, Essenes, Zealots, or even, despite everything, on behalf of Jesus. However, the more passionate the claim to ultimacy, the less scope there was for mutual tolerance, and tensions were now rising swiftly towards breaking-point.

The Pharisees by and large stood for the absolute authority of the Torah. Its identification with Wisdom helped to provide a conceptual basis for their claims. The followers of Jesus made equivalent claims for him, and could do so on the conceptual basis that the new age had after all broken in with him. To contrast these conceptual bases is not in either case to imply a narrowly intellectualist quality of religion, but to make the point that the response to the Torah or to Jesus as the revelatory form of God was not in either case an arbitrary decision or purely emotional reaction, or the result of some sort of magical intervention overriding human minds. Whatever else was involved on the part of God or the human spirit, these were truly human responses occurring within a truly human frame of reference, in which human understanding and rational reflection were fully involved. Such responses would not have been possible without the slow, painful process which had brought the people of that place and that time face to face with the question of ultimacy in these terms.

What was not possible on logical and theological grounds was for two contrasting claims to ultimacy to coexist. Each would put the ultimacy of the other in question. Each was bound to challenge the claim of the other. Both confronted

[2] Hayes and Miller, 663–7.

their generation with the inescapable necessity of radical decision.

Thus, a break between Judaism as it had been and the Jesus-centred movement was not inevitable, but a break between a Jesus-centred and a Torah-centred movement was.

The interval before the actual break might have been longer than it was, with Jesus' followers continuing to interact with the wider Jewish community. Despite the anti-Pharisaic polemic in the Gospels, there is evidence too, especially in Luke/Acts, of a degree of tolerance between Pharisees and the followers of Jesus (Luke 7: 36; Acts 5: 34). In the event, historical circumstances hastened on the moment of crisis. The destruction of Jerusalem and its Temple not only shattered hopes for the speedy inauguration of God's holy rule in terms of Zealot and apocalyptic expectation; it left the Pharisaic way, especially in the tradition of Hillel, as one of the only two ways of holiness still viable in the continuing course of history for the heirs of the Jewish tradition. The other was the way of Jesus. With the disappearance of other movements, and the break with the followers of Jesus, Judaism came to be defined in terms of the Pharisaic tradition.

According to Josephus, some eminent Pharisees did take an active part in the conduct of the war.[3] Yet a fundamental difference existed between the apocalyptic–Zealot and those who saw the purpose of existence as piety under the Torah. It comes as no surprise, therefore, to find Pharisees opposing the rebellion against Rome. Outstanding among these, and reportedly a disciple of Hillel, was Rabbi Yohanan ben Zakkai. We have already encountered him lamenting the lack of respect for the Torah in Galilee. Before Jerusalem fell, as legend has it, he was smuggled out of the doomed city in a coffin.[4] However he escaped, he was allowed by the Romans to found a school for the study of the Torah in Jamnia (about 50 miles west of Jerusalem).[5]

---

[3] Josephus, *Life*, 191. Cf. Neusner, *Politics*, 47, 66.

[4] J. Neusner, *Development of a Legend: Studies on the Traditions concerning Yohanan ben Zakkai* (Leiden, 1970), 28 ff. For ben Zakkai's dedication to peace (in the tradition of Hillel: see above, p. 117 n. 42) cf. Neusner, *Life of ben Zakkai*, 20, 114.

[5] Davies, 256 ff.; Neusner, *Politics*, chap. 6.

Like-minded scholars who survived the war joined ben
Zakkai there and laid the foundations of Judaism as it has
survived to the present. The honorific title of Rabbi was
institutionalized by a form of ordination. Thus, teaching
authority could be regulated, and the dangers of individualistic speculation and, of course, prophecy could be
avoided.[6] In effect, the Rabbi took over from the priest; and
the House of Study or Synagogue replaced the Temple.[7]

Davies writes of the 'school in Jamnia where Judaism
could preserve its continuity' (p. 256). However, it could as
well be claimed, as above, that Jamnia saw the preservation
of *one of two* possible lines of continuity with Israelite–Jewish
tradition, and a continuity that was matched by a very considerable element of discontinuity.

Continuity of a different kind could be found in commitment to Jesus. That way too was certainly matched by a
radical discontinuity, but its discontinuity with the prophetic
past was not as acute as with its Pharisaic–Rabbinic contemporary. The two branches grew away from each other,
but neither could or can claim exclusive rights to the trunk.

In the aftermath of the Jewish rebellion, the two movements found their respective identities in the objects of their
ultimate concern—the Torah or Jesus. As the basis of differentiation grew sharper, a complete break soon became
inevitable. The same distinction lies today between Christianity and Judaism, particularly orthodox Judaism. It is
too fundamental to be disregarded without doing both an
injustice; yet one may still hope not only for increasing mutual respect between the two offspring of early Judaism, but
for the rediscovery of a vision of God in which they both
share to a greater extent than either commonly realizes.[8]

It is, however, with those who historically came to be
excluded from Judaism, but who in effect excluded themselves from the form which Judaism took, that our inquiry

[6] Davies, 271.
[7] Ibid. 258.
[8] Dow Marmur, in *Beyond Survival* (London, 1982), discloses an understanding
of Judaism with which I find an affinity to an unexpected degree. See p. 40 for his
understanding of 'the Torah as an inspired human response to God's self-disclosure
to the people of Israel', and p. 122, '. . . our concern for Jewish purpose prompts
us to look at the whole body of Jewish teaching in its true light, i.e. as the product
of the tension between the prophetic and the priestly'.

must now proceed. It will involve an examination of the
theoretical and practical implications of acknowledging Jesus
rather than the Torah to be the form of God. We begin by
considering the significance of the fact that such a claim was
made in the context of the Torah.

2. THE TORAH AS THE CONTEXT OF THE QUESTION OF JESUS

In the context within which Jesus' own life was set, the
admission that he was right about God and was truly the
form of God would have revolutionary implications. This
would be so especially for those who had set highest store
on the Torah as God's revelation. Their hallowed preconceptions concerning it and its relationship to God, and
hence their ideas about God and themselves, would be shattered.[9] At the same time, the displacement of the sovereign
Torah by an actual human being would involve claims being
made for that person which would break through the limits
of what it had hitherto been possible to claim for any human
being, from Moses to David or the prophets.

We may better understand the character of this crisis if
we briefly retrace our steps. The revered prophets had attacked and overthrown idols and every localized deity in the
name of a supreme Lord of all history and creation, who was
God and not man. They had given impetus to the creation
of a book which witnessed to the sovereignty, universality,
and ultimacy of the God who had made himself known in
Israel. The book itself, inasmuch as it was believed to bring
God to light, his purposes and his will, served as the visible
form of God, the *locus* of revelation. As such it was imbued
with the holiness and authority of God himself.[10] If the
Torah was God's word, what more could be said, beyond
repeating it and at most translating it or interpreting it?
What God was, the book was.

The ascription of divine value to a visible representation

[9] See W. Pannenberg, *Jesus: God and Man* (London, 1968), 251-8; also Hengel, *Son of God*, 68.

[10] Schürer, 315, 'As a result of the acknowledgement of the divine origin of the Torah, the book containing it also soon became sacrosanct and inspired.'

of God is in fact contingent on two factors. First, only that which could be intelligibly thought of as deriving directly from God (such as his words) could plausibly be credited with the status and dignity of God. Secondly, the transcendent value of any visible representation of God can only be commensurate with the transcendence accorded to God himself. It may well be argued that nowhere had there been a profounder sense of God's transcendence than in Judaism, and hence nowhere else could a higher degree of holiness be attached to the *locus* of his revelation than was attached to the Torah. In short, only within the context of Jewish monotheism could a revelatory form have such ultimate significance and sacred value. Conversely, nowhere else were competing claims to ultimacy likely to be resisted with such uncompromising vigour, whether these came from idols or emperors, prophets or priests. Such threats coming from outside had already been faced with unyielding courage, and it would happen again.

For a man within the context of Judaism to challenge the supremacy of the Torah created an unprecedented crisis.[11] Jesus could not as a prophet have posed such a challenge for two reasons. First, his status as a prophet in the Judaism of his day would have had to be defined by the Torah which constituted Judaism, and his challenge would have automatically disqualified him. In other words, even if he saw himself as a prophet, he was bound to be dismissed as a false prophet by upholders of the Torah. Secondly, the Torah itself stood between Jesus and the great prophets of old. They could offer no precedent for Jesus' challenge to the Torah because, historically, their witness to God antedated its creation, and in later practice their recorded words were subordinated to it.

Ironically, while concrete forms of God had yielded to the prophets' spoken word, the prophets themselves had yielded to the written word. But now this written form was challenged by a concrete form. True, this was not an impersonal

---

[11] The difference between Jesus and John the Baptist may be found in the fact that, while John provoked questions, he offered no overt challenge to the authority of the Torah. He was executed as a result of his threat to secular authority (cf. Vermes, *Jesus*, 50). John lived and died under the Torah, before the inauguration of the 'new age' (Matt. 11: 11; Luke 16: 16).

form fashioned by a man—an idol such as the prophets had themselves condemned—but something they had never even needed to condemn in their own tradition, and scorned in others, the divine in a human form.

We are not here concerned with the question of whether Jesus himself claimed explicitly to be divine (though on the present argument this would be scarcely conceivable).[12] Our concern is rather with what would have to be said and thought about Jesus if he was believed to have superseded the Torah with its virtually divine status. As we have seen, such an idea could only begin to make sense in the context of Judaism if Jesus was the Messiah. That at least had to be said, but it did not go far enough. Such a claim still confronted the positive claims made for the Torah. Could even the Messiah really be conceived of as superseding the Torah, when virtually every other symbol of transcendence was to be found within its own pages in its witness to God, and was already being drawn into the service of the Torah itself to convey its godly status? Pre-eminent among the symbols signifying the outreach of God himself to the world and humankind were terms such as 'Word', 'Wisdom', and 'Spirit of God', which we shall be examining further below. Already in Jesus' day these symbols of God's self-expression had begun to be assimilated to the Torah to show it to be God's self-expression.

The best and perhaps the only way to articulate the conviction that Jesus rather than the Torah was God's true self-expression was to transfer the familiar symbols of ultimacy from the one to the other. As a result, where these symbols were to be found within the writings of the Torah they would be understood to signify Jesus and not the Torah itself.[13] Hence the Torah would appear as a witness not to itself but to the ultimacy of Jesus, and its witness to a coming Messiah would be immeasurably strengthened. As seen in

[12] Dunn, *Christology*, 32, '*But if we are to submit our speculations to the text and build our theology only with the bricks provided by careful exegesis we cannot say with any confidence that Jesus knew himself to be divine, the pre-existent Son of God*' (emphasis original).

[13] Ibid. 196, '. . . *the first Christians were ransacking the vocabulary available to them in order that they might express as fully as possible the significance of Jesus*' (emphasis original).

this changed but still positive role in the cause of God, its authenticity and holiness were to a very large extent preserved, but no longer absolute. That it should function in this way was necessary, since the possible alternative way of expressing Jesus' superiority, by denying altogether the holiness of the Torah, was dangerous. First, if the book about God and his dealings with his people in history was judged not to be holy and so not about God, the result would be to divorce the God of history from the history of God's people. Secondly, if the Torah counted for nothing before God, Jesus could be supposed to be superior to the Torah and yet still very far from God. The question of ultimacy would be left wide open and the seriousness of Jesus' challenge would be lost.[14]

Thus, the symbols of ultimacy found in or serving the Torah would have to play a crucial role in expressing the significance of Jesus. In due course, the case could be strengthened by employing every other available symbol of ultimacy to this purpose. The danger would remain that the sense of transcendence which these symbols derived from their various backgrounds would be deficient. In that case, higher connotations would have to be imparted to them if the one to whom they were applied was not to be dragged down to their level. The struggle would be long and hard and arguably could not have succeeded without constant recourse to the symbols found in and fashioned by the Torah. In that case again, the seriousness of Jesus' challenge would have been lost.

However, despite the sacred value still to be ascribed to the Torah, it ceased to be ultimate when its divine attributes were transferred to Jesus. Those whose understanding of themselves and God had been shaped by the Torah were

[14] These dangerous developments manifested themselves in Gnosticism (the name derived from the Greek *gnosis* 'knowledge', and given to the varied syncretistic religious movements which flourished in the second century AD). It took time for the early Church to recognize its threat. For a comprehensive survey, see K. Rudolph, *Gnosis* (Edinburgh, 1983); for a brief account, see R. A. Norris, *God and the World in Early Christian Theology* (London, 1966), chap. 3; see also R. McL. Wilson, *The Gnostic Problem* (London, 1958); E. Pagels, *The Gnostic Gospels* (London, 1980).

now confronted with the task of reconstructing those understandings and all life's meanings and purposes in the light
of Jesus. Such a task is never completed.

At the same time, in the perspective of commitment to
Jesus, another acute problem arose. The spoken and recorded word could without too much difficulty be supposed
to come directly from God. But how could a human being,
an offspring of the natural created order, be supposed to have
derived directly from God without straining intelligibility to
breaking-point?

The symbol 'Messiah' could serve to represent Jesus as
the direct agent of God, but still leave too many questions
open as to the true nature of that relationship. Furthermore,
when translated into Greek as *Christos*, it came to function
surprisingly soon as a proper name, leaving the question still
more open (see below, chap. 7, sect. 1).

Yet somehow Jesus' direct derivation from God would
have to be maintained if he were to be acknowledged as the
form of God in place of the Torah. Those committed to
Jesus as the Christ (and so later called Christians, Acts 11:
26) had to find a way of expressing his immediate relationship to God.

The difficulty of expressing such a connection intelligibly
is witnessed to from earliest times. On the one hand, Jesus'
relationship to God was depicted in quasi-biological terms.
The stories of his conception and birth taken literally pose
far more problems now in the light of a scientific understanding of human reproduction than they would have done
when they were first told; but it is in fact most unlikely that
such stories were intended primarily to explain Jesus' birth
in the first place. They can be seen rather as attempts in the
light of subsequent events to express convictions concerning
the immediacy and uniqueness of Jesus' relationship to God.
This intention is compatible with supposing, as I do, that
Joseph was Jesus' natural, biological father.[15]

[15] For discussion of the virgin birth, see Dunn, *Christology*; also R. E. Brown,
The Birth of the Messiah (London, 1977), and id., *The Virginal Conception and
Bodily Resurrection of Jesus* (New York, 1973); E. Schweitzer, *The Good News
according to Matthew* (London, 1975), 29–35; I. Howard Marshall, *The Gospel of
Luke* (Exeter, 1978), 62–77. The remark by the last-mentioned (p. 76), 'From the
historical point of view acceptance of the virgin birth is not unreasonable granted the

On the other hand, in the Greek world especially, there was widespread aversion to any idea of God being involved in materiality. Hence, in almost complete contrast to the New Testament birth-stories, the acknowledgement of Jesus' relationship to God seemed possible at a later date only at the expense of his genuine humanity and physical existence. The influence of this outlook is still with us, and so is the task of continuing to try to find the right words and concepts to express this relationship.

Despite the difficulties we face in this task, and although at first sight it might seem easier to stick to words as the form of God's direct self-expression (since they are our prime means of self-expression), it may nevertheless be the case that the truth of God can be more adequately brought to light in human form than by any other means.[16]

The basis of the argument is recognition of the fact that the actual forms in which God may be (and in human history has been) represented are many and various, so that within the logic of formal revelation it is important to distinguish between the logics of different forms of revelation. To be specific, revelation in the form of a book, which in its concrete form as a verbal construct is an impersonal object, differs in kind from revelation in the form of a person, and the logical implications of the former are different from those of the latter.

Where God is believed to be revealed in the form of any impersonal object, relationship with and commitment to God will be governed by the kind of commitment and relationship appropriate to an object. By its nature, it cannot respond, but only define in terms of what it must itself always be in the immobility of its objectivity. If a personal God is believed to be revealed in an impersonal form, acute tension is generated between the kind of commitment appropriate to an object and the kind of commitment appropriate to a person. This tension is taken into the Torah itself precisely because of its own witness to a personal God. It points to

possibility of the incarnation', represents an understanding of God's relationship to this world diametrically opposed to the one on which this book rests. See below, p. 200.

[16] See above, p. 39.

God in the form of a person, while remaining in itself an impersonal symbolic form. As such it cannot be what by its own testimony God is (Isa. 55: 8-9). We can recognize here the positive significance of its uninhibited anthropomorphisms.[17]

If a personal God is believed to be revealed in a personal form, such tension is no longer entailed. A personal form is capable in principle of representing the personal qualities of a personal God, and of being related to in the freedom and mutuality appropriate to a personal relationship. Of course, since historical persons differ in their characteristics and qualities, much would depend in the context of history on which person was acknowledged to be the form of God. But again, in principle, provided that it was the case that a given person truly represented the qualities of the personal God, commitment to that person in visible form would be conducive to, rather than in conflict with, a right relationship with a personal God. So, although the idea of Jesus as the form of God presented acute conceptual problems, nevertheless the response to Jesus as the form of God opened up radically new and creative possibilities for a personal and loving relationship with God. The reality of this experience took hold of Jesus' followers. Language had to catch up and as far as possible communicate this reality. It did not have the right to dictate to it or imprison it.

In conclusion, we may readily understand how the attempt to speak of the ultimacy of Jesus would offend from the start. Most ordinary, pious Jews would be scandalized at the attribution of their hallowed symbols of transcendence to anything other than the Torah, let alone to a historical man condemned under it. Secondly, any rational person was likely to be confused, if not repelled, by the application of so many different and apparently contradictory images to one objective reality, more especially if well-established symbols of transcendence—conceived of as suprahuman, supranatural, and eternal—were applied to a concrete human being who lived and died.

Yet the impulse behind it all is not the desire to offend or

---

[17] Ibid.

confuse, but the conviction that ultimacy in fact belongs to a human figure of history, Jesus from Palestine. To put it differently, it stems from the belief that the clue to the meaning of existence is to be found in the story of Jesus. Hence he lies at the heart of what Christians want to say about God (theology), about human destiny and fulfilment, or salvation (soteriology). How Jesus could be that is the question of Christology. It is a serious question only for those who believe he is—or at least might be—that.

Of the greatest significance is the fact that Jesus not only gave concrete and visible expression to an alternative account of God in contrast to the Torah, but that he did so in the context of the Torah. The latter had not only shaped his understanding and experience of God, but had raised the question of ultimacy in a unique and profound way; apart from it, Jesus' impact on his world and potentially on all human worlds could not have been what it was. At the same time, many of the symbols which enabled the ultimate significance of Jesus to be grasped and communicated were not only to be derived from the written words of the Torah, but had been forged and tempered in the community which had lived and died for the Torah, and which in doing so had shown what total commitment in practice could mean, whatever the odds and whatever the cost.

Nevertheless, if ultimacy belonged to Jesus as the form of God, it could not still belong to the Torah.[18] In terms of the polarity model, either the Torah or Jesus would have to be acknowledged as the *locus* of revelation in the formal mode.

The question we come to now is whether commitment to Jesus as the form of God could and can escape the negative consequences which, it has been argued, spring from the isolation of revelation in the formal mode or exclusive reliance on it. In terms of the polarity model, the final question will be whether in Jesus the polarities of revelation are so held in balance as to avoid both tyrannical and anarchical distortion and to preserve a creative life-giving harmony.

[18] G. W. H. Lampe, *God as Spirit* (Oxford, 1977), 125, '[For Paul,] instead of the Torah, it is Christ who is the expression of God's creative mind.'

2. THE POLARITIES OF REVELATION AND
THE FORM OF JESUS

When Jesus died, various things might have happened. We have explored some of the theoretical consequences of the response to him as the form of God. But such a response had to come from human beings, whose freedom and responsibility, we have argued, cannot be overridden and yet are always fallible. We may now look at the way things might have developed through the free response of Jesus' contemporaries. At the same time, we may also come to see how the inner logic of a response to Jesus will point to certain possibilities and exclude others. In other words, a response which is not only free but also rationally coherent will disclose a path whose general direction is clear, even if not precisely marked out; one which will not branch out in all directions at random.

So we may begin with the real historical possibility that, when Jesus died, what he claimed to be true about God might have been successfully suppressed then and there and his cause defeated—as his opponents no doubt hoped, wishing their own concept of God to remain unchallenged.

However, that did not happen; and where it did not happen the response to Jesus could, in terms of the polarity model, lead in three different directions, resulting from three different emphases. One course would result from an over-emphasis of revelation in the formal mode in Jesus; another from overemphasis of subjective revelation; and a third from a recovery of a true balance of the polar dialectic in him. There would, however, be no absolute hard and fast distinction between these emphases, and in the event we see developments in the response to Jesus occurring right across the polar spectrum.

It is obvious, in terms of the present argument, that what one would wish to see and uphold is the third possibility— the recovery of the polar dialectic—but our task is not merely to acclaim it but to try to show how it in fact springs from the inner logic both of Jesus' own response to God, and the response to him as the form of God. The related task is to show how the alternatives, though hypothetically possible in the context of human freedom, would nevertheless be self-contradictory and so ultimately intolerable for beings that participate in reason as well as freedom.

Our emphasis so far has been on the response to Jesus as the form of God, and so we may consider first the possibility of overemphasizing formal revelation in him. Having displaced the Torah, Jesus himself might have been treated as the unique source and expression of formal revelation, and so have become the fixed and exclusive point of revelatory reference for those who acknowledged the genuineness of the revelatory activity of God in him. He might then have been treated as the other founders of new religions have been treated; after his death, every detail of his life, every saying, every judgement might have been collected and accorded supreme revelatory authority, second only to what he might have written himself, as in the case of Muhammad.[19]

However, this did not happen; and here we may appreciate the significance of the remarkable fact that Jesus appears to have written nothing himself. By not doing so, whether by intention or happy chance, he avoided the risk of conferring on any secondary, impersonal, symbolic form the revelatory authority he claimed for himself in personal relationship. It was entirely in keeping with his own reliance on an immediate relationship with God that he should declare that possibility to be open to all other persons. By that declaration and promise he prevented commitment to himself as the form of God from involving the loss of subjective revelation. In fact he achieved the opposite. To acknowledge Jesus to be the *locus* of revelatory authority must mean accepting what he says and promises about the possibilities of relationship with God. To acknowledge Jesus thus and to deny the possibility of an immediate, living, responsible relationship with God would be self-contradictory. It would in effect mean applying a criterion other than Jesus for judging what could be accepted from Jesus. Jesus himself not only witnessed to the dynamic interaction of the form and vitality of God in his own life, but opened the way to a similar experience of the vitality of God through response to himself as the form of God.

[19] K. Cragg, *The Call of the Minaret* (New York, 1964), 94 ff.

Hence commitment to Jesus in person would be incompatible with the notion that revelation is limited exclusively to the formal mode. It means rather to be open to an experience, already anticipated in the traditions of Judaism, of an immediate relationship with God, spoken of in terms of the coming or the presence of the Spirit. Accordingly, the coming of the Spirit, in the language of the New Testament, may be interpreted as expressing a new experience of a living personal relationship with God.[20] This, according to the Gospels, was what Jesus promised to those who related to God through him; it is hardly surprising that when it came it caused no embarrassment to his followers. Their new experience of the immediacy of God in personal relationship, with the personal freedom and responsibility it brought, could be joyfully acknowledged without in any way putting the revelatory authority of Jesus in question. On the contrary, if the expectation of this experience derived from Jesus, its occurrence would reinforce his revelatory authority and commitment to him.

The Fourth Gospel especially may be looked to in support of the case that has been argued here. It is most probably a reflection on the significance of Jesus, rather than an accurate portrayal of how he would have appeared to his contemporaries.[21] It may nevertheless paint an accurate picture of him as at once asserting the authority of his own representation of God and yet firmly denying that his visible formal representation was sufficient in itself; it would be completed in an experience of the living presence of God, which itself could not stand alone but would be informed by Jesus (John 16).

In exploring the revelatory significance of Jesus, the author of the Fourth Gospel went beyond the 'bare facts' of history and resorted to language and imagery from beyond the mainstream of Judaism. In doing so, he exercised the responsible freedom derived from Jesus to interpret his experience, informed by what he had heard concerning Jesus but not bound by the secondary forms in which the message

[20] Lampe, 95, '. . . the tendency is stronger in the New Testament than the Old to understand "Spirit" to mean personal God in his relation to man.'
[21] See C. K. Barrett, *The Gospel according to St. John* (2nd edn., London, 1978).

came. He was free to draw on the language-resources of Judaism, and perhaps was doing so more than has often been conceded.[22] At the same time he was free to exploit the language-resources of the Graeco-Roman thought-world. This he and other followers of Jesus were free to do, because, as we have seen, if the Torah was no longer held to be the definitive form of representing God, then its language and imagery were no longer definitive. If no single language had to be used to represent God's relationship to humankind, then all languages could be used to that purpose, and yet no language as such could ever rightly supersede the person Jesus as the definitive form of God.

So we may understand why in the New Testament Jesus was never treated as other great religious leaders have been treated. The author of the Fourth Gospel was certainly not alone in thinking that the listing of endless facts about Jesus was pointless (John 20: 30). But he and others realized that some were needed in order to give a content and character to that name, so that he did not altogether lose his foothold in historical reality. This was a very real danger, as we shall shortly see.

The danger was serious precisely because it arose out of the new experience of the immediacy of God, which is what we mean by the recovery of subjective revelation. The whole of the New Testament bears witness to this, though already in its pages there are hints, and more than hints, of dangers in store. The Spirit, as the dominant but not the only symbol of God's immediate presence and the freedom of human response, is associated with various phenomena which point to the reality of this experience.

We may notice first the return of prophecy, implying an intuitive recovery of the right to speak out of an immediate experience of God (Acts 11: 27-8; 1 Cor. 12: 28); secondly, ecstatic utterance, signifying in an extreme (and hence potentially dangerous) way a direct experience of God unmediated and unformed by words, on which hitherto revelation had so much depended;[23] thirdly, the recovery of

[22] Hengel has shown how far Greek ideas had flowed into Jewish thought before the time of Jesus; see his *Judaism, passim.*

[23] Paul acknowledges the gift but is very concerned about its anarchic potential (1 Cor. 14: 13-19; cf. Acts 2).

initiative for action, without recourse to formalized authority. Thus, we have the remarkable phrase, in Acts 15: 28,
'It seemed good to the Holy Spirit and to us . . .'. At the
same time, the very occurrence of controversies which could
only with the greatest difficulty be resolved points to a lack
of reliance on any entrenched, fixed, and formal revelation.

It may be said, however, that it was the stress generated
at this point which led the Church away from the Scylla of
anarchy towards and even into the Charybdis of tyranny.
We must see first how the early community of Christians
was sailing towards a formless anarchic freedom, and yet
how again this unbalanced extreme contradicted the inner
logic of the response to Jesus.

We have noted various manifestations of the freedom of
subjective revelation, springing without contradiction from
a response to Jesus as the form of God. The danger lay in
responding to the recovered freedom without further recourse to the person in whom it was grounded. The danger
was greatest at two points, in relation to practical (that is,
moral) behaviour, and in relation to leadership.

There is evidence that at a very early date there were some
who supposed that to follow Jesus into freedom from the
Law or Torah was to follow him into freedom for anything.[24]
That would imply that his function was to break the power
of formal revelation and to open the door to freedom, but
that he had no part to play in the expression and shaping of
that freedom. Such a view in effect limits the significance of
Jesus in time and place and so denies him ultimacy; it is
completely self-contradictory, when the acknowledgement
of his ultimacy is the only condition on which the loosening
of the constraints of formal revelation can be justified and
make sense in the first place. Where Jesus' ultimacy is truly
acknowledged, the expression of freedom derived from him
must conform to its expression in him. For this to be possible, it must rest on the same foundation.

Jesus did not claim freedom for himself as a self-centred
individual human being, but in order to live his life centred
on God, with whose character his own understanding was
so fully informed that he could conform his life to it as to

[24] For Paul's attack on such 'antinomianism', see Rom. 6; 1 Cor. 5.

another personal centre of selfhood. That, at least, is the conviction of faith; if it were not the case, it would be inappropriate to claim ultimacy for Jesus. If it is so, it means that Jesus did not offer freedom from the Torah to others for the sake of self-centred human freedom—the anarchic freedom of self-will—but for the sake of freedom for God, as he himself represented him. Thus, while Jesus lived in the strength of the immediacy of his own relationship to God, he offered to others a relationship to God in terms of a relationship to himself. He called for a relationship to himself in order to form a right relationship with God, providing in himself a clear and far from anarchic criterion of the character and constraints of holy love.

The second danger lay in the fragmentation of authority arising out of the freedom found in Jesus. No community can continue in existence without developing forms of authority and structures of leadership. It is extremely significant that, as the movement centred on Jesus took root in different places within different cultures, various forms of organization and leadership emerged.[25] This demonstrates once again the exercise of responsibility in response to Jesus, as opposed to dependence on any secondary, fixed form of authority.

However, the recovery of subjective revelation which created the risk of moral anarchy by the same token created the risk of political anarchy. The danger arose of a reaction determined by a distorted response to Jesus, preventing the recovery of a right response. In other words, if the danger of anarchy seemed to arise from the unrestricted claim to subjective revelation on the part of *all* those committed to Jesus, a solution might seem to lie in restricting claims to revelations in that mode to *one* person. Leadership would then naturally be vested in that person, and for practical purposes he would supersede the no longer physically present Jesus as the norm of truth. Problems arise here which will occupy us at length below. The only immediate point to be made is that such a claim to divine authority, resting on subjective revelation but isolated from the form of Jesus

[25] See H. von Campenhausen, *Ecclesiastical Authority and Spiritual Power* (London, 1969).

himself, could not in fact avert the risk of anarchy, because there was no way in which such a claim could be legitimated for one person rather than another at any given time. All that was likely was that there would be fragmentation at the community level instead of at the individual level, as different leaders became the central point of reference within different circles.

Total commitment to any individual on the basis of his or her claim to subjective revelation could only be offered at the expense of the ultimacy of Jesus, and hence once again would be self-contradictory.[26] At the same time, since such a claim had little alternative but to rest on a monopoly of subjective revelation, it could only be made at the price of denying to others that free and responsible relationship to God which it was the whole object of Jesus' life and death to make possible.

Thus, on the one hand, the recovery of subjective revelation through Jesus could lead to anarchy, but only where there was a failure to accord true recognition to Jesus as the form of God. Similarly, the danger of tyranny could arise in reaction to anarchy, but only where the failure to recognize the ultimacy of Jesus was perpetuated.

The dangers of anarchy and tyranny do not arise out of the recognition of the ultimacy of Jesus, but could arise out of the failure to treat his ultimacy seriously enough. In commitment to him as the form of God, revelation in the formal mode and in the subjective mode is integrated with all its creative potential, while the demonic consequences of isolating one from the other are averted.

In conclusion, we must accept that after Jesus' execution leaders were bound to arise and would have to exercise authority in the Christian communities. In whatever form they did so, to the extent that they conformed to Jesus they would represent the normativeness of Jesus. If they differed from him and presented themselves as the true representation of God, then a stark choice would arise between continuing to acknowledge Jesus to be the form of God, or acknowledging someone or something else to be so. Whatever that other

---

[26] In 1 Cor. 1: 10-17 Paul shows himself to be aware of this. (See also above, chap. 2, sect. 2.)

object of commitment might be, commitment to it would give shape to a way of existence as different from that informed by Jesus as the object of commitment happened to differ from him. A community constituted by acknowledging Jesus to be the form of God could not recognize as a member a person who acknowledged another to be the form of God. Nor could such a person with consistency profess to be part of the community centred on Jesus. This would not mean that God was not related to other persons or communities or was inaccessible to them; that would be contrary to the logic of divine love, which requires of its source, as of those who acknowledge it, an unrestrained outreach. Yet love cannot compel. Though present, it is powerless where it is rejected or denied. Lives not open or conformed to love as seen in the form of Jesus (whether his name is known or not) are to a greater or lesser extent not conformed to God. To that extent they lose the creative potential of right relationship with God and suffer the consequences of disordered being.

It remains the case that within the overarching community of commitment to Jesus the responsibility of working out the implications of commitment must give rise to many different forms of practical, social, and intellectual expression, as well as to different forms of leadership and authority. So far from being the cause of disunity, such variety would not only be inevitable but of positive creative value within the diverse circumstances of historical existence. The different ways in which the logic of divine love as disclosed in Jesus was expressed concretely would represent in visible form to the inquirer at any time what recognition of Jesus as the form of God can mean. But neither any single expression nor the combined whole could properly claim to be itself the form of God. These derivative forms separately and together would, or should, be illustrative of the quality and potential of the love of God disclosed in Jesus, but cannot claim to be definitive without claiming more than their due.

Hence, diversity of expression should pose no more threat to the underlying unity of those committed to God in the form of Jesus than the different clothes, or indeed the different faces, of the members of one family undermine its

unity. The danger of disunity would only arise if one particular form was treated as definitive in itself, the uniform
which all must wear. This could only arise if it was regarded
as somehow in itself the form of God, though other than
Jesus himself and excluding the creative freedom which he
represented. The fact and the tragedy of developments of
this sort will be explored below.

Before proceeding further, however, we must face up to
one further difficult question. We have argued that recovery
of the polar dialectic, and hence the possibility of a right
relationship with God, springs from commitment to the person of Jesus as the form of God. But though Jesus' friends
had begun to apprehend that he might indeed truly represent
God, none of them responded unequivocally to him as the
form of God in his lifetime. Nor, we shall argue below (sect.
5), could they have done so without being guilty of idolatry.
But then, what possibility of personal relationship could
there be for these friends, let alone for others who had never
met Jesus, after his death? At that point it might seem that
knowledge of Jesus could after all only be knowledge *about*
Jesus, of facts fixed in history and in oral and written records.
The relationship of these derivative verbal constructs, impersonal symbolic objects in themselves, to a personal God
would seem to be analogous to the relationship we saw above
of the Torah to God. Even if Jesus was the form of God,
how could commitment to him now in symbolic form escape
the criticisms raised in the former case? How could commitment to Jesus in symbolic form be integrated with the
experience of the living God?

The problem here is in some ways more acute than in the
case of the Torah. The book was at least to hand and concretely visible to those committed to it, and in their eyes it
witnessed to its own status as the form of God. Hence its
acknowledgement as such posed no logical problem. In contrast, the record of Jesus was there, orally and soon in visible
written form (the Gospels), but it witnessed not to itself but
to Jesus in person as the form of God. Thus, the visible
record neither called for nor was entitled to total commitment, while what was so entitled was no longer visibly
present. It would not, perhaps, have been surprising if the

emphasis had fallen completely on subjective revelation, on the immediate experience of God's living presence, contingent upon but no longer dynamically integrated with commitment to Jesus as the form of God. He and his wonderful achievement lay out of sight in the past. To claim otherwise, to maintain that he was still present in a living personal relationship with his followers, would be extraordinary and have profound implications. Even so, making such a claim would not of itself preserve the human and historical integrity of Jesus, and could paradoxically lead to a continuing distortion of the polar dialectic.

3. JESUS AND THE VITALITY OF GOD

The question that confronts us is how Jesus, who died, could conceivably remain in a living personal relationship with his followers.

We are engaged here with matters which are ultimately mysterious, the being of God, the person of Jesus, and not least the mystery of human life itself. It would certainly be presumptuous to expect to comprehend such things completely. Yet the natural impetus of human reason drives us on to make as coherent as possible our understanding of the whole of life, not excluding our life in relationship to God. In the second place, on the basis of our own experience of being persons, and on the premiss of the reality of Jesus' personal existence and the authenticity of his relationship with God, we may be able to move on a little further in the attempt to show how human beings may relate to God through the form of Jesus.

We must begin by distinguishing a number of different questions which bear on the central issue, which is our concern with commitment to Jesus as the form of God and with what this means. Two alternatives confront us here, each with its own problems.

First, from the normal perspective of history Jesus is dead, and can only be known about through the written record. How, then, can commitment to him be anything other than commitment to a verbal form, to which persons, as we have argued, cannot be committed without violence to the true nature of personal existence? In short, how can commitment to God in the form of a dead person or a verbal record generate the creative power of a living personal relationship?

The Christian response, of course, is that Jesus is not dead; despite his execution and burial, he is alive and open to personal relationship. This has been the fundamental assertion of Christians from the beginning and may ultimately be true; but even if it is true it does not eliminate every difficulty. We are faced with two further questions. First, how can the claim that Jesus is alive now be true without doing violence to the wider understanding of reality with which we are presently working? Mystery may, or rather will, remain, but blatant contradiction is intolerable to rational creatures. Secondly, how might the Jesus alive now relate to the historical person of whom the story tells? This is by no means as simple and straightforward an issue as is sometimes assumed.

To begin with the first question. The claim that Jesus is still alive challenges our basic assumption that his life in its totality was integrally woven into the web of human evolutionary and historical existence. That this awesome whole stands in relationship to God has also been assumed, and that Jesus stood in special relationship to God has been put forward as a reasonable supposition and as the premiss of Christianity. But what we have attempted to avoid has been imputing to Jesus any special factor or attribute that would be incompatible with the insight we have obtained into what it is to be human. This understanding comes from the scientific work of biologists, psychologists, sociologists, and others, whose integrity we can trust and whose insights have helped us to realize what we are. Admittedly, they disagree among themselves and could be wrong on many counts; but the point is whether in the last resort Jesus was truly one of us, or differed in some fundamental way, so that he was never as we are and we could never be as he was. It is a difference of this kind that has been rejected so far in this inquiry in the attempt to take Jesus seriously as a human being, and hence as the clue to the meaning of our being. The assertion 'Jesus is alive' now seems necessary to meet the requirements of commitment to God in the form of a person. Must it mean abandoning the position we have taken, and having to argue that the effects of death on Jesus were wholly unlike what we accept to be the effects of death on all other human beings?

In facing this basic issue we must make one further important distinction. The claim is that Jesus is alive, and is known to be alive in the personal experience of his followers. But is the experienced aliveness in fact the living presence of Jesus in some way distinct from God, and as he was in his human selfhood on earth? Or is it rather the living presence of God who is eternally in the form of Jesus? A further question is whether ultimately these are mutually exclusive alternatives, or only appear to be so from our present perspective. Either way, we have no option but to start from our present perspective and all the varied questions that confront us there.

These issues can only be approached with reservation; but they cannot be avoided, precisely because the claim that Jesus is alive is so central to the tradition of commitment to Jesus, and yet so hard for many of Jesus' followers or potential followers to comprehend today. Our starting-point will be to examine further the meaning of personhood (as generally conceived in the West). A person bears within himself the dynamic of form and vitality. To encounter a person is to encounter a visible form about which true facts can be stated, as to immediate appearance and also as to character as revealed in past and present words and acts. At the same time, it is to be confronted by a living and creative centre, capable of personal response and of bringing into existence as yet unrealized possibilities, which nevertheless, in the case of an integrated personality, will not be out of keeping with the character already disclosed.[27] Thus, while a person may share certain visible characteristics with a marble statue, unlike the latter—however well executed—a person is also a centre of vitality. The life fills and gives character to the form, and the form bears and renders accessible to others the character of the life. But whence comes the character of the life? Many factors play a part, but it is perhaps

[27] For the idea of 'character' in relation to doctrinal development, see S. W. Sykes, *Christian Theology Today* (London and Oxford, 1971), chap. 8, 'The Character of Christ'.

clearer today than ever before that the character of personal
life is the product above all of personal relationships, from
earliest infancy.[28]

One can acknowledge here the significant role that Mary
and Joseph may well have played in imparting the reality
of love to Jesus in his infancy—something which, we may
suppose, they could only do because they were open to and
pointed to a love beyond themselves. Yet however great the
part they played, the mystery of Jesus is still the reality and
constancy in his experience, as witnessed to in the Gospels,
of a personal relationship with God. Within this relationship
of love, one might say that Jesus' own life conformed to or
took on the character of God's life without violence to his
humanity. Hence, under the conditions of human existence
he gave visible expression to the eternal character of God
and at the same time to God's creative life-giving power,
which overflowed in the love Jesus showed (cf. John 15:
9).[29] This would mean, on the present argument, that to
encounter Jesus historically would be to encounter both the
form and vitality of God, in the dynamic and creative unity
of human personhood. Thus might one understand language
concerning the Spirit of God in Jesus, who himself in distinction from God shows such fundamental affinity with
God as to be appropriately described as his son.[30] Response
to this person would open the door to a new understanding
and a new experience of God within a personal relationship.
Jesus looked on his fellow human beings with the eyes of
God, and those who looked on him would see God in his
gaze.

We find, then, that to acknowledge God in the form of
Jesus does not mean divorcing God's form from his vitality,
nor does it mean reducing God to the limits of that visible
form at the expense of his own eternal, indestructible life

[28] See Bowlby and Shotter in Harré, *Personality*. Also Lampe, 19, 'Creation
itself is a process of personal development, and the creation of man in God's image
and likeness, as a son of God, means the making of a human spirit *in relationship*'
(emphasis original).

[29] Cf. J. Hick, *God and the Universe of Faiths* (London, 1973), 163, 'The divine
agape [love] exerting itself in relation to mankind and operating on earth as the
agape of Jesus, forms one continuous event in virtue of which we can say that Jesus
was God's attitude to mankind incarnate.'

[30] See Lampe, 24; also above, p. 136 n. 102.

and sovereign freedom. The life of God that filled the life of Jesus in the intimacy of personal relationship was neither exclusive to nor exhausted in that particular life under the conditions of historical existence, nor was it ever withdrawn or isolated from the rest of God's creation. At the same time, if Jesus was the form of God, the life of God which fills the rest of creation could never and can never be otherwise in character than as disclosed in Jesus, even if apart from that disclosure it has only been more or less clearly apprehended as such in the history of humankind's experience and awareness of God.

It was argued in Part I that form and vitality can never in fact exist autonomously and independently of each other. We have now found that the form of God was never isolated from the vitality of God in the personal life of Jesus; and if Jesus was the form of God become visible in history, it cannot be supposed that the vitality of God in eternity could ever be isolated or divorced from that form. The life of God was never and will never be other in character than as expressed in the form of Jesus. Just as to encounter the form of Jesus historically was to encounter the form and vitality of God, so to encounter the vitality of God in the immediacy of personal experience today or any day is to encounter a vitality whose form is that of Jesus (whether apprehended to be so or not). The life of Jesus, shaped under conditions of history, finitude, and death, was conformed to the life that transcends those conditions, the life of God. In the circle of those who saw Jesus as the form of God, the life of God would be experienced thereafter as nothing else than the life of Jesus. The response to that personal life would not be a response to a dead person, cut off and immobilized in the past. In fact the life of Jesus would be experienced in the immediacy of personal relationship with God in a more intimate way than was open to Jesus' friends during his historical life, when he was physically separate from them. With the form of Jesus taken up into the life of God, or rather, found to belong eternally to that life, this concrete separation was eliminated, because it is in the nature of God to be present to persons in the immediacy of experience. Thus the life of Jesus as the life of God becomes available not only to those who had known Jesus during his ministry, but to those who never knew him personally during his lifetime—and not least to those who have known God in other forms outside the confines of Judaism in any time or place.

To sum up. Commitment to Jesus as the form of God entails commitment to God in the form of Jesus. Hence, the way is opened to a living relationship with a personal God who transcends the limitations of death. In this informed experience, the creative possibilities of life within the dynamic interaction of form and vitality are established. The polar dialectic is preserved and an understanding of revelation emerges which, it may be claimed, does justice to the concept of a God who is the living personal ground of all that exists.[31]

We find, then, that commitment to Jesus as the form of God is not commitment to a dead person or a verbal form but to the living God. Through that commitment a person experiences the aliveness of God who is eternally in the form of Jesus. But one very important question remains. What actually has become of Jesus, the historical person who may thus be said to have opened the door to a living relationship with God? Is he personally, in terms of his own selfhood, excluded from that relationship, dead and gone? It seems doubtful whether any understanding of God as the ultimate ground and goal of personal life is compatible with the total negation of persons at death, whether that person is Jesus or any other human being. Only that would be negated which was incompatible with God's holiness in eternity.[32] This may include physical corporeality, which may be thought of as the means of person-making within creation and good for that reason. It would not then be a denial of the goodness of creation to deny that physical bodies will be taken into God's eternal existence,[33] and it would not be essential to believe that Jesus' physical body was reconstituted for eternity any more than most people expect this for their own bodies. A

[31] Niebuhr, 13, 'God is both vitality and form and the source of all existence.'

[32] Cf. Tillich, *Systematic Theology*, iii. 398, 'The elevation of the positive in existence into eternal life implies liberation of the positive from its ambiguous mixture with the negative, which characterises life under conditions of existence.'

[33] 1 Cor. 15: 50, 'Flesh and blood can never possess the kingdom of God, and the perishable cannot possess immortality.'

person's destiny with God is not contradicted by the presence of his or her skeleton in a grave. To suppose, then, that Jesus' skeleton may lie somewhere in Palestine is not incompatible with faith in him as the form of God, or with experience of the life of Jesus, or with the conviction that he shares God's life.

Whatever one's conclusions on this issue, it is more important to recognize that whatever is incompatible with God's holiness is incompatible with God's life in eternity, whether it is self-excluded or excluded by God. Conversely, the person whose life was perfectly conformed to God would have nothing to lose that mattered when transposed into his eternity (1 Cor. 3: 13–15). In the manner appropriate to that mode of existence, that person would, we may suppose, be perfectly united with and active with God in his continuing outreach towards creation. Thus Jesus, having perfectly performed God's work and fulfilled his purpose on earth, would be caught up into God's eternal creative activity.

As far as the experience of Jesus' followers on earth is concerned, no sharp distinction would need to be drawn between their experience of the aliveness of Jesus and the aliveness of God. Hence, the New Testament's ambiguity at this point is positively significant rather than misleading or careless.

However, the distinction between Jesus and God still needs to be affirmed for two reasons. First, it must be upheld even in the realm of eternity, if the selfhood of Jesus and hence of all other human selves is not to be thought of as lost in an all-absorbing, impersonal, pantheistic oneness.

Secondly, though here we touch on the most difficult questions, the principle still applies that we do not predicate of Jesus himself that which would deny his common humanity with us. The fact that the living presence of Jesus experienced by his followers transcends the limitations of human personal relationships has led some commentators to argue that this transcendent quality belonged to Jesus in his own essential being. If so, he was not as we are. We would rather suggest that the experience of the transcendent life of Jesus is the experience of the aliveness of God, who is eternally in the form of Jesus to which Jesus opened the door and within which his life is embraced. The distinction may seem too fine to dwell upon, and yet bears strongly on what Christians will think it right to say about Jesus in his historical existence.

We have attempted to meet some of the difficulties raised by speaking of commitment to Jesus as the form of God. Without compromising the reality of Jesus' historical life and genuine humanity, we have suggested a way of seeing how the particularity of that life may be seen as the bodying out of the eternal truth of God, and how the personal subject of that life need not be thought of as excluded from the eternal life of God, but is, rather, intimately bound up with it. Hence commitment to Jesus as the form of God is not isolated from the vitality of God. The polar dialectic is preserved and the possibility of a living personal relationship with God is opened up to Jesus' fellow human beings.

Yet a problem remains. If the distinction between the selfhood of Jesus and the selfhood of God is upheld in the realm of eternity, then the second question posed above confronts us. How does the Jesus alive now relate to the historical person? In the following section we shall argue that a very natural emphasis on Jesus alive now can, paradoxically, be construed in terms that tend to divorce him from the historical figure. Emphasis then shifts to subjective revelation in such a way as to detract from Jesus' revelatory significance as the form of God. In the last section of this chapter we shall pursue further what it means to speak of Jesus as the form of God, and shall reaffirm the importance of commitment to him as that, within Christian commitment to God.

4. THE SPIRITUAL JESUS MISCONCEIVED

The possibility that Jesus might be superseded by someone else claiming to draw on the same subjective source with equal authority was considered in sect. 2, and rejected as being incompatible with commitment to Jesus. However, the position is changed, and not necessarily for the good, when commitment is offered to Jesus as a spiritual being rather than as to the person he was. It is the nature and implications of this shift of focus that we must now explore.

During his life Jesus was certainly a 'creative spirit', a person able to enlarge upon, qualify, revise, and in theory even contradict what he had previously expressed about God, and hence the revelation attributed to him. To his followers he was available as a source of subject-dependent formal revelation as defined in Part I (in theory at least: we shall see that his revelatory authority could not in practice supersede that of the Torah until after his death).

The forms in which he represented God were only contingently binding during his lifetime. As long as he lived, the situation was open, the limits were not drawn. He might change his mind, freely or under pressure. But with his death this openness ended. His followers could not look for something new or something more, nor was Jesus any longer a human subject free to give it. At that moment, his whole life consisting of the totality of his words, actions, reactions, and impact on others became a revelatory datum irrevocably fixed in history.

However, if the personal subject of that historical life could be conceived to exist independently of it, in a suprahistorical way, and yet as still able to engage in revelatory activity in the sphere of history, then the revelatory value of Jesus' historical existence is put in question. In other words, in so far as the heavenly subject could be thought of as engaging in revelatory activity before or after or apart from that person who bore the name of Jesus in history, the unique revelatory significance of that person's historical life would be undermined.

We have argued that Jesus, in the course of his historical life within the total process of evolution, brought God to light in a new (and, to a Christian, true) way. That he could do this and, conversely, that he could have such revelatory value attributed to him, was contingent not only upon what he was in himself but on the historical context within which he lived. Without that he could not have interpreted his own life or become the man he was in the way he did. Equally, apart from that milieu, with its traditions and the Torah at the centre, the response to him as the ultimate revelation—

as the form of God—would not have been possible; at least
it could not have borne the meaning and implications which
it did bear. His revelatory value was forged in the creative
interaction between himself, his God, his world, and his
fellow human beings. He was the point at which the evolutionary world through a historical man converged with the
outreach of God towards the world and humankind. As the
point of convergence, he who in every way was a human
being like us could be acknowledged as the form of God,
without violence being done to the truth of God and without
loss to human freedom and responsibility. One human life,
grounded in the world and history, was at the same time
so grounded in the reality of God in a relationship of love
that it could then and there disclose the truth of God and of
what it means to be human.

That could not be so if the subject of that life existed apart
from and before its historical expression. He would not then
have been a human being like us, or the point at which the
lines of evolution and history converged with the ground of
all being, God. The gap between creation and its source
would not be bridged. By the same token, the revelatory
value of that historical life would be diminished, or rendered
arbitrary and absurd.

A transcendent pre-existent subject, who entered historical existence at one point in time to reveal heavenly truth
unrelated to earthly existence, could logically have entered
history at any other place and at any other time, or in many
places many times. Were he supposed to have done so, then
no particular form in which he appeared or spoke could be
claimed to be of ultimate revelatory value. In other words,
the utterances of prophets or saints or other spokesmen for
God could claim to have equal revelatory value.[34]

Such a diffusion of revelatory authority we have already

---

[34] For example, see J. Daniélou, *Origen* (London, 1955), 117–27. On the one
hand, Origen follows Irenaeus in seeing history as a time of preparation for the
pre-existent Logos' full self-disclosure in the Incarnation. On the other hand, he
can write that prophets and patriarchs 'were taught by God's Word before he
became flesh' (*Comm. John*). Origen's intention is to uphold the uniqueness of the
Incarnation, but his attitude, according to Molland (quoted by Daniélou), 'implies
a concept of history difficult to reconcile with the significance attaching to the
Incarnation as a unique event'.

seen to be incompatible with the ultimacy of Jesus. It can be avoided to some extent by the claim that the revealing subject appeared, if not exclusively, nevertheless uniquely and completely and definitively, in Jesus, and that he had not fully expressed himself before and would not do so again in the course of history. Other supposed expressions of divine truth before or apart from Jesus could then be treated as only more or less adequate or valid. But the greater the emphasis on Jesus' transcendent subjectivity, the harder it would be to see why his revelatory activity should not continue to be expressed through the historical mouthpieces of his followers, as it was through the mouth of the man who bore his name and who was first recognized as the form of God. In short, if the subject who spoke was unshaped by the unique configurations of his history, why should he only speak at one moment in history? And if he did speak and act uniquely in Jesus, why then and there and not elsewhere? No convincing answer can be given and it has to be left to the inscrutable and seemingly arbitrary decrees of God.[35] Yet if it were arbitrary, unrelated to the actual course of history, then the course of history as such would remain meaningless; the concrete phenomena of history, including human beings, would have no significance in themselves, if they could be seized upon or spoken through at random by a transcendent subject. It is perhaps no accident that Gnostics and cult-leaders to the present day who have taken advantage of such revelatory loopholes have also attached little significance to history.

It also follows from the arbitrary nature of revelatory intervention that those persons to whom revelatory words have been attributed cease to have the limited and yet authentic value of human subjects responding in sincerity to their awareness and understanding of God. They gain instead the revelatory value due to a suprahuman heavenly being. If that source was called Jesus or God, then what others expressed

---

[35] See R. E. Brown, 'The Community of the Beloved Disciple' (London, 1979), 113 f., concerning the party attacked in the Johannine epistles: 'For the secessionists the human existence was only a stage in the career of the divine Word and not an intrinsic component in redemption. Salvation would not be different if the Word had become incarnate in a totally different human representative who lived a different life and died a different death.'

would claim the revelatory authority due to Jesus alone as the form of God, whether or not such later revelations were compatible with the historical Jesus. Conversely, the revelatory value of the visible, historical Jesus would be reduced to that of other visible mouthpieces of the one transcendent subjective source, and its human authenticity would equally be lost. The same would apply to the future. The words and acts of those who followed Jesus could then have a revelatory value equal to that of Jesus attributed to them; and there would be equal lack of recognition of human creativity in the expression of what was believed to be true about God.

It is perhaps necessary to emphasize here that the value of other people's words and actions in witnessing to the presence and power of God known in the form of Jesus is not in any way to be denied. The question is whether any can claim equal revelatory value, or perhaps even superiority, in virtue of their contemporary expression, in contrast to the apparent remoteness of Jesus' historical life.

If the revelatory value due to Jesus is attributed equally to other persons, whether before or after him, then the significance of his own historical existence is put in question. Either it becomes part of a larger whole, or it is in danger of being totally superseded.

On the one hand, it is no longer the life of Jesus as a coherent whole which serves to constitute revelation in the formal mode; his life becomes just one element in a larger and inevitably contradictory whole. The whole will comprise many lives in which the transcendent subjective source has supposedly come to expression. But inasmuch as these expressions are different and yet all supposedly of equal standing in relation to this source, there can be no resolution of the conflict inherent in their differences. In fact, since total commitment to different persons in the uniqueness of their individuality is impossible, the attempt to combine the revelatory authority of different lives can only proceed on the basis of abstracting what appears to be common to all of them. In the process of abstraction, the revelatory object is depersonalized and the characteristics of commitment to God revealed in the form of a person, as defined above, are lost. Little can survive apart from an unformed, contextless, mystical awareness of spiritual reality.

On the other hand, emphasis may be placed not so much on the totality of the accumulated sequence (the total revelation accumulated from the many sources), but on the immediate and present expression of the heavenly subject. In that case, although commitment to the form of a person is preserved, all past persons in whom the heavenly subject may be supposed to have expressed himself will be superseded, including the historical person Jesus. This will appear legitimate if the ever-active, transcendent, subjective source is itself called Jesus, and hence is considered entitled to enlarge or modify his original revelatory expression.

Whatever the plea, the effect in either case is that the distinctive features of Jesus' own life and response to God are set alongside other responses to God and lose their definitive value. In particular, his death stands in uneasy and almost meaningless relationship to a heavenly subject which, in its suprahistorical and boundless revelatory activity, can never have been truly exposed to the reality and bounds of death.[36] Revelation as such verges on the anarchy of unconstrained subjectivity.

It may therefore be concluded that in commitment to Jesus as a spiritual being there is a serious risk not only of jeopardizing his humanity and revelatory significance, but of undermining the value of worldly existence. This would conflict with the belief that God is the creator of our world and the ground of its meaning. An interpretation of Jesus' revelatory role which contradicts this belief cannot be satisfactory. So we return now to the acknowledgement of him as the form of God, and in the following section we shall attempt to show what this must mean.

5. JESUS THE FORM OF GOD

We have argued that both the form and vitality of God were manifested in Jesus' life. However, those who actually met him encountered an objectively real person external to themselves. In his objectivity, as we have seen, he challenged the

[36] For further consequences in christology and soteriology, see Dunn, *Christology*, 128, '. . . the pre-supposition of a pre-existent heavenly redeemer resulted in a critical shift in Adam christology—a shift from a christology of death and resurrection to a christology of incarnation—and not only in christology, but also in the concept of redemption which goes with it.'

claim of the Torah to be the form of God, and explicitly or implicitly offered himself as the alternative.

The question that confronts us now is, 'What is the *himself* of Jesus? What of Jesus is for us the form of God?' If the answer is, as is traditionally given, his whole self in the totality of his being, then this could not be available to us in its entirety before its completion in him. In other words, just as the meaning of a story cannot be grasped before its ending, so the meaning of the story of Jesus could not be grasped before his death.[37] If Jesus was to supersede the Torah as the form of God, it could only happen when the meaning of the name could be defined not only by his life but by the fact and the manner of the ending of his life. Precisely because his death was the fruit of his life, and not just an accident, it set the seal on the meaning of his life.

So it was in the moment of his destruction that the truth was rendered complete for the first time. Only after his death, *only as given and taken away*, could Jesus be un-equivocally the form of God for humankind. Christianity never has escaped and never can escape this tension implicit in its own foundation; it exists as the movement that ac-knowledges this Jesus to be the form of God, and lives within the personal response to God in the form of Jesus.

It is in this light that we may view what has been called the supreme paradox of Christianity,[38] the Incarnation ('en-fleshment' of God). 'Paradox' is often too readily employed to conceal contradiction and avoid hard work, but it is, per-haps, true paradox to affirm that it was just when Jesus was no longer available in bodily form that he became the embodiment of the truth of God. For this reason, as sug-gested above, it would not only have been unthinkable for his fellow Jews, but in fact idolatrous for anyone, to have worshipped Jesus as God in the course of his lifetime. (It would have meant ascribing ultimacy to partial, un-completed truth.) Equally, those responsible for his death cannot be held guilty of deicide. The truth of God in Jesus could only be complete when his life was completed. The

---

[37] See A. E. Harvey, ed., *God Incarnate: Story and Belief* (London, 1981), for the use of 'story' in the interpretation of doctrine.
[38] Cf. Tillich, *Systematic Theology*, ii. 90.

truth became visible only when he was rendered invisible. Its full meaning and implications could only be grasped when he was no longer concretely present. Only this truth could supersede the Torah as the *locus* of revelation, the truth of God made visible.

It was in the totality of Jesus' life, extended in time but grasped intuitively after his death as a meaningful whole, that the truth of God was bodied out. In this sense he was the incarnation of God. In so far as that symbol furnishes the story of Jesus' birth with a pointer to the ultimate significance of his whole life, it has positive religious value. However, when 'incarnation' is viewed as occurring in a quasi-biological way at one particular moment in time—in the moment of his birth—it is, I suggest, a dangerously misleading concept. It not only threatens the reality of Jesus' humanity but generates insuperable intellectual difficulties if that consequence is denied. It also imputes to Jesus in the course of his lifetime the divine status and worship-worthiness which he himself is said to have rejected (Mark 10: 17 f.), and which we may now judge to be the cause of unnecessary difficulty and offence to his fellow Jews, Muslims, and other theists. The call for a decision as to whether Jesus is indeed the form of God or not is a sufficient challenge to all human beings, without requiring consent to a questionable way of expressing how this could be so.[39]

We may now consider further some of the implications of acknowledging Jesus to be the form of God, the criterion of truth. There can only be one ultimate criterion, and if that status is claimed for Jesus, it must be denied to any other possible claimants, personal or impersonal. More especially, the most elevated forms in which human beings have attempted to represent God to their minds can be seen as barriers between themselves and God precisely when they are mistaken for God himself and not seen as pointers to him.

All such barriers are lifted by Jesus, and are lifted for ever from the lives of those who take their stand with Jesus; the

---

[39] The question will nevertheless arise, 'What is the "ontological corollary" of the confession that Jesus is the form of God? What must reality be like for it to be possible for that statement to be true?' See below, p. 327.

way is open not only to become aware of the reality of God's presence and love in a new way, but to recover the freedom and responsibility of human personhood. Above all, the responsibility is recovered of working out the implications of God's love as expressed in Jesus in each situation as it confronts us. We are free to learn and grow in the light of new experiences and of new possibilities for personal relationship in a changing world, and in their interaction with the story of Jesus and our response to him as the form of God.

The claim that it is Jesus, as seen in the whole of his life and death, who is the form of God, will qualify but also reinforce what has been said about the Spirit as the vitality of God. Jesus during his lifetime in his external physical form could not at the same time be the vitality of God for others, even if, as we have maintained, they could experience something of that vitality in their relationship to him. However, any experience of the vitality—of the immediate presence—of God that was shaped by and conformed to knowledge about Jesus as brought to completion by his death would, if the claim for him is true, be nothing less than the experience of God as God really is. It was only natural, then, that after Jesus' death the experience of vitality which came to those who responded to him should have been spoken of almost interchangeably in terms of the risen Lord, the Holy Spirit, the Spirit of God or Christ, or simply in terms of the presence and power of God himself.[40] The source is one and the same. Different verbal symbols used to signify it should not be allowed to imply the operation of different agents.

However, some distinction in speaking of God in the Spirit still needs to be maintained if the significance of Jesus is not to be lost sight of. If the source of vitality in the experience of Christians is indeed God himself, it is not therefore to be supposed that he is cut off from the living experience of those who have not committed themselves to Jesus as the form of God. Yet in so far as their experience is

---

[40] Cf. Matt. 28: 16–20; John 14: 18, 23; 16: 7, 13; Rom. 8: 9–10; 1 Cor. 15: 45. See Lampe, 3–11, 61–94; also Dunn, *Christology*, 5, 'The relation between Christ and the Spirit becomes clearer when we realize that Paul regards Jesus as now in some sense *the definition of the Spirit*; it is the Jesus-character of his and his converts' experiences of the Spirit which marks them out as authentic.'

interpreted through forms other than Jesus, it will be received and will express itself in various ways which to a greater or lesser extent conform to him. There are, then, differences in human experience of the Spirit, but the distinction pertains not to the source, but to the way the Spirit is apprehended and received. His reception is governed in part at least by conscious human response and the availability of various interpretative resources.

Different religions have their different interpretative symbols, and usually one which functions as the focus and organizing centre of all available symbols of ultimacy and transcendence. Christians, who no longer have Jesus concretely present, nevertheless have in his name their central organizing symbol. Thus, we may say that God in the Spirit is accessible to all human beings in the immediacy of experience, but that the character of this experience will be shaped by the interpretative symbols through which it is channelled. Where Jesus is the supreme interpretative symbol, the experience of God will have its own distinctive character, without being totally unrelated to the experience of God in other religions and contexts of interpretation.

However, it is important to add here that the distinction being drawn is not merely a matter of terminology or private experience, but of practical consequence. We have previously asserted the importance of a right representation of God in relation to experience of God, since a right relationship with God, the ground of existence, is the condition for the right ordering of human existence in every dimension of it, and for the avoidance of the destructive consequences of disorder. In other words, only a right relationship with God can bring about the full realization and enjoyment of the creative possibilities of human existence at every level, and this, Christians believe, comes about through recognition of and commitment to Jesus as the form of God. If this belief is true, practical consequences would flow in two directions, negatively and positively. On the one hand, it would follow that, if the vitality of God was experienced and construed in a manner contrary to the form of Jesus, then at best tensions must arise, in which lie the risk of potentially destructive conflicts within the lives of individuals or society. At worst, vitality would be integrated with a form contrary to Jesus. To the degree that this contradicted the normativeness of Jesus and repressed or distorted the true character of God's vitality, it would give rise to an objectively real and dynamic integration of form and vitality opposed to God himself.

It is in this light that we may view the powerfully destructive movements of history. Whether they advance under the banner of religion or ideology, God or anti-God, makes little difference in practice. Their dynamism has no other ultimate source than that which is the ground of all vitality. It is when human beings, in the exercise of their freedom (and often because of their ignorance), construe it in a form contrary to its essential nature that vitality rebounds in a negative and destructive way against the form imposed upon it.[41] To those identified with the contrary forms, this negative effect will be experienced as evil and perhaps be seen as the work of a personal Devil, but belief in an autonomous, free-ranging Devil is ultimately incompatible with belief in one God. Christian tradition has more appropriately attributed negative consequences of wrong belief to the wrath of God, though all too often Christians have made nonsense of the work of Jesus by depicting wrath to be virtually the essence of God. On the contrary, the seemingly destructive interaction of vitality and distorted forms of God can be seen as one side of the creative work of God. This is perhaps why even the most horrifically destructive movements of history have not been wholly devoid of creative elements and creative after-effects. But these are achieved along a hard and painful road. A loving and creative God might be looked upon to open up a path that led positively and joyfully to the achievement of his goals.

It is the claim of Christianity that the inner conflicts and destructive consequences of tension between vitality and distorted forms are overcome when the vitality of God is apprehended in the form of Jesus. At least such tension is in principle overcome, even if within the limitations of human life a perfect resolution is not possible. In the struggle to advance towards it, Christians are by no means exempt from

[41] See above, p. 2 n. 4.

setbacks and failures. Damaging conflicts between individuals and communities are clear proof of this. Yet those
who acknowledge Jesus to be the truth of God do have a
resource that saves them from being overwhelmed by failure—quite simply, the knowledge of God's unconditional
love (Rom. 8: 38-9).[42] Even so, it would be well to minimize
the scope for failure, and we may here briefly anticipate some
of the problems which will concern us more fully below.

The name 'Jesus' was described above as the central organizing symbol of Christianity. It is a symbol rich in content and yet elusive. Its very elusiveness is productive of
inexhaustible depths of meaning, and is at the same time a
warning. The fact that for us Jesus is not concretely present,
but is mediated through our minds in the symbol of his
name, warns us against presuming to have an absolute claim
on the truth of God in any tangible form—human, verbal,
institutional, or whatever—such as would imply that not
only non-Christians but all other Christians who spoke or
acted differently were wrong. By the same token, it warns
us against presuming to be free from misinterpretations and
misconceptions and their potentially destructive consequences.[43] Yet in so far as within our understanding the
name, or symbol, of Jesus conforms to the person who bore
that name, we may be confident that it conforms us towards
the truth and vitality of the one to whom he conformed in a
personal relationship of love.

Here above all the practical consequences can or should
be seen. Persons released into a relationship of love with the
God of Jesus, whatever has previously informed their lives,
are not let loose into a world of formlessness, but are freed
to be transformed into the form of God. In the process
they will render concretely visible in the world around them
something of the form of God himself, which is the form of
Jesus, and in offering themselves in love in relationship to
other persons they may open the door to them for a true
relationship with God. Thus, they may continue the formative and creative work of Jesus in different ages and cultures, but can never supersede the foundation on which that
work rests.

[42] See above, p. 167, for an interpretation of the urgency of Jesus' warnings
which would not see them as putting God's unconditional love in doubt.

[43] See above, p. 2 n. 4.

So, in conclusion, Jesus' task of bringing God to light in his own person could not be completed before his death. Only then and only if he were true to his vocation, could he be fully and rightly apprehended as the form of God, and only then could any experience of the presence and vitality of God be rightly construed and hence conform to God as he really is. The Spirit of God could not be *known* as the Spirit of God before Jesus' death, any more than Jesus could be the form of God. At that moment it became possible for human beings to know God in truth and in power in the creative interaction of understanding and life, form and vitality—the form of Jesus and the vitality of the Spirit.[44] In this way we may interpret the symbol of the Trinity as witnessing to the essential conviction of Christians that God, the personal ground of all, is disclosed in the visible form of Jesus and the inner vitality of the Spirit, each necessary to the other.

This necessity is not arbitrarily decreed by supernatural revelation, but is required by belief in God as the ground of our evolutionary world and as open to personal relationship with human beings. The very idea of God would be self-contradictory and nonsensical if what we grasp through the symbols 'truth and life' could not be predicated of him. A relationship between God and humankind which did not embrace the modes of form and vitality in dialectical unity could not embrace human beings as personal and evolutionary creatures and could not therefore establish the conditions for creative existence in a changing world.

So a person who lived and died two thousand years ago is not necessarily dead and gone; and an event, though seemingly remote in time, is far from remote in its significance for the shaping of human life and the realization of its creative potential at all times. Under conditions of human existence in an evolutionary world, at a certain point in the history of humankind, in one person's life, the true terms and character of God's relatedness—the meaning of holiness—were disclosed and proved to be for the good of all. Hence the possibility and desirability of a right relationship with the living

---

[44] Cf. John 16: 7, 'I tell you the truth: it is for your good that I am leaving you. If I do not go, your Advocate will not come, whereas if I go, I will send him to you.'

God was opened up, a relationship like that which Jesus had himself enjoyed, free and creative, governed only by the logic of eternal holy love, a living relationship set within the structures of evolutionary and historical existence, yet transcending the limits of finitude as God's life transcends creation. The way was opened for the entry of the human spirit into the life of God without loss of its humanity, and for the life of God to be constantly re-expressed in the forms of human persons, without loss of his divinity.

IV

THE RESPONSE TO JESUS
WORKED OUT IN HISTORY

INTRODUCTION

THE followers of Jesus found that their own living relationship with him was not broken by his death. A community came into being which found its identity in its
commitment to him as the form of God, and in its claim to a
continuing experience of his living, personal presence. For
those involved, this was somehow nothing less than the creative presence of God himself.

In the preceding pages some account has been given of
the theoretical implications of acknowledging Jesus to be the
form of God in the context of the Torah. At the same time,
it has been argued, in terms of the polarity model, that the
revelation of God in the formal mode and in the vital or
subjective mode was integrated in the person of Jesus. Because the truth of God came to light in that person, the
significance of what was seen there transcended the limits of
that person's historical existence, without in any way de-
tracting from his genuine humanity. From this it would
follow that it is possible for the human Jesus to meet the
demands of God's revelation in an evolutionary world. In
other words, a case may reasonably be presented that commitment to the man Jesus as the form of God is the first and
crucial step towards a right relationship with God. Within
this relationship destructive tensions and distortions are or
can begin to be overcome, and the highest creative potentials
of human beings may be realized.

However, the experiences which opened up these possibilities were open to interpretations that were, perhaps

inevitably, to impede their realization. In brief, the disappearance of the objectively present, physical Jesus was
matched by a new experience of his spiritual presence. He
had moved off the stage of history and was no longer present
in person as a revelatory point of reference—the concrete
locus of formal revelation. At the same time, he moves on to
the spiritual stage. But that stage is already occupied, by the
Holy Spirit. In other words, there already exists a symbol
for God in his spiritual outreach.[1] To change the metaphor,
it is almost as if we had two North Poles and no South Pole.
But how can two North Poles be postulated, let alone related
to each other intelligibly? Such a problem could generate
centuries of dispute.

Initially, there was the tendency witnessed to in the New
Testament[2] and a few other early Christian writings towards
identifying Jesus with the Holy Spirit—two names for the
same spiritual reality. But most of the early fathers veered
away from this. As a result, the Holy Spirit seemed to be
increasingly redundant. It had no specific and necessary part
to play in God's revelatory activity, since its role was taken
over by Jesus conceived of as a spiritual heavenly being. The
different positions were by no means always clearly worked
out, but the result either way in doctrinal terms is virtual
binitarianism[3] (in the sense that it only appears necessary to
speak of God in terms of Father and Son, and not of the Holy
Spirit as well). However, the Holy Spirit did not completely
disappear from view. The reasons for this, and the problems
posed by his persistence, will occupy us later.

It cannot be denied that, in the absence of the concrete,

---

[1] Dunn, *Christology*, 144, '*for Paul as much as for the earlier Jewish writers the
Spirit is the dynamic power of God himself reaching out to and having its effect on
men*' (emphasis original).

[2] See above, p. 214 n. 40; also Lampe, 114; A. Grillmeier, *Christ in Christian
Tradition*, i (2nd, rev. edn., London and Oxford, 1975), 56 (quoting the second-
century Apostolic Father, Hermas), 'The Holy Spirit, which was there beforehand,
which created all creation, was made by God to dwell in the fleshly nature which
he willed' (*Similitudes*, v. 6. 5). Cf. also Cyprian's description of the Incarnation,
'The Holy Spirit puts on flesh, God is mingled with man' (*Idol.* 11), quoted by
Lampe, 211.

[3] 'The thought of the earliest Fathers about God was at least as much binitarian
as trinitarian' (M. F. Wiles, *Working Papers in Doctrine* (London, 1976), 9). See
also id., *The Making of Christian Doctrine* (Cambridge, 1967), 79 f.

visible Jesus as the *locus* of formal revelation in the subsequent course of history, his followers had to find some
form of substitute authoritative reference-point, if anarchy
was to be avoided. Alternative *loci* of revelation and hence
norms of holiness were found in, for example, holy book,
holy bishop, holy council, holy pope, holy tradition, holy
congregation or elders, holy reformer, or whatever. So far
as any of these witnessed or still witness to Jesus as the form
of God, they serve their proper purpose. As soon as any
one of them is conceived to be the absolute *locus* of formal
revelation, and so in effect the form of God in itself, it becomes idolatrous and demonic. Such developments and their
destructive consequences (not least the loss of the polar dialectic) will be considered in Part V.

In this Part our concern will be with the immediate problems facing the community which acknowledged the revelation of God in the form of Jesus. How was it to express
its convictions about Jesus, and interpret its experience, in
terms that would do justice to what it had been given and
wished to offer to others?

Paradoxically, the very thing Christians wished to affirm,
namely Jesus' continuing life-transforming spiritual presence, could, as we have seen, serve to detract from the
reality and significance of his historical life (see above, chap.
6, sect. 4). Yet the conviction that Jesus' human life was real
and important was too firmly embedded in the tradition to
be relinquished, despite the intellectual problems this posed
in relation to other claims that had to be made for Jesus.
The problem already noted of the duplication of terms for
the subjective pole of revelation (Jesus and Spirit) was thus
further aggravated by the fact that one term, 'Jesus', still
carried connotations of formal revelation, even if he was no
longer visibly present. Thus, the very name 'Jesus' functioned ambiguously. It could be used to signify God's revelation in the formal or subjective mode, and if the
distinction was not drawn, confusion if not contradiction
could result. In more direct terms, the question posed itself,
What was the relationship between Jesus now alive in the
spirit and the Jesus who had lived a genuine human life? We

must pursue these problems as they took shape within the community committed to Jesus.

7. Faith and the Symbols of Faith

I. PROCLAIMING JESUS AS THE REVELATION OF GOD

(a) The search for symbols

WE must consider now what it was that Jesus' followers were attempting to do, and what their motives were. With the experience of Jesus' living presence came the conviction that he was indeed right with God, the true representation of God, and the agent of his purpose, and hence the key to a right understanding of God's relatedness to all human persons and creation—in short, the form of God. He could only be that in virtue of his perfect response to God. That meant he was not only the form of God, but the form of human personhood, the blueprint for the human response to God, disclosing what God had always intended his human creation to be in true relationship to himself. These convictions constituted the Christian Church. How that person *could* be truly human and at the same time the truth of God has, from the beginning, stretched Christian understanding to the limit, and always will.

These new convictions and this experience were bound to find expression in new forms, both institutional and verbal. Those who acknowledged Jesus rather than anything else to be the form of God in virtue of that fact constituted a new community, which would have to take shape in some form or other in history. Its members were bound to attempt to articulate their convictions and experience, and to identify the new centre of their existence and their relationship to it. Just as the language of ultimacy was transferred from the Torah to Jesus, so the language to express the new identity in Jesus was drawn naturally for the most part from the language employed to express the old identity in the Torah. Thus, the community centred on Jesus spoke of itself as the new Israel in contrast to the old Israel, as related to God in a new covenant, or new testament, in contrast to the old covenant. Other words took on new connotations, in particular *ecclesia*, which, although used in the Septuagint for the assembly of God's people at the time of the Exodus, had not previously acquired a clearly defined, technical meaning. It was now adopted by Jesus' followers as the name for the community centred on him, and in English is translated as 'Church'. However varied the forms and symbols in which the new community expressed itself, commitment to Jesus was the unifying factor of the Church as a whole, just as commitment to the Torah was the unifying factor within the diversity of Judaism.

Not only was it necessary for members of the Church to articulate their own convictions to each other, but the content of these convictions was such as to compel their proclamation to those outside its community. So it would be necessary to find words that would serve the purpose of communication not only in Palestine, but in the ever wider world into which the community extended itself, where the value-laden symbols of Judaism would not necessarily have the same impact.

The basic issue was, to repeat, the question of God's relationship to the world and humankind. Jesus' followers believed that Jesus had established the true terms of this relationship, which meant that he stood in a very special and indeed unique relationship to God and by the same token was of universal and ultimate significance. The overriding need was, then, to express and to communicate to others this belief in Jesus' special relationship, on which all else hinged.[1]

Words and concepts to serve this purpose were, as we have seen, already available within Judaism, and we must now explore them further. They may be roughly divided into two categories. On the one hand, there were those which symbolized man in his transcendence—that is, they were used of human beings who stood out as special agents of God's purposes, who were exalted in their relationship to God but of necessity distinct from him in virtue of their human status (e.g. prophet, priest, Messiah). On the other

---

[1] See above, p. 184 n. 13.

hand, there were the symbols of God's immanence—that is, of his outreach towards and activity within creation (e.g. word, wisdom, spirit, power). These two ways of thinking about God's relatedness converged in the attempt to interpret the significance of Jesus, and that convergence was the source not only of richly creative symbolism, but of acute tension in the history of his followers' attempts to speak about him. To appreciate the course the debate took, it is necessary to distinguish one further factor which affected the symbols of God's immanence.

Within the course of Jewish history an increasing sense of God's transcendence emerged. But transcendence can mean different things. If the generalization can be permitted, it might be said that the emphasis in Judaism lay on the transcendent sovereignty, power, and moral holiness of God, in contrast to the characteristic Greek idea of transcendent being, by definition utterly divorced from the realm of becoming. In the latter case, it was logically necessary to postulate distinct, spiritual realities or metaphysical principles as mediators between the world and the remote, supreme God. But in the mainstream of Jewish thought, God, though transcendent, was not remote.[2] Even if as creator he was 'wholly other than his creation', he was not by definition excluded from direct involvement in the scenes of worldly action; and Judaism was more concerned to affirm the expression of God's power and purpose in the world than to ask how his divine essence stood in relation to material existence.

Accordingly, words and concepts were brought into service within Judaism to express God's active involvement in the world and in history, and his close relationship to humankind, without infringing his transcendence as properly understood. These terms, appropriately described as 'bridge' words,[3] served in their original context as symbols of divine presence or direct agency, in contrast to the idea of 'bridge' beings as separate entities standing between God and the world. This distinction cannot be said to have been

[2] See above, p. 37 n. 1.
[3] Lampe, 35.

maintained unequivocally in early Judaism, but the exceptions prove the rule, inasmuch as 'bridge' beings appear where the influence of Greek (and Persian) thought seems strongest. However, it is often not clear whether a term points to God in his immanence or identifies a separate heavenly mediator; but perhaps such a clear-cut distinction was foreign to the author's own way of thinking.

We are left with two broad categories of symbols: on the one hand those which express God's outreach or immanence in the world; and on the other those which serve to identify human agents acting or destined to act on God's behalf, who in their humanity are clearly distinct from God. But the picture is not static. A widespread concern in the Graeco-Roman world to protect the absolute oneness of the supreme God led increasingly to the differentiation of the symbols of divine outreach into distinct spiritual realities or principles. Thus, 'bridge' words tended to become 'bridge' beings, hovering uncertainly within a realm of existence between the transcendent God and the material world. Their ill-defined character would open up new possibilities and pose new problems for Christians as they moved into the wider world. On the one hand, differentiation would facilitate their identification with human agents; they at least had this in common, that they were other than the one Lord of Jewish worship. On the other hand, the lack of precise definition left open the question of just how distinct they were, or how close to God himself.

It was the various concepts and images which belonged to these different categories which were, for reasons already given, utilized by the followers of Jesus to convey the idea of his closeness to God and the belief that his activity in the world was on God's behalf. We must now return to these images, or the most important of them.

(b) 'Messiah/Christ', 'Spirit', 'Lord'

The word 'Messiah', as we have seen,[4] stood for the human agent of God's purposes. Thus, to designate anyone as Messiah in the traditional sense would be to attribute unique and supreme status to him as God's representative, the executor

[4] See above, p. 131; for *Christos* as the Greek equivalent, see p. 186.

of the divine plan, without raising any question as to the genuineness of his humanity. Jesus was so designated, at least after his death if not before.[5] However, a problem in interpreting the significance of his designation as Messiah is posed by the fact that in later Jewish thought ideas occur of a pre-existent Messiah, who was believed to exist incorporeally in heaven pending the moment when he should be sent into action.[6] The problem is compounded by the fact that it is not at all clear when these ideas originally emerged. Hence it is difficult to be sure whether 'Messiah', when applied to Jesus, was simply a supremely honorific title or already carried in itself connotations of pre-existence. Even if it is claimed that both senses are represented in the New Testament, it does not seem that, with the possible exception of the Fourth Gospel, there was any doubt about the genuineness of Jesus' human experience; and certainly nowhere is the reality of his death put in question. However, where the connotations of pre-existence were introduced, whether through the concept of 'Messiah' directly or its association with other concepts of pre-existence, as may be the case with Paul,[7] the problems posed by the identification of Jesus with a transcendent spiritual subject, as described in chap. 6, sect. 4 above, would begin to arise.

In its original sense the word 'Messiah' could be applied to a visible, historical figure who was expected to give concrete expression to God's purpose. It can thus be understood to symbolize the revelation of God in the formal mode. In that sense it could not represent the immediate experience of God, which the word 'Spirit' could symbolize. The two terms 'Messiah' and 'Spirit' separately could, then, serve to symbolize the form and vitality of God. Conjoined to Jesus, they would witness to the form and vitality of God in him. This balance would not necessarily be disturbed by the representation of Messiah as a pre-existent heavenly reality,

[5] See A. E. Harvey, *Constraints*, 78.

[6] Schürer, 505; also Dunn, *Christology*, 72, 75–82. (Jer. 1: 4 shows how the sense of a divinely foreordained destiny can be expressed in language that might suggest pre-existence.)

[7] Dunn holds that there is no idea of a pre-existent Christ in Paul's thought, even in Phil. 2: 6–11 (*Christology*, 114–21). For a contrary view, see Hengel, *Son of God*, 66 ff.

except in so far as that idea would lead more readily towards the total assimilation of Messiah to Spirit. This development would, in any case, probably owe more to the attribution to Jesus as Messiah of other terms with even stronger connotations of incorporeal transcendent existence.

The balance of form and vitality in Jesus was, however, more likely to be weakened when 'Messiah' lost its positive content and historical reference and became, in its Greek form, 'Christ', simply another name for Jesus known in the spirit. Remarkably, this seems to have occurred as early as the writings of Paul. Perhaps it was the very strength of Paul's identification of Jesus as Messiah that rendered the title synonymous with the person (and hence in effect more nearly a proper name than was the case with 'Lord'; see below). With Jesus surnamed as Christ and known in the spirit, 'Christ' and 'Spirit' would seem virtually interchangeable.

However, it may be doubted whether the positive content of 'Christ' was entirely lost with Paul. The word 'Christ' represented something which the word 'Spirit' could not. The important thing about 'Messiah', whether viewed as a title or pre-existent being, was its specific application. The doctrine of the pre-existent Messiah was coupled with the doctrine of hiddenness, which implied that he could only be manifested in one form and was hidden or absent till then. In the same way, the title 'Messiah' could only be bestowed on one agent, when the right person appeared. Hence 'Messiah', whether viewed as a title or pre-existent being, could only have a single referent. True, where a division of functions was envisaged, there might be talk of two Messiahs, as at Qumran, where the kingly Messiah of David and the priestly Messiah of Aaron had complementary roles.[8] But only one Messiah could perform a single role. If any person was designated 'Messiah' or 'Christ', then no one else present and active in history before him or after him could properly lay claim to the same status. Such claimants could only be false Messiahs, or anti-Christs. If Jesus is Messiah, then the Messiah/Christ is indeed Jesus and no one else, and

---

[8] Vermes, *Scrolls*, 184 ff.

Jesus in his particularity stands in unique relationship with God.

We see here the important distinctions between 'Messiah' and 'prophet'. The designation 'prophet' was not exclusive. Many could speak for God out of their experience of him in the spirit. Prophecy represents the activity of the Spirit, which itself symbolizes the breadth and continuity of God's relatedness, the outreach of his creative power. The Messiah of God could not conceivably be thought of as unrelated to God, cut off from his outreach in the spirit. On the contrary, the language of the Spirit would be necessary to convey the closeness of his relationship, on which all else would hinge; but the designation 'Messiah/Christ' would still represent something distinct, so that it could not become entirely interchangeable with 'Spirit'.

In the non-Jewish world the title 'Lord' could serve a purpose very similar to that of 'Messiah' (and so will not require lengthy consideration). Though open to a wider range of meanings, 'Lord' (Gk. *kurios*) was used specifically of the Roman emperors, who were accorded divine status and who tolerated no opposition or competition. Thus, to hail Jesus as 'Lord' was to make an exalted and exclusive claim for him, and to risk martyrdom at the hands of emperors who recognized the implications (especially when accompanied by refusal to sacrifice to the emperor or to the gods of Rome).[9] The use of the title for saviour-figures in pagan mystery cults no doubt contributed to the religious significance of 'Lord', but it gained deeper meaning and its exclusiveness was reinforced when references to 'the Lord' in the Old Testament were taken to apply to Jesus. However, the word remained too ambiguous and widely used to serve as well as 'Messiah' could in identifying Jesus. It was for that reason, perhaps, that it had to remain a title.

The close assimilation of 'Christ' with 'Spirit' in the language of the early Church effectively witnesses to the belief that in one person the two facets of God's relatedness are integrated. Jesus is, then, to be seen as the source of true

---

[9] R. M. Grant, *From Augustus to Constantine* (London, 1971), 106. Cf. R. L. Wilken, *The Christians as the Romans saw them* (New Haven and London, 1984), 118–21.

understanding of God, and of a living vital experience in personal relationship with him.[10] The Spirit informed by Jesus Christ the Lord and Jesus Christ the Lord experienced in the spirit are indeed the one God known and experienced. Each of the two basic terms, 'Christ' and 'Spirit', carries a distinct meaning and hence performs a distinct conceptual function in disclosing God. Neither in isolation can adequately convey the reality of God in his relatedness. To treat them as interchangeable is to risk losing the content and force of each one.[11] Only in their dynamic interaction is God adequately disclosed.

The New Testament hardly represents the case exactly in these terms, but it may be for fundamental reasons of this kind rather than by chance that the contributors to the New Testament did not go further in rendering 'Christ' and 'Spirit' interchangeable, even when their immediate concern was with the living presence of Jesus. The power that flows from a generator may be one and the same and ready to flow out instantly wherever a connection is made, but the two wires cannot be reduced to one. No more can the poles of form and vitality be reduced to one, and a wiring diagram that depicts the contrary is, to say the least, misleading. Once the New Testament was formed, no theologian who acknowledged its authority could overlook the fact that within it Jesus was represented as Lord and Christ and as distinct from the Holy Spirit. This more than anything else was likely to hinder the identification of Jesus Christ with the Spirit, even though 'Spirit' had positive value already in the Greek world as a symbol of divine reality in relation to humanity.[12]

We may now sum up the position reached. Jesus after the resurrection is apprehended by his followers as a spiritual reality and he is this as Messiah/Christ and Lord. The tendency to assimilate him with the Spirit is, indeed, strong, but complete identification is avoided in the New Testament,

[10] Dunn, *Christology*, 182 and *passim*.
[11] Lampe might seem to run this risk (e.g. p. 145), and as a result be exposed to a charge of unitarianism, but in terms of the present argument his repeated emphasis on the normativeness of Jesus defends him from this charge (pp. 34, 64, 106, 114, 181).
[12] Grillmeier, 88 n. 183.

and with rare exceptions outside it. This leaves the status of the Spirit *vis-à-vis* the historical Jesus seemingly clear, but *vis-à-vis* Jesus alive in the spirit very unclear, because he cannot be completely identified with or unequivocally differentiated from Jesus the Christ. At the same time, the collocation of the symbols of man's transcendence and of God's immanence in the person of Jesus will inevitably pose a problem for understanding the being of Jesus, as to whether he was essentially man-transcendent, or God-immanent.

The question seems to have been raised at a very early date. The writer of the letters of John opposed those who appeared to hold that Jesus was God immanent as spirit, and only *seemed* to live a human life[13] (hence they are called 'docetics' from the Greek word *dokein* 'to seem'). On the other hand, an early group of Jewish Christians, called Ebionites,[14] held that Jesus was essentially man-transcendent, a man inspired by God. However, the debate would be pursued in somewhat different terms in later generations, where different symbols achieved currency. Their introduction can be associated both with the failure of 'Spirit' as a term with which to identify Jesus and with the fact that 'Christ' did become to all intents and purposes simply another name, while 'Lord' could still be used of God or man and so remained too ambiguous to serve the required purpose.

Where 'Christ' came simply to mean Jesus—experienced as risen and living Lord and hence at one with God in his personal outreach to the world and humankind—a different word would have to be used to distinguish the historical figure, and, of course, the name Jesus is available for this purpose. This leads to the contrast drawn in nineteenth- and twentieth-century theology between the Jesus of history and the Christ of faith, where 'Christ' has become synonymous with the presence and activity of Jesus in the spirit.[15] Paul

[13] 2 John 7. See above, p. 209 n. 35; also Grillmeier, 78 f.
[14] Grillmeier, 76 f.
[15] M. Kähler, *The So-called Historical Jesus and the Historic, Biblical Christ* (Philadelphia, 1964), 66, '*The real Christ is the Christ who is preached*' (emphasis original); quoted in W. G. Kümmel, *The New Testament* (London, 1973), 224. See also V. Harvey, *The Historian and the Believer* (London, 1967), 173-9.

could recognize the distinction but hardly the discontinuity often associated with the phrase.

At the same time, if 'Christ' seemed to be just another name for Jesus in the spirit, which appears to have been increasingly the case in the Hellenistic world after Paul, then some term other than 'Christ' (and not 'Spirit' or 'Lord' on its own) would be needed to convey positively his high standing before God. This task presented itself in different terms from those which applied during or with reference to Jesus' historical life. At that stage 'Messiah' was the highest designation available for a human being. After the Resurrection, the question concerned the relationship to God not just of an exceptional human being, but of someone apprehended as existing in the manner of God himself, in the spirit, with a claim to nothing less than the ultimacy of God. The right terms to define the relationship of Jesus in the spirit to God would then be those appropriate to spiritual reality, but not 'Spirit' itself. As remarked above, other terms had already emerged within Judaism in the attempt to express the relatedness of the transcendent God to his world. As such they all carried more or less of the connotations of God in his outreach. This would render them highly appropriate to those who saw and experienced in Jesus the outreach of God. Such terms indeed were essential. The experience itself of Jesus in the spirit carried implications for the understanding of Jesus and God which neither the symbol 'Messiah' on its own nor even 'Spirit' could convey. 'Messiah' defined Jesus as God's representative. By implication, it defined God as Jesus represented him, because Jesus was truly Messiah only if his representation of God was true.

However, though the designation of Jesus as 'Messiah' may have carried such implications, the word itself did not convey them explicitly even as a title, let alone as a name. Other symbols would therefore have to be found to express the conviction that God was definitively revealed in Jesus.

At the same time, if God *was* definitively revealed in Jesus, it followed that God was not only like that then, but must always have been like that, and would always be like that (because God is eternal and unchanging in his nature). This would be so whether recognized to be so or not, and even when there could or can be no possibility of human acknowledgement, as at the beginning of the universe or the end. If it were not so, Jesus would not be the definitive revelation of God. (The aim here is not to prove that he was, but to examine the implications of confessing him to be so.)

It follows from this that whatever symbols were used to portray God's creative activity, his all-embracing, providential care for creation and humankind, or the fulfilment of his purposes, these symbols must hereafter be tied to Jesus, if they are to be apprehended and interpreted aright. If Jesus defines God, he defines the symbols of God. Conversely, tying such symbols to Jesus makes it possible to express what 'Messiah' partially but imperfectly expressed, namely, that Jesus is the true representation of God, the definition of God.

The traditional symbols of God's self-expression and outreach would serve this purpose effectively when linked to Jesus, after the full force of 'Messiah' was weakened or lost. However, despite their positive value, these symbols of God's relatedness as applied to Jesus could also pose problems if they were treated as more than symbols, and rather as 'bridge' beings[16] and personal agents of God's relatedness, in some way distinct from God. Such a view might arise, as we have remarked, under the influence of Greek thought, but it would be reinforced, as Lampe suggests, by the complete identification of Jesus with such concepts.[17] Not only would they then impart to him a unique relationship to God of universal significance, but Jesus would impart to them the personal characteristics and differentiation from God which were his as a human being, and which constitute the fundamental conditions of personal existence in history. The question then arises of whether such differentiation is a fundamental condition of God's existence in eternity, as usually supposed in traditional understandings of the doctrine of the Trinity. However, that issue cannot be considered yet. We must turn now to three symbols which were employed in the attempt to express Jesus' unique relationship to God, and hence his supreme revelatory significance, and which might thus serve to identify him as effectively as 'Messiah' had previously.

2. WISDOM, SON, AND LOGOS

(a) 'Wisdom' and 'Son'

We have already encountered the concept of Wisdom and seen how it played a key role in the elevation of the Torah to revelatory supremacy.[18] It would play a similar role in the elevation of Jesus within Christianity.[19] As in the case of Spirit, the authority of use in the Old Testament scriptures could be claimed for Wisdom. In the key passage from the book of Proverbs (8: 22; see above, p. 114), and in many other passages where Wisdom appears in the Old Testament, it is very unlikely that there is any conception of a spiritual reality distinct from God.[20] However, in the book known as the Wisdom of Solomon, written in Greek probably not long before Jesus' day, Wisdom does appear more clearly delineated as a mediating figure. Not surprisingly, perhaps, the influence of Greek thought is generally acknowledged in this work. The Wisdom of Solomon and also the Wisdom of Ben Sira (Ecclesiasticus) were both included in the Septuagint; where it was used, these later writings were accorded the same sacred authority as the rest of the Old Testament.

Thus, by the time of Jesus, 'Wisdom' was already established as a symbol of God's relatedness, and was perhaps already on the way to being conceived as a spiritual mediator carrying out God's creative purposes.[21] Either way, in so far as Wisdom was associated with the divine plan for creation and believed to be the source of life-giving power, the image combined in dynamic personal terms elements of both form and vitality in creative interaction. The emphasis fell more

---

[18] See above, chap. 4, sect. 2.

[19] Dunn, *Christology*, 163–212.

[20] Ibid. 176.

[21] Dunn rejects even this possibility: ibid. 210, '*Wisdom never really became more than a convenient way of speaking about God acting in creation, revelation and salvation*' (emphasis original).

heavily on form when Wisdom came to be identified with the Torah, so that the latter was seen as the embodiment or visible form of Wisdom. Such an identification said much for the Torah in associating it so closely with God and his purpose for creation. Equally, it said much that Jesus' followers wished to say about him in preference to the Torah, as the inspirational source of right understanding and right practice—the definitive clue to God's purpose in creation.

The Epistle to the Colossians draws the profoundest conclusions concerning Jesus' relationship to God through applying to him the imagery commonly associated with Wisdom, though not the word itself (Col. 1: 15-20). Doubts over the authorship of this letter render it uncertain whether Paul's viewpoint is represented there. It seems very probable, however, that Paul was familiar with the Wisdom of Solomon. He was prepared, at least in opposition to contrary views such as seem to have been expressed at Corinth, to proclaim Christ rather than anyone or anything else to be the Wisdom of God (1 Cor. 1: 20-5). In doing so, he was most probably 'asserting the finality of Christ's role in God's purposes for man and creation', to quote Dunn (p. 194), rather than intending 'to assert the pre-existence of Christ, or to affirm that Jesus was a divine being personally active in creation'. The connotation of pre-existence, or rather coeternity with God, belonged naturally to the symbol of Wisdom. Its application to Jesus to express his ultimate significance opened the way to thinking of him as personally pre-existent.

Despite applying the image of Wisdom to Jesus, Paul more commonly speaks of him explicitly as Son rather than Wisdom. 'Son' had long been used as a symbol of close relationship and service to God in Jewish tradition. It is hardly surprising that Paul preferred this personal symbol. It had, of course, the obvious advantage of being masculine, while 'Wisdom' (*Sophia*) was feminine. The gender of *Sophia* would create no real difficulty where the word was used metaphorically, whether in the New Testament or in later writers. However, if it was taken to designate a mediating figure, that figure would seem to be female. This could and did lead to the vivid mythological representation of the divine in terms of sexual differentiation, i.e. of God and a

female offspring or consort. The philosophers and theologians of this period appear to have been strongly averse to
this (not so the Gnostics[22] and other popular religious teachers, which perhaps added to the word's disrepute). As a
result, ways of representing the divine in which both mas-
culinity and femininity could be embraced were lost.

However, apart from such considerations, the feminine
gender hindered the identification of Wisdom with the man
Jesus beyond the Pauline metaphorical level, and limited the
possibility of personal identification with him. The attributes but not the name of Wisdom could be transferred to
the person who perhaps even in his lifetime was called 'Son
of God'. The result would be to transform the meaning of
'Son' as applied to Jesus. In his lifetime it could have been
used of Jesus as of Charismatics and other servants of God.
But none of these was thought of as the Wisdom of God. To
think of Jesus in the spirit as the Wisdom of God (as in
Colossians), and still to call him 'Son', was to lift his sonship
on to a totally different, supraworldly, suprahistorical plane.
Wisdom elevated and conferred pre-existence on Son; Son
differentiated and personalized Wisdom.[23] The two images
in harness bore Jesus up to heaven and into eternity. More
prosaically, in our terms, they served to express faith in the
universal and ultimate significance of that person.

However, even in Paul's writings, 'Son' was not adequate
in itself to define Jesus' relationship to God. In Jewish and
Greek thought it remained full of ambiguities and potentially
misleading connotations. A clearer designation was needed.
The term 'Logos' seemed best suited for the purpose. It
would itself in due course have its own misleading connotations corrected by the reapplication of the symbol 'Son',
and would have its meaning enlarged by association with the
imagery of Wisdom.

(h) 'Logos'

'Logos' is a Greek word which has no exact English equivalent. In everyday usage it can often be adequately translated as 'word', signifying 'the outward form by which the

[22] See above, p. 185 n. 14.
[23] If ideas of pre-existent sonship already existed (cf. Hengel, *Son of God*), at
the very least these would have been strongly reinforced by the collocation of
symbols in Jesus.

inward thought is expressed'.[24] But it might equally signify 'the inward thought itself', or both thought and expression together, or again 'reason'—the rational principle underlying thought and speech. In the period with which we are concerned, 'logos' had gained a wide range of meanings from its use in different philosophical and theological circles.

On the one hand, having been used in Greek versions of the Old Testament to translate the 'word' of God,[25] it could stand for the expression of God's power and purpose in creation, and so be closely associated with Spirit in the activity of the prophets. As such, it would scarcely be differentiated from God himself in his active outreach to the world. Hence, its meaning would be very close to that of 'Wisdom', its gender much to be preferred.

On the other hand, it acquired significantly different connotations within the syncretistic philosophical movements commonly known as Middle Platonism,[26] which drew on the varied resources provided by Plato,[27] Aristotle,[28] the Stoics, and the Neopythagoreans.

Plato had distinguished between the worlds of being and becoming, the former immaterial and unchanging, accessible to the mind, the latter material and changing, accessible to the senses. In making this distinction he was wrestling with the problem of knowledge.[29] He asked how rational beings can know what is. This led him to explore the relation of universals to particulars. How, for example, is the concept

[24] H. G. Liddell and R. Scott, *A Greek-English Lexicon* (7th edn., 1883). *Logos* can mean verbal expression, particular utterance, or divine oracle; it is rarely used for a single word (ibid., 9th edn., 1940).

[25] See Dunn, *Christology*, 217-20.

[26] These movements stemmed from the revival of Platonism in the first century BC, and flourished in the second century AD until the emergence of Neoplatonism with Plotinus. For a full account, see J. Dillon, *The Middle Platonists: A Study of Platonism 80 BC to AD 220* (London, 1977). For a brief introduction, see Norris, 8-32; also A. H. Armstrong, *An Introduction to Ancient Philosophy* (3rd edn., London, 1957), 147-55.

[27] For an exhaustive treatment of Plato, see W. K. C. Guthrie, *A History of Greek Philosophy*, iv, *Plato the Man and his Dialogues: Earlier Period* (Cambridge, 1975), v, *The Later Plato and the Academy* (Cambridge, 1978). For a concise introduction, see R. M. Hare, *Plato* (Oxford, 1982).

[28] See Guthrie, vol. vi, *Aristotle: An Encounter* (Cambridge, 1981). Also J. Barnes, *Aristotle* (Oxford, 1982).

[29] Hare, 30, 'One of Plato's chief incentives to metaphysics was a nest of problems which he thought he had encountered about knowledge.'

or 'idea' of a table to be related to particular tables? The latter can be chopped up as firewood and disappear. But the 'idea' remains, non-physical in itself and immune to the processes of physical change and corruption, and, so it would seem, more real. Plato concluded that all things in the world, not only concrete objects, but concepts such as virtue and goodness,[30] are but pale fleeting copies of the immaterial, imperishable ideas, or forms. These he conceived of as not merely products of the human mind, but as existing in their own right in a realm more truly real than the only seemingly real physical world.[31]

Already posited in this account is the human being as knower, tied to the material world in virtue of his body, yet having access to the immaterial real world. This he had in virtue of his soul or mind. Although its destiny was to be embodied, and to impart energy and rational order to the body, its true home was in the immortal realm of imperishable being. Here philosophical and religious interests converge, and one can see how Plato came to exert such a powerful influence on the later history of philosophy and theology.

The function of the soul already described—to energize and order the body—and its intermediate place between the realms of being and becoming would seem to have suggested to Plato a way of interpreting reality as a whole. In the *Timaeus*, he postulated as the organizing principle of the material universe a World Soul[32]—a sort of creator god— which contemplated the world of forms and reproduced them as well as it could in the far from ideal conditions of material existence. Though Plato was not a fully systematic thinker and left many loose ends, he offered a comprehensive view of reality that was to have lasting influence.

[30] Guthrie, iv. 507, 'Absolute standards of right and wrong could only be restored along with belief in a world of stable and comprehensible reality . . . supreme reality is supreme goodness.' Also Hare, 18.

[31] Guthrie, v. 378, 'By the theory of Forms I mean the idea that what we call universals are not simply concepts in the mind, but objective realities displaying their character to perfection and eternally, invisible to the senses, but grasped after intensive preparation by a sort of intellectual vision, with an existence independent of their unstable and imperfect instances or copies which are all that we experience in this life.' Also Hare, 32-7.

[32] *Timaeus*, 3-4 (trans. D. Lee, Harmondsworth, 1965). Also Norris, 16-22; Guthrie, v. 253 ff.

Platonism did not, however, monopolize ancient thought. A different account of reality comes from the Stoics (who took their name from the *Stoa*, or porch, where their founder Zeno taught in Athens).[33] Although they posited two interacting principles, spirit and matter, unlike Plato they taught that both were bodies, with spirit as a rarefied substance pervading the grosser material of the body, as the soul in a human being. In contrast to Plato's radical distinction between being and becoming, they portrayed the universe as a great ensouled animal, hence a living organism. Human souls were portions or sparks of the rational power governing the whole. This all-pervasive spirit of reason, the source of the harmonies of nature and of understanding in human minds, was called 'Logos'.

The Middle Platonists drew the Platonic and Stoic strands of thought together. The Logos and World Soul were equated, in some writers explicitly;[34] in others the idea of the Logos/World Soul is present, though the word 'Logos' is not used of it.[35]

There remains one further contribution to the 'amalgam'[36] of Middle Platonism to be noted, which according to Dillon imparted to it its distinctive quality. This came from Neo-pythagoreanism, with its 'postulation of a supreme, utterly transcendent First Principle, which is also termed God'.[37]

Plato himself had been much influenced by the early Pythagoreans—by their communal life, their fascination with numbers, and their 'mystical approach to the soul and its place in the material world'.[38] But here was something new. In combination with Aristotle's Unmoved Mover[39] and Plato's allusions to the idea (form) of the Good,[40] the Neopythagoreans contributed to Middle Platonism a profound sense of God's absolute transcendence.

[33] See Norris, 22 f.; also Armstrong, *Introduction*, 119-29.
[34] e.g. Antiochus of Ascalon—a philosopher of the first century BC (Dillon, 83). Philo and Plutarch (first and early second centuries AD) frequently refer to the Logos in this sense (Dillon, 159, 200).
[35] e.g. Atticus and Albinus (second century AD) (Dillon, 252, 284).
[36] Ibid. 115.
[37] Ibid. 127 f.
[38] Hare, 10 f.
[39] Guthrie, vi. 252-62 (p. 259, 'The first Unmoved Mover is God'). Also Dillon, 13; Armstrong, *Introduction*, 88-91.
[40] Guthrie, iv. 503-21.

Early Christian thinking developed in this milieu and could hardly have escaped its influence; in fact, there was much in the Middle Platonic vision of reality that was positively appealing to Christian ideas and interests. God was represented as supremely transcendent. In the perfection of his immutable being, he could not be implicated directly in the material world of becoming; but the spiritual world of forms (ideas) could be represented as existing in the mind of God,[41] as his inward thoughts prior to their expression in the creation—and the agent of expression was none other than the Logos, God's Word. Inasmuch as human beings, despite their material bodies, had a stake in the spiritual world in virtue of their reason (*logos*), the Logos (rational principle) could be seen to function appropriately not only as the agent of creation, but as the agent of reconciliation that would reunite estranged human reason with divine reason— humanity with God.

The Logos thus emerges as a key concept. It is the intermediary between God and the world. Like Wisdom, it is spiritual; but unlike Wisdom—at least in more orthodox Jewish thought—it is conceived in Middle Platonism to be distinct in being from the transcendent God, relating to him and expressing his mind and will, but relating also to the material world from which the pure essence of God was by definition excluded.[42] Yet, with that difference, the Logos in Middle Platonism plays a comparable role to that of the Spirit in Judaism, by signifying both the relatedness of God as far as that was possible in the immediacy of experience, and the world-creating and sustaining power of God. At the same time, as in the case of Wisdom, and more so than Spirit, the Logos represents the principle of order and harmony in creation.

With the Logos of Middle Platonism a concept became available of enormous value for Christians in their task of expressing the significance of Jesus. It was only to be expected that they would seize on it not merely as a vivid

[41] Dillon, 48, 'With the assimilation of the Platonic Demiurge (World Soul) to the Stoic Logos, the situating of the Ideas in the mind of God becomes more or less inevitable.' This probably occurred with Antiochus of Ascalon or even earlier.

[42] In its philosophical context, the Logos is a metaphysical principle rather than a personal being, though metaphorical language could blur the distinction.

symbol of transcendence, but as signifying the true identity—the underlying reality—of that person who was called
Logos in the Fourth Gospel and to whom, it was supposed,
the Old Testament witnessed.

The question that now confronts us is the adequacy of the
symbol 'Logos' for Christian purposes, as seen against its
Old Testament and Middle Platonic background. On the
one hand, in the Old Testament sense, it served as a symbol
of God's self-expression. Even allowing for some variation
of usage, the less the differentiation of Logos from God, the
greater was its value as a symbol of transcendence. On the
other hand, as a spiritual reality distinct from the supreme
God, in the Middle Platonic sense, 'Logos' could more
readily than 'Spirit' lend itself to complete identification
with Jesus as a spiritual being distinct from the God whom,
in his earthly life, he had addressed as 'Father'.

With these advantages Logos nevertheless introduced into
Christian thought a complementary set of disadvantages.
These sprang, first, from the limitations of the Old Testament meaning of 'Logos' as a symbol of Jesus; secondly,
from the limitations of the Middle Platonic sense of 'Logos'
as a symbol for Jesus; and thirdly, from the complications
created by the application of 'Logos' in both senses to Jesus,
and their interaction with other symbols of transcendence
applied to him.

In the first case, to call Jesus 'Logos' in the Old Testament
sense served well to convey the conviction that in him the
truth of God was expressed. 'Logos' in this sense could
function as a vivid metaphor like 'Wisdom', and in this context had connotations not merely of verbal expression, but
of active power, very close to 'Spirit'. But Logos so understood as the Word of God could scarcely be conceived of as
an independent being able to enter into a personal relationship with God as Father. To speak of Jesus in this way
as the Logos of God in a more than metaphorical sense
would place the reality of his personal existence in question
(by identifying Jesus with a non-personal Logos); on the
other hand, if Jesus' personhood was still affirmed, a wedge
would be driven between this non-personal Logos and the
real person, Jesus himself.

In contrast, the Middle Platonic conception of hierarchies of being meant that the Logos was not only distinguished from, but necessarily set below, the supreme God. It could be associated with the world of becoming, with history, concrete existence, and manifestations in material form, from which God in his perfect being was by definition excluded. But that he was so superior, separate, and inaccessible was not what Christians ultimately wished to say about God the Father. Moreover, though 'Logos' in this sense allowed them to say much that they wanted to say about Jesus, ultimately it did not say enough.

The problems would have to be faced in due course, but it can hardly be doubted that, in the first instance, 'Logos' was the most powerful symbol available to convey to a non-Jewish world the closeness of Jesus' relationship to God, and the conviction that in him the form and vitality of God were expressed in the sphere of creation. The disadvantage of the distinction of the Logos from God could to some extent be qualified by emphasizing the basic (and Stoic) meaning of 'Logos' as thought in the mind prior to outward expression. Thus, the early Christian Apologists, such as Justin Martyr and Tertullian, could argue that the Logos originated within but became differentiated from the Father.[43] On this understanding, Jesus as the Logos could be thought of as standing as close to the mind and being of the Father as possible. (The actual designation of God as 'Father' was not unfamiliar to Greek ears, though it had the connotation 'Father of the Universe' rather than 'Father of the Logos as Son'.) 'Logos' also shared with 'Spirit' the authority of scriptural usage, but had a further advantage. In the Fourth Gospel the Logos was already explicitly identified with Jesus, in distinction from the Spirit. Whatever uncertainties still remain concerning the precise meaning of 'Logos' in that Gospel compared with later usage, and however hard it may be in practice to perceive clear distinctions in meaning between 'Logos', 'risen Lord', and 'Spirit', the logical problem posed by identifying Jesus with Spirit, from which he is explicitly distinguished in the sacred and authoritative writings, would not arise in the case of Logos.

The term had also already been developed in the sphere

    [43] J. N. D. Kelly, *Early Christian Doctrines* (5th, rev. edn., London, 1977), 95–9, 111 f.

of Judaism by Philo of Alexandria as a way of linking the Old Testament to Platonism.[44] In the process, he came very close indeed to transforming 'Logos' from a bridge word into a bridge being (without apparently seeing any great problem in doing so). Philo's influence within Judaism was not great, but by linking the Old Testament 'Word of God' with the 'Logos' of Middle Platonism, he served the interests of Christian theologians very well. Aided by Philo, they could attribute what was said of the undifferentiated word of God himself in the Old Testament to the differentiated Logos of Middle Platonism as identified with Jesus. Meanings never originally intended could then be read into scripture, more or less unconsciously. In other words, Christians could treat references to the 'Word of God' as references to Jesus the Logos; just as references to the 'Lord' in the Old Testament had been taken as references to the Lord Jesus.

However, it is here that we see the source of further difficulties. The use of the one word 'Logos', which served to unite Jewish and Greek ideas of transcendence in Jesus, could also serve to conceal serious underlying differences of interpretation. The semblance of agreement would be shattered when different ways of understanding Jesus and his significance developed according to different presuppositions over the meaning of 'Logos', and matching differences concerning his redemptive work. Out of this would arise violent controversies concerning the relationship of the Logos to God the Father on the one hand, and on the other its relationship to Jesus the man. The former issue came to a head in the Arian dispute, which will concern us in the following section. The latter gave rise to the Christological controversies between the Platonically minded theologians of Alexandria in Egypt and the more traditionalist, biblically minded theologians of Antioch in Syria;[45] these will be considered in sect. 4 below. All parties

[44] For Philo as a Middle Platonist, see Dillon, 139–83. For the place of Logos in Gnostic speculations, see Rudolph. He attaches more importance to Gnostic influences on early Christian theology than I do.

[45] For the contrasting approaches to biblical exegesis, see Wiles on Origen and Theodore of Mopsuestia, in P. R. Ackroyd and C. F. Evans, eds., *The Cambridge History of the Bible*, i, *From the Beginnings to Jerome* (Cambridge, 1970), 454–510 (p. 489, '[Antiochene] emphasis on the biblical text, on historical fact and on the

would be challenged not only by their direct opponents, but by the tension generated between the connotations of their own understanding of the Logos-symbol and what the faith and worship of the Church required to be said of Jesus who was identified with the Logos.

3. THE LOGOS AS JESUS IN RELATION TO GOD

I have tried to show how the symbol 'Logos' could serve better than any other symbol available at the time to convey Jesus' unique standing in relation to God, and hence his unique authority and revelatory significance. Other well-established symbols of transcendence or divine outreach, such as 'Spirit' or 'Wisdom', could not, for reasons already discussed, be applied exclusively or without qualification to Jesus, though they might be used metaphorically. 'Logos', however, seemed free of such limitations and so capable of being applied not merely metaphorically but literally to Jesus. In so far as Jesus was identified with the Logos, the Logos could serve to identify Jesus, to disclose his relationship to God and hence to everything else. Its importance within the Christian tradition is that, even when the term 'Logos', and the way of thinking associated with it, fell more or less into disuse, it had already laid down the terms for talking about Jesus and God. It had, perhaps more than any other word, fixed the rules for theological play, rules which it seems can still hardly be questioned without provoking indignant protest.

However, we have already seen that the symbol 'Logos' itself is of mixed parentage, and this alone makes it hard to see what applying it literally to Jesus should mean, quite apart from the problem raised by any attempt to speak of the things of God literally. Such difficulties were not long in making themselves felt in the early Church. Problems arose specifically over the role and status of Spirit, and the relationship of the Logos as Jesus to God. We shall examine these two questions in this section, and in the next the question of the relationship of the Logos as God to the historical figure Jesus.

humanity of Jesus'). See also D. S. Wallace-Hadrill, *Christian Antioch* (Cambridge, 1982), 31 f.

We begin with the Spirit. Once Jesus was identified with the Logos, the tendency we noticed before in the New Testament to assimilate him to the Spirit was checked. What then happens to the Spirit? We have understood the word as a symbol of God in his outreach to the world, and to human beings in particular in the immediacy of experience. Hence the Spirit represents subjective revelation. Grillmeier maintains that ways of speaking about Jesus which relate him to Spirit or Logos, to be found in certain early theologians, are 'identical in point of content of ideas'.[46] We have suggested here that 'Logos' conveys the idea of form as well as vitality to a greater degree than does 'Spirit'. But even if this is so, it does not affect the issue. If 'Logos' embraces the meaning of 'Spirit', the latter would seem to be superfluous.

However, in the New Testament (by this time recognized as sacred revelation), and also in traditional rites, Jesus and the Holy Spirit were both named separately in relation to God. This awkward anomaly would have significant consequences in due course. Before turning to them, we must consider the other important consequences of identifying Jesus with the Logos, as this bore on his relationship to God and the understanding of him as a man. The problem shaped itself differently according to whether Old Testament or Middle Platonic connotations of 'Logos' predominated, and was further complicated by the fact that the different points of view interacted on each other.[47]

The Old Testament sense of 'Logos' was originally predominant among those who stood in the theological tradition of Antioch. Its advantage was that it signified God expressing himself. So if Jesus was Logos in this sense, it meant he really was God's direct self-expression. This Logos, however, could hardly be differentiated from God in any real way, least of all in terms of the personal relationship which the Gospels portrayed between Jesus and the Father. Those who set great store by that relationship and by the whole of Jesus' earthly life, as the Antiochenes did, would therefore find it virtually impossible to identify Jesus completely with the Logos, however close a relationship might

[46] Grillmeier, 88 n. 183, with reference to Justin, Hippolytus, and Tertullian.
[47] Detailed treatment of the development of Logos-theology can be found in Grillmeier and Kelly.

otherwise be asserted. Yet without that identification the supreme revelatory significance of Jesus could seem in doubt.

The understanding of Logos derived from Middle Platonism was more characteristic of Alexandrian theology (though not of all Alexandrian theologians). We have already noted above some of its advantages and disadvantages. Logos in this sense could be fully identified with Jesus and so help to maintain his distinction from the Father. But it could only do this at the price of setting him on a lower plane. Once again his supreme revelatory significance could seem to be in doubt.

Such an identification posed a two-sided problem. The Logos distinct from God must either be equal to him or inferior. If he was equal, there would appear to be two Gods; but to postulate two first causes was absurd, and in any case Christians had died for their rejection of polytheism. On the other hand, if the Logos was inferior, then he could be more readily identified with Jesus (who experienced the various limitations of life on earth) as well as posing less of a problem for belief in one God. But if Jesus was the Logos who was inferior to God, how could he be worthy of worship? Yet Christians had died for refusing to abandon worship of Jesus the Messiah. Somehow he was entitled to more than the Logos from this perspective could give.

Thus, whether from the biblical or Platonic point of view, the problems posed by the identification of Jesus with the Logos were acute. Any kind of identification would strike non-Christian thinkers, Jew and pagan alike, as absurd. Jews could hardly tolerate the personification of the word of the Lord. For Middle Platonists, the assertion that the Logos was immanent in the world was one thing; to say that he was fully present, or worse, enfleshed (incarnate), in one particular human being was very much another.

The early Christian theologians inevitably shared many of the philosophical and theological presuppositions of their critics, and so would have felt the force of their objections. They were faced with the task of making sense to themselves, as well as to others, of what the Church claimed about Jesus. In pursuing this task, they were working with symbols and

ideas which were not only more or less the common stock of
their world, but had also already been worked over,
stretched, and refashioned within their own tradition. In this
continuous dynamic process, many factors were at work.[48]
Not the least significant was the interplay of symbols on each
other resulting from their common application to Jesus, as
we saw in the case of 'Wisdom' and 'Son'. This interplay
can be seen to embrace 'Logos' as well, and to extend between the two senses of 'Logos', with both positive and
negative consequences. The different configurations can be
briefly described.

The subordinationist implications of the Middle Platonic
Logos could be compensated for in two ways. On the one
hand, it could be combined with Logos-language drawn
from the Old Testament. On the other, the gap could be
closed or at least narrowed by transferring the symbol 'Son'
to the Logos.

In the first case, the undifferentiated Logos (word of God)
could counterbalance the over-differentiated Logos (World
Soul). Both Logos-symbols could serve in their different
ways to convey the revelatory significance of Jesus, and used
together they would affirm him to be one with and yet distinct from the Father. As an expression of the paradox of
faith calling for further reflection, this could serve a valid
purpose. However, where such language was thought to describe who and what Jesus was, the use of the single term
'Logos' concealed rather than resolved the logical difficulties
and obscured the paradox. A likely consequence was over-
confidence in the language used, and an unsympathetic hostility towards those who would not gloss over the underlying
problems.

In the second case, the symbol 'Son' could serve to draw
the Logos into a 'natural relationship', and hence on to the
same plane as the Father. But 'Son' affected 'Logos' in more
than one way. In the first place, it personified the metaphysical concept of Logos (in similar fashion to Wisdom)
and placed it within a personal relationship to the Father.
In so doing, it helped to displace the Platonic connotations
of God's fatherhood in Christian theology, so that God as

[48] See Wiles, *Doctrine*.

'Father of the Universe' gave way to God as 'Father of the pre-existent Logos-Son'. More than this, 'Son' was also the channel through which the connotations of Wisdom could flow freely into 'Logos', and so strengthen its link with Old Testament usage.

The interplay of Son and Wisdom began, as we have seen, at least as early as Paul. It was most probably this which originally raised Jesus on to the same plane as the Father. The Son-metaphor in the Old Testament sense could not have achieved this on its own. As traditionally used of a man in relation to God, 'Son' never had the implication of natural biological kinship, but rather of adoption, signifying election and obedient response in a close relationship of love. The biological aspect of the metaphor, however, played an increasingly important part in later discussion, where the precise relationship, not of the historical Jesus, but of the Logos-Son with the Father, was at issue.[49] Then the combination of biological connotations with Wisdom-imagery in the symbol of 'Son' served effectively to pull the Middle Platonic Logos on to the same plane as the Father, and so into equality with him. By this means, conceptual thought could catch up with the demands of faith, which insisted that Jesus was a worthy object of worship and therefore not less than God. Yet, though the imagery could serve this purpose, it was still more an expression of faith than an explanation. The mystery of the relationship between Father and Son, and the problem of the ultimate oneness of God, remained unresolved.

The symbol 'Son' functioned in a contrasting way where the biblical sense of 'Logos' was dominant, as in the Antiochene tradition. Here 'Son' imparted differentiation which was otherwise lacking. The Word of God, which in the Old Testament was the expressive power of God directly at work, as in the prophets, became as Son a mediating personal agent, not identical with God (neither was it identical with the human Jesus; this raised problems which will be considered in the next section).

[49] The shift of meaning from adoption to natural sonship in the case of Jesus may have already begun with Paul, perhaps under the pressure of Wisdom imagery; cf. Gal. 4: 1.

The same word, then, could mean very different things, and the same symbol could function in contrasting ways according to the particular context of theological discussion. It is not surprising that disputes were often fuelled by widespread misunderstandings.[50] These disputes may be reckoned to fall into two basic categories. On the one hand, there were those where different language and different traditions of thought raised the often mutual suspicion in different quarters that the ultimate and universal significance of Jesus was being put in question by those who professed to be Christians. Where that was not the intention or the implication recognized by those accused, the issue could in the end often be resolved, even if bitter hostility and mutual excommunication marked the route. The qualifying of symbols and balancing of statements as described above would have their place in disputes of this kind, and open the way to mutual recognition.

On the other hand, there were disputes where, in our terms, the heart of the matter was whether Jesus really was of universal and ultimate significance or not, in short, whether he was God. We must here recognize that, whatever else it means, the word 'God' itself functions as the supreme symbol of ultimate and universal significance. As a symbol, it was open to the same dynamic interplay as the others we have discussed. However difficult it might be to fathom its meaning and proper application, failure in the last resort to designate Jesus as God would entail the denial of his universal and ultimate significance, and hence the betrayal of the conviction on which the Church was founded. However significant Jesus was otherwise deemed to be, to call him less than God was to say too little. If Jesus was believed to be the Logos-Son, then equally the Logos-Son must be called 'God', even if such a claim raised insuperable intellectual problems.

This, we may hold, was the issue at stake in what was perhaps the most bitter controversy in the early Church, the Arian dispute. Arius was a presbyter of Alexandria, and heir to the traditional identification of Jesus with the Logos. But

[50] '. . . like a battle by night', according to the historian Socrates (c.380–c.450), *Hist. eccl.* i. 23.

he qualified that identification, and distinguished between the Logos which was eternally in God as his immanent reason, and a 'certain one'[51] whom God created to be his agent in creation and redemption, who could be called 'Logos' or 'Son' by courtesy rather than by right.[52] By identifying Jesus with this Logos-Son, Arius acknowledged him to be supreme over all creation and uniquely close to the transcendent God. Only someone within the circle of Christianity could make such an exalted claim for Jesus. Nevertheless, Arius was ready to accept the implication discussed above that Jesus as Logos-Son was less than and indeed wholly other than God. He broke out of the concealed ambiguities of the Logos-tradition by refusing to resort to the counterbalancing 'Word of God' language of the Old Testament. On his terms it could not be used in that way. In opposition to current trends, he re-emphasized the biblical idea of sonship, as implying a moral relationship of love and obedience rather than natural kinship. Jesus the Logos was adopted Son rather than Son by nature.[53]

Arius' solution had two great advantages. He was able to avoid the problems of having to show how the Logos-Son could be God without there being two Gods, or the one God being divided or changing. Secondly, his Jesus-Logos, as a creaturely being, was logically free to conform to or not to conform to God's will. His actual love and obedience were therefore morally authentic, and not of necessity. Arius could thus do justice to the New Testament account of Jesus' experience of temptation and suffering, something which the defenders of Jesus' divinity were hard-pressed to explain. It remains the case that Arius' Jesus was not really human like us, because the pre-existent Logos, even if not God, was nevertheless far above humanity and in Jesus displaced his human soul or rationality. This aspect of Arius' teaching left a surprising number of his contemporaries undisturbed, including his famous opponent Athanasius (but, interestingly, not Eustathius, Bishop of Antioch). But perhaps

[51] Athanasius, *De Synodis*, 15. See R. C. Gregg and D. E. Groh, *Early Arianism* (London, 1981), 96 and *passim*.
[52] Gregg and Groh, 102 f.; Kelly, 229.
[53] Gregg and Groh, 84.

the lack of criticism at this point is not so very surprising, since Arius' Logos was at least like us in being a rational creature, and in his creaturely freedom was able to achieve through his obedience to God a genuine moral victory over sin. By thus showing other rational creatures the way, he could secure their salvation. It has been recently argued that soteriology was in fact Arius' primary concern,[54] rather than anxiety to protect the transcendent oneness of God.

Whatever his main concern may have been, Arius' solution won considerable but not unanimous support. The protracted controversy he set in motion threatened to divide the Church just when the Roman emperor Constantine was looking to it to help unite the empire. Constantine summoned a general council of the Church in AD 325 at Nicaea, by the Sea of Marmora, in what is now Turkey. Among those who attended were Bishop Alexander of Alexandria and his deacon Athanasius, who would later succeed him as bishop. It was not long since the Church had been subjected to severe persecution by Constantine's predecessors. For the 220 bishops assembled at Nicaea[55] to be received with great honour by an emperor, who refused even to take his seat before them, would have been an awesome experience.[56] It would also make it very hard for them to oppose his wishes. A creed was approved at the Council which all the bishops present were required to sign. A word had been introduced into it, possibly at the emperor's own suggestion, which was designed to exclude Arius' viewpoint. The word, *homoousios*,[57] meaning 'of the same substance', was not scriptural and was therefore suspect to many, but it seemed to be the best term available to establish Jesus the Logos-Son's position on the side of God rather than of creation, as Son by nature rather than by adoption. It scarcely explained how the two, Father and Son, could be one God, and it was open to different interpretations, but at least it appeared to establish Jesus' worship-worthiness as God. Arius' own

[54] This is Gregg and Groh's main thesis.
[55] H. Chadwick, *The Early Church* (Harmondsworth, 1967), 130.
[56] H. Lietzman, *A History of the Early Church*, iii, *From Constantine to Julian* (London, 1950), 117.
[57] See Kelly, 233–7.

teaching was explicitly condemned. All the bishops signed
the creed except two (and their motives were not, it seems,
primarily theological).

But the Council did not succeed in unifying the Church.
The controversy broke out with even greater intensity and
lasted for many more decades.[58] Somewhat surprisingly, the
keyword *homoousios* was at first more or less ignored even by
supporters of the Nicene position, till Athanasius in particular re-employed it to maintain the full divinity of the
Son. His cause finally triumphed at the Council of Constantinople in AD 381. It is the creed believed to have been
promulgated there which is still used in most Christian
Churches and called the Nicene Creed. It differs from the
original creed of Nicaea in having an expanded section on
the Holy Spirit. Otherwise its significance lies in its reaffirmation of *homoousios* and so of the Son's full divinity.
The Council marked the virtual end of Arianism, except on
the borders of the Roman Empire.

For all the complexities of the debate, the clash of personalities and the interference of emperors, the conclusion
of the dispute with the defeat of Arianism ought not to be
regarded as a historical accident which might easily have
gone the other way. The logic of Christian commitment
required otherwise; the defeat of Arianism was inevitable,
if the Christian Church was not to surrender the central
conviction by which it was constituted. Arianism could do
more justice than many of its opponents to the moral character of Jesus' life, but it failed to do justice to the conviction,
witnessed to in the New Testament and upheld by the earliest Christians, that Jesus was of ultimate and universal
significance. Arius' failure to maintain the absolute uniqueness of Jesus' sonship in principle is precisely the point at
which the inadequacy of his account emerges.[59] In our terms,
Jesus, as represented by Arius, was not the form of God.

[58] The views of later Arians differed in important respects from those of Arius,
but they shared his concern to preserve the transcendent oneness of God. For a
detailed account, see Kelly, 237–69; Chadwick, 133–51; and F. Young, *From Nicaea
to Chalcedon* (London, 1983), 109–15 and *passim*. The last enlarges very usefully
on the background and personalities of the protagonists.

[59] Gregg and Groh, 30, 49, 52, and esp. 56, 'One equal to the Son, the Superior
is able to beget' (quoted from Arius' *Thalia*).

One must add, however, that on Arius' own account Jesus came nearer to being that than anything or anyone else had been or ever, perhaps, could be. His intentions in faith may well have been more adequate than the language he employed to express them. Unfortunately, in that age, inadequacy of language was almost universally assumed to represent inadequacy of faith, if not sheer perversity. But at the end of the day, for Jesus to be above creation but below God, as Arius suggested, was not good enough for the worshipping church.[60]

It is of particular interest here to note that in order to make the point that needed to be made the Church was driven beyond the symbols of transcendence derived from scripture. The language of philosophy had already been harnessed alongside biblical language in the task of apologetic and teaching about God, but, before Nicaea, no blatantly philosophical, non-scriptural terms had been incorporated into the central confessions of the Christian faith. We have already noted the suspicion which the term *homoousios* aroused on this account. Yet the expression 'of the same substance as the Father' had to take its place alongside 'Son' if the ambiguities of traditional symbols were to be overcome and the ultimacy of Jesus maintained.

The language of substance, nature, and person was to acquire increasing significance from now on. But though such terms might counter the ambiguities of traditional symbols, they introduced new sets of ambiguities themselves, not readily apparent in English. The Greek terms employed could not only mean different things, but different words might or might not mean the same thing. This was so in everyday usage. When used of God, their meaning would be even harder to determine. The scope for confusion and misunderstanding between Greeks—let alone between Greeks and Latins—was enormous, and the Church took full advantage of it. The new language could scarcely begin to serve its intended purpose till the various ambiguities were ironed out. Yet its employment is profoundly significant. A precedent was set for the use of non-biblical language in the Christian confession of faith. This shows

[60] Cf. Wiles, *Doctrine*, 96.

that what matters is not what language is used but how well it can serve to express the ultimacy of Jesus. Scriptural or non-scriptural language can be employed, whichever serves this purpose best.

For all the turmoil of the fourth century—with pagans complaining of the serious disruption of public transport because of so many priests hurrying to and from councils[61]—it might seem that the Church had advanced little further than the point reached in New Testament times. In other words, at Nicaea, and more especially at Constantinople, the patristic Church arrived at the point almost reached in the New Testament, when the risen Jesus, the Messiah, was all but identified with the Holy Spirit. Such language implied that the bearer of the name Jesus was none other than God in his continuing outreach. But the Church could scarcely advance much further. In the intervening years the Fathers had wrestled with the question—raised but not answered in the New Testament itself—of how Jesus could be one with God and yet distinct. Had his virtual identification with the Holy Spirit been pursued further, the same sort of problems would have had to be faced over how the Spirit of God (rather than the Word of God) could be so differentiated as to accord with the distinction between Jesus and God witnessed to in scripture. It was this witness and the memory of Jesus' historical life, rather than the Logos' ancestry in Middle Platonism, which required the distinction to be maintained once the Logos was identified with Jesus.

But in fact the identification of Jesus with the Spirit could not have proceeded further. As we saw, the witness of scripture told against it. Jesus himself simply was not Spirit without remainder; to think that was the mistake of docetism. Even as risen Lord he could only be 'all but' identified with the Spirit. In the gap created by the 'all but' he was not only distinguished from but still below God the Father. Another symbol was therefore needed which had the potential to

---

[61] The emperor Constantine II was held responsible, 'He ruined the establishment of public conveyances by devoting them to the service of crowds of priests, who went to and fro to different synods, as they call the meetings at which they endeavour to settle everything according to their own fancy' (Ammianus Marcellinus, *Res Gestae*, xxi. 16. 18, quoted in J. Stevenson, ed., *Councils, Creeds and Controversies* (London, 1966), 3).

bridge the gap in status without blurring the distinction, with reference to Jesus exclusively and uniquely, not just as another inspired prophet. 'Logos', for all its problems, ambiguities, and deficiencies, could serve that purpose. Combined with 'Son', it could lift Jesus to the orbit of Godhead, the point of unconditional ultimacy and universality.

The question now is whether, having served that purpose, this symbolic vehicle of exaltation must remain locked to Jesus as the essential and eternal condition of his remaining in the heights, or whether it can be jettisoned and allowed to fall back to earth. It may be argued that it not only can but must be allowed to fall back, if the true and enduring meaning of Jesus' ultimacy is not to be obscured.

Right from the start the Logos-Son symbolism, for all its positive value, was never entirely free from negative implications. The Fathers, on their own assumptions concerning the inspiration of scripture, were committed to the identification of Jesus with the Logos as expressed in the Fourth Gospel. Given that fact, we can recognize that they struggled hard and at great cost to adjust their symbols to what they were convinced needed to be said about Jesus, rather than letting the symbols dictate and so distort the message. But it does not follow that they were entirely successful. Even after Nicaea and Constantinople, acute problems remained.

The Logos-Son symbol served the Church's need in pointing to Jesus' exalted status and hence his unique revelatory significance. But at the same time its incorporation into talk about Jesus introduced a complication into the originally straightforward picture in the Synoptic Gospels of Jesus' personal relationship with God his Father. In fact it would seem to have made such a relationship logically inconceivable. What could be said of Jesus the Son in relation to the Father could not at all easily be said of the pre-existent, divine Logos-Son and the Father. The freedom of Jesus' response to God was the authentic expression of his humanity, without which he could have little to say to his fellow human beings.

The virtue of Arius' account was that at least his creaturely Logos had this freedom (hence his appeal, perhaps). But how could the freedom to turn from God, the corollary of the freedom to turn *to* God in love, be attributed to the co-eternal Logos-Son who was God himself by nature? To suggest such a thing would be to imply the possibility of self-contradiction in God, which is intolerable. At the same time, a genuine personal distinction within the eternal being of God would, as we have seen, either imply the existence of two Gods or require the subordination of one to the other. The divine, eternally coexistent Logos had to be distinct because it was Jesus the Son, and yet could not be distinct in real personal terms without destroying the oneness of God and hence the principle of monotheism. The Church was reduced to affirming the distinction in terms of subtly defined, metaphysical relationships, which excluded the possibility of real, mutual, personal relationship. Though it would continue to employ the language of personal relationship between Son and Father, particularly in the context of devotion, it had lost the logical basis for such language to be intelligible, or for such a relationship to be possible between the divine pre-existent Logos-Son and the Father.

That being the case, it was not very difficult at this point to include the Holy Spirit as the third party to the relationship. The real grounds for including the Spirit as a symbol of God's outreach were once again scriptural authority and the worshipping-practice of the Church, especially the Spirit's inclusion in the baptismal rite.[62] But the effect of doing so as an appendix to the debate about the Logos-Son was to incorporate the Spirit in very similar terms. The Logos had had to be differentiated from God and personalized because of its identification with Jesus and consequent designation as Son in relation to Father. There was no real need to individuate the Spirit in this sort of way, but the idea of distinction in unity postulated of the Logos-Son set a precedent for a similar distinction between the Spirit and God. Since the scriptural image of 'Son' was hardly appropriate in this case, some other differentiating term needed to be found, if possible one supported by the scriptures. So, while the Logos was described as *begotten*, the Spirit was described as *proceeding* (cf. John 15: 26); and the

---

[62] Wiles, *Doctrine*, 80 f.

distinction between begottenness and procession was left as
the only differentiation between the Logos-Son and the Spirit, and also between these and the Father in his
unbegottenness.

All three were described as persons, that is, individuated
realities. The word did not then have the connotation of
personality or self-conscious identity, which in this context
would imply three Gods. The meaning of such distinctions
was conceded to be an impenetrable mystery.[63] In all other
respects, the three persons were indissoluble and in-
distinguishable. The bare fact of their differentiation had to
be accepted on the authority of scripture and Church councils. The potentially destructive consequence of this intellectual impasse must be examined in due course, but first
we must consider the relationship of the Logos as God to
Jesus. This will bring us to the question of whether, here
also, the interpolation of the Logos–Son symbol threatens
the reality of Jesus' relationship with the Father, and
whether we shall have to conclude that the reality of this
relationship, and its centrality for faith, can only be recovered if the Logos–Son symbol is relinquished, or at least,
if it is seen as a symbol expressing faith in Jesus' ultimacy,
and no longer as designating a pre-existent divine being.

4. THE LOGOS AS GOD IN RELATION TO JESUS

The Church's refusal to let Jesus be less than God raised
the intractable question of the relationship of the Logos-Son
to the Father. Its refusal to let go of Jesus' genuine humanity
would raise an equally intractable question. How could the
pre-existent Logos-Son who was God be identified with a
man who was born and lived at a particular time?

We have already discussed the problems which arise when
the subject of a historical life is imagined to be a transcendent, spiritual, subjective reality (see above, chap. 6,

---

[63] 'The begetting of God must be honoured by silence. It is a great thing for
you to learn that he was begotten. But the manner of his generation we will not
admit that even angels can conceive, much less you' (Gregory of Nazianzus, *3rd
Theol. Oration*, 8; in E. R. Hardy, ed., *The Christology of the Later Fathers* (London
and Philadelphia, 1954), 165).

sect. 4). The identification of the Logos with Jesus raised this problem in an acute way.

Different lines of thought developed in the Church, which once again may be associated with the traditional outlooks of Alexandria and Antioch.

(a) The Antiochenes

We have already mentioned the difficulty that the Antiochene theologians had in differentiating the Logos of God in Old Testament usage from God himself. To the extent that they could not distinguish the Logos from God, they could not identify it wholly with the historical Jesus. Their advantage then was that they could take seriously the reality of Jesus' human subjectivity, his life under the conditions and humiliations of historical existence and his free and authentic human response to God. Had the more Jewish sense of 'Logos' as a symbol of God's purposive activity been preserved, the term might still have been available to them to express Jesus' revelatory uniqueness. By the time of Nicaea, however, the Antiochenes had allowed the symbol 'Son' to move from Jesus himself to the Logos,[64] so that the symbol of God's eternal purpose was transformed into a pre-existent, coeternal, personal being.[65] This Logos-Son was distinct from the Father by definition; yet, as sharing the Father's divinity, he could not be the subject of the very human experiences ascribed to Jesus in the New Testament, such as being tired, hungry, and ignorant, and facing temptation. These experiences could not be predicated of God; but if they were unreal for Jesus—the Antiochenes were convinced—his true humanity would be denied, and consequently his redemptive work would count for nothing. The Logos-Son, distinct from the Father yet immune to human limitation, intervened awkwardly between Jesus and the Father, and could not be wholly identified with either. As their opponents were eager to point out, it was not easy for

---

[64] T. E. Pollard, *Johannine Christology and the Early Church* (Cambridge, 1970), 119, on Eustathius of Antioch.

[65] Gregg and Groh, 2, 'Dr. Robert Sample has shown . . . that one of the major results of the Synod of Antioch of AD 268 was to render automatically suspect any theological system without a pre-existent cosmological Christ.'

the Antiochenes to do full justice to the identification of
Jesus and the Logos in the Fourth Gospel.

The question which arises from this is whether the Antiochenes, whatever their intentions, failed to establish the
ultimate and universal significance of Jesus as the revelation
of God. Could he be that, if he was not the Logos? Could he
be anything more than an exceptionally inspired man at best?
Or a kind of split personality with a dual subjectivity at
worst, as the Alexandrians suspected?

The Antiochenes in fact tried very hard to meet objections,
and to uphold Jesus' unique revelatory significance, by
maintaining that the Logos was present and active in Jesus'
life fully and continuously, whereas it was only present in
other lives partially or temporarily.[66] Hence Jesus'
uniqueness lay in the unique degree to which the Logos
related to him and he to the Logos, and the degree was such
that it amounted in effect to a qualitative distinction. It was
in virtue of the presence and activity of the Logos in him
from the very beginning of his life that Jesus could do God's
work and be the true, final, and definitive revelation of God,
without ceasing to be a truly human being.

If one were simply to substitute 'God' for 'Logos' here,
or understand 'Logos' as a symbol for God in his outreach
(which was more or less how the word was understood originally in the Antiochene tradition), the position summarized above would be very close to that put forward in
this book. It has been argued here that, as a consequence of
his uniquely close and personal relationship with God, Jesus
represented God faithfully, and in doing so confronted his
own and later generations as the form of God (see above,
pp. 202 ff. and chap. 6, sect. 5).

However, the symbol 'Logos', tied to the pre-existent Son,
was no longer available to express the unique revelatory
value of Jesus himself (in the way that 'Messiah' could originally). The Logos-Son had somehow to be a different subject from the subject of Jesus' historical human life. The
Alexandrians, though their motives were less than generous

---

[66] Grillmeier, 429–39 (on Theodore of Mopsuestia), 457–63 (on Nestorius); also
Young, *Nicaea*, 199–213, 229–40.

and they could do little better themselves, nevertheless correctly perceived the gap and concluded that in the Antiochene account there were either two subjects—two sons— in Jesus, or else he was a mere man.[67]

The accusation contained an element of truth, but was less than fair to Antiochene intentions and to another important aspect of their position. Unable to employ the Logos-symbol to identify Jesus as the revelation of God, the Antiochenes were left with the alternatives of denying this claim, which they did not wish to do, or of developing another term to serve this purpose. This they attempted to do with the Greek word *prosopon*. As argued above in the case of *homoousios*, it was a legitimate undertaking to resort to philosophical language to try to express the ultimate revelatory significance of Jesus, and not just to rely on traditional symbols. The later Antiochenes, in particular Theodore of Mopsuestia and Nestorius, came very close to success with *prosopon*,[68] and might perhaps have succeeded if their efforts had met with the serious theological attention they deserved instead of bitter personal vendettas and political manoeuvres, instigated primarily by Cyril of Alexandria.

The basic meaning of *prosopon* was 'face', and hence it had connotations of outward appearance, expression, and ultimately, of individual person as confronted. In other words, *prosopon* is virtually the equivalent of 'form' as we are using it. The import of Antiochene teaching was that to encounter the truly human historical person Jesus was to encounter the *prosopon* of God himself—the invisible God visibly expressed in that human form. This, as an expression of faith in the revelatory significance of Jesus, clearly comes very close to our claim that the genuinely human Jesus was and is the form of God. One difference is that for the Antiochenes Jesus was the form of God during his lifetime and not, as we have argued here, only in the totality of his life,

[67] Cyril, *Letter to Acacius*, 15, 'Nestorius . . . makes a pretence of affirming that the Word was incarnate and became man whilst being God, and failing to recognize the meaning of being incarnate he uses the words 'two natures' but sunders them from each other, isolating God and a separate man connected with God in a relation only of equal honour or sovereignty' (L. R. Wickham, *Cyril of Alexandria: Select Letters* (Oxford, 1983), p. 51; cf. p. 65, 'To Eulogius').

[68] Grillmeier, 431, 459–63.

seen after his death (see above, chap. 6, sect. 5). However, the great value of their account is that it came very close to establishing that God can be represented in a human body and personal life—in other words, can be embodied or 'incarnated'—without the sacrifice of human authenticity.

Unfortunately, the Antiochenes lacked the courage of their convictions. They tended in practice to divide up the activity and words of Jesus as recorded in the New Testament between the personal Logos-Son and the man, implying after all a kind of split personality and divorcing God from what was truly human. The form of God was, it seems, to be seen not so much in the totality as in the parts. This practice seemed to confirm their opponents' worst fears. Perhaps the Antiochenes had little option, committed as they were to a pre-existent personified Logos, as well as to the reality of Jesus' human life.

They were also under another constraint, that of a pre-critical approach to biblical exegesis. We can recognize now the problems this posed for them and for all their contemporaries. The difficulties of exegesis are still far from removed, but at least we can acknowledge now the human role in the creation of the New Testament. We can recognize that the combination and interweaving of historical record and theological interpretation in the pages of scripture does not necessarily represent the combination of a natural and a supernatural subject, as it were in harness in the one person of Jesus. This bears particularly on the interpretation of the Fourth Gospel, which was central to the debate.[69] Anyone compelled by his assumptions to take literally every word and experience attributed to Jesus in all the Gospels can hardly avoid either separating out what is human from what is divine in him, or treating the human as more or less a pretence. That the Alexandrians leaned in the latter direction is not therefore something blameworthy, but neither are they to be considered exempt from criticism. Their grounds for criticizing the Antiochenes' failure to identify Jesus with the Logos may seem less valid now than in the past.

[69] See above, p. 192 n. 21.

(b) The Alexandrians

In considering the Alexandrians' position, we find that their strength was the converse of the Antiochenes' weakness. There is, perhaps, even greater risk in generalizing about the former than the latter, but a number of shared convictions can be discerned in those who stood in the tradition of Athanasius. They agreed in condemning Arianism and in affirming that the Logos-Son was equal with God the Father and was born as Jesus. Hence Jesus had the full, unequivocal value of God, as the saving and revelatory figure of universal and ultimate significance. But he was that because the divine Logos-Son was deemed to be the subject of his life. Hence, in contrast to the Antiochenes, the Alexandrians found it virtually impossible to take seriously, or at least to affirm intelligibly, the reality of Jesus' human existence.[70] At worst, a supernatural being simply took to himself human flesh, not human existence, and his so-called human life was no more than a charade. His purpose would either be to use his fleshly disguise to fool and defeat the enemies of God, natural or supernatural, in order to save humankind (though it was very hard indeed to find convincing reasons why it should be done that way); or else through his divine power to divinize the flesh and/or the mind and so secure our salvation (but salvation in this account is at worst magical and subhuman, and at best divorced from the social and physical structures of earthly existence).

Two factors in this tradition stood in the way of complete denial of the reality of Jesus' human existence. One was the New Testament itself; the other was the slogan 'That which he has not assumed he has not healed'. The former witnessed to Jesus as a man, a particular person. The latter, in contrast, served rather to affirm his humanity. The distinction is subtle but significant. The slogan, as formulated by Gregory of Nazianzus,[71] one of the Cappadocian fathers, was effective

[70] Young, *Nicaea*, 261, 'Basically, however, Cyril regarded the whole matter as beyond human explanation and yet still true; paradox is the best way of stating such truths.' See pp. 213–29, 240–65, for a fuller account of Cyril; also Grillmeier, 414–17, 473–83.

[71] Gregory of Nazianzus, 'Letter to Cledonius against Apollinaris' (Epistle 101), in Hardy, *Christology* (n. 63 above). See Kelly, 297.

in combating the extreme views of Apollinaris,[72] who frankly denied that Jesus had a human soul or, at least, a human mind; its place was taken by the Logos. But Gregory's rejoinder affirmed it more as a matter of definition than as a dynamic reality. In this Christian Platonic tradition, the emphasis lay more on the Logos taking human nature or humanity to himself,[73] rather than becoming a man. A soul was a necessary constituent of human nature, and so part of the definition of humanity. Therefore the humanity which the Logos took must have included a soul. Where 'soul' is merely part of a definition, its role is passive. This leaves the Logos free to be the active subject of Jesus' life.

This neat solution could not, however, satisfy Apollinaris or the Antiochenes. Despite their opposition to each other, they agreed that a passive soul is no real soul at all. In this account, the Logos did the work and the human soul, like the Holy Spirit, could have nothing in particular to do apart from just being there. Least of all could it be conceived of as a genuine subject capable of a free and mutual personal relationship with the Logos-Son or God the Father. To imagine that, or to ascribe any special functions to 'it', apart from those ascribed to the Logos in Jesus, would at once conjure up an image of a split personality in him, or at least a strange sort of double life. This is exactly what the Alexandrians objected to in the Antiochenes; yet in the end even Cyril began to admit a specific role for Jesus' human soul.[74] The difficulty of avoiding such an implication, where there was still concern to affirm Jesus' humanity, is a symptom of the tension generated by the conflict between the logic of the Logos-symbol and the New Testament picture of Jesus as a real man.

In the last resort, the idea of a duality of subjective identities in Jesus was as intolerable as a duality of subjective identities in God. Yet without this, though Jesus' humanity might be affirmed in theory, no real or active role could be conceded to it for fear of displacing his 'Godness' as Logos

[72] See Kelly, 289–95; Young, *Nicaea*, 182–91.

[73] Hare, 46, 'Whereas for us a definition is one kind of analytically or necessarily true proposition, for [Plato] it was a description of a mentally visible and eternally true object.'

[74] '2nd letter to Successus' (Wickham, 84–93). Cf. Grillmeier, 474 ff.

or of splitting his personality. In practice, in the later history of the Church the reality of Jesus' human existence has constantly tended to give way to the idea that the subject of his historical life was a supernatural pre-existent being, the Logos-Son, distinct from God the Father but sharing with him such attributes of divinity as omnipotence and omniscience, far removed from the limitations of human life as we experience it. His mother could seem more real and approachable as a fellow human being.

(c) Chalcedon

The debate about Jesus' person came to a head in AD 451 at the Council of Chalcedon (across the Bosporus, opposite Constantinople). The reality of his humanity and of his divinity was affirmed in the definition issued at the Council, but without explanation as to how humanity and divinity were integrated in the life and person of Jesus. Further disputes arose subsequently as to whether one or two wills were present and operative in Jesus. This only serves to underline the inherent problem posed by attributing to Jesus a transcendent subjectivity distinct from a genuine human subjectivity.

We have already seen how the Logos identified with Jesus was held to be distinct from God, and yet incapable of a fully personal relationship with God of the kind which the Synoptic Gospels particularly depict between Jesus and the Father. Still less could there be a reciprocal personal relationship between the human nature and the divine nature in the person of the historical Jesus as defined after Chalcedon.

Thus we see how in the course of the Church's debate about Jesus the question of the relationship between Jesus and his heavenly Father became two questions concerning the relationship between the Logos-Son and God, and the Logos-Son and Jesus. Neither relationship could be truly free and personal. The Logos-Son identified with Jesus and equal with God could indeed serve to uphold Jesus' revelatory significance, and through him God's free, personal, and loving outreach to all humankind and the whole of creation. But this primary objective of faith could, it seems, only be purchased at the price of Jesus' genuine, evolutionary, historical reality, and his freedom to respond as an authentic human being to God. Without that, the case for Jesus' revelatory significance today falls to pieces.

The word 'Logos', better than 'Spirit' or 'Wisdom', could serve a purpose in the Greek world analogous to the idea of 'Messiah' in the Jewish world in identifying Jesus as the definitive revelation of God. The symbol 'Logos' with its different connotations, in conjunction with 'Son' and enriched by 'Wisdom', created a picture of Jesus as God's agent and representative in the sphere of creation, yet not as a subordinate being but equal with God himself. It may be suggested that the underlying conviction represented here is identical with that expressed in the phrases 'Jesus is the form of God' or 'God is in the form of Jesus'. However, the personification of the Logos-symbol generated acute problems, both conceptual and practical. Further problems may be seen to arise from the fact that, though 'Logos' could take the place of 'Messiah', their connotations were by no means identical. 'Logos' could symbolize not only Jesus as the form of God, but Jesus in his spiritual role as the life-giving source of divine power in human experience. The use of 'Logos' with this wider meaning instead of 'Messiah' meant that the equilibrium of 'Messiah' and 'Spirit' as symbols of the form and vitality of God in Jesus was upset. The combination of both poles in 'Logos' left 'Spirit' in an equivocal position. At the same time, though the designation 'only begotten Son' had marked Jesus out as unique, the transference of Son to Logos weakened the uniqueness of Jesus inasmuch as the Logos-Son could 'speak' in others. Another consequence of identifying Jesus as Logos rather than Messiah was equally serious, if not more so.

The term 'Messiah' had a meaning, but had not hitherto had personal application, and so could without too much difficulty be assimilated to Jesus and redefined in terms of what he actually was. That the difficulty was not entirely negligible may be gathered from the episode recorded in Mark 8: 27–33. Peter's acknowledgement of Jesus as Messiah, as God's special agent, was accepted by Jesus, it seems; but Peter's subsequent insistence that Jesus as Messiah must not suffer was sharply rebuked—'Get thee behind me, Satan!' Perhaps we have here the first clear example of a symbol of transcendence being used to good effect to convey the significance of Jesus, and yet of the preconceptions associated with it imposing improper constraints on the understanding of Jesus and his vocation.[75] Jesus could rightly be called 'Messiah' if that signified that he was God's representative and was doing God's work; but to imagine that in doing God's work he must not risk suffering and death, because no one thought the Messiah would suffer, was to think as men think, and not to understand the logic of divine love.

In comparison, Logos could be assimilated with the risen Lord—Jesus in the Spirit—relatively easily, but the assimilation of Logos, conceived of as a pre-existent being, with the historical Jesus was almost impossible. The resulting paradox was that the risen Jesus-Logos could scarcely be identified with the Jesus who lived a human life and died. 'Logos' served a positive purpose in a way analogous to 'Messiah' in signifying the closeness of Jesus' relationship to God and his role as the expression of God's creative purpose. But latter-day Peters would take Jesus-Logos aside and rebuke him, saying he could not even be a human being, let alone suffer and die, and Jesus was not there to rebuke them.

The New Testament was there, however, as an obstinate witness to Jesus' genuine human life and death. It still is. Those who imagine that the role of expressing God's creative purpose could not be fulfilled in a truly human life are still rebuked for thinking as men think, and not allowing their thoughts to be reshaped radically enough by what Jesus was and did. They fail to take the Incarnation seriously enough, even when their intention is to uphold the conviction that God was in Jesus.

To conclude. The temptation to conform Jesus to presuppositions concerning Logos was very strong. The symbol 'Son', through its assimilation to 'Wisdom', had all but slipped its historical moorings, and so could do little to keep

[75] Cf. Pannenberg's distinction between Christology 'from below' and 'from above': *Jesus: God and Man*, 33–7.

Logos subject to historical reality. As a result, the continuity between the human Jesus and the risen Lord represented by the resurrection stories was all but broken. The identification of Jesus' selfhood with the selfhood of a pre-existent spiritual being (Logos-Son) tended to divorce Jesus worshipped as Logos-Son from the concrete figure of flesh and blood portrayed in the Gospels. His experience of human life, his freedom as a responsible human being to wrestle with and take difficult decisions, even his suffering and death, have been rendered so unreal by generations of Christian piety that the impact of his originality, integrity, courage, and inspiring dedication to God has all too often been virtually lost to sight. Alternatively, where these things were counted real, it was as though the suffering he was ready to bear was real for the man but not for God, as though it was not precisely there, in the form of Jesus who was and is the form of God, that the quality of God's love was disclosed. If these criticisms have any validity, then we cannot rest content with the attempts of the early Fathers to express the ultimacy of Jesus. The utter seriousness of their commitment is witnessed to by their constant willingness to undergo suffering, exile, or martyrdom, rather than deny their convictions.[76] But this does not of itself guarantee the adequacy of their words and language to convey what needed to be conveyed.

Commitment to the ultimacy of Jesus today requires, therefore, that we try as hard as they did to communicate what we believe to be true about him as best we can in our world and in terms of our way of thinking. We must also recognize that we have less excuse than our Christian forebears for refusing to re-examine or to let go of symbols or images that are not adequate to their purpose, which is to witness to the ultimacy of the man Jesus. If need be, even the most hallowed symbols, such as 'Logos-Son', must be relinquished, or at least submitted to stringent re-examination. But whatever symbols we may resort to in

[76] In the words of one of the most famous 'heretics'—Nestorius, who suffered worse than most—'Now my death approaches and every day I pray to God to dismiss me—me whose eyes have seen the salvation of God. Rejoice with me, Desert, thou my friend, my nurse, my home; and thou exile, my mother, who after my death will keep my body until the resurrection by the grace of God' (quoted in Young, *Nicaea*, 240).

order to express Jesus' ultimacy, however positive their value, we must allow them to be rebuked by what Jesus was, if they are to serve his purposes.

5. CHALCEDON REAPPRAISED

It would be impossible in the space available here to pursue our historical inquiry further, but neither is it really necessary, for two reasons. In the first place, we have argued that the fundamental compulsion of the first disciples and their successors in the early Church was to proclaim the ultimacy of Jesus. If that view is valid, then we may hope that our examination of their attempts to articulate and communicate their convictions will have served to identify some of the principles and problems which will attend any attempt to express Jesus' ultimacy, and are not only relevant to the early period of the Church's history. In the second place, though the Church's struggle to articulate its convictions did not end when the patristic period drew to a close (and never can end), nevertheless the Council of Chalcedon was a major watershed. The definition of faith promulgated there drew together in terms of the prevailing symbol-system the essential elements of commitment to Jesus. It affirmed his historical reality (humanity) and his ultimacy (divinity), but denied division in God or in Jesus himself.

As we have seen, the terms in which these convictions were expressed generated acute intellectual problems, but nevertheless they were to serve as the main basis for the articulation of Christian conviction in the future, especially in the West. This fact means that a reassessment of the position reached at Chalcedon, and the way it was arrived at, creates a new point of departure for theological reflection. Our task now, therefore, is to complete our reassessment and to draw out its implications, both theological and practical. We will consider some of the practical implications in Part V. This chapter will conclude with an attempt to answer the immediate question, 'What should those who respond to Jesus today say about him, about God, and about the Holy Spirit?'

It is our contention that the patristic Church upheld the

fundamental commitment to Jesus which it inherited from his first followers, but that it failed to resolve the contradictions into which it was drawn by the symbols it employed within the prevailing conceptual framework. But even its failure witnesses to its primary commitment. It preferred the embarrassment of unresolved contradiction to the respectability of a coherent but one-sided representation of its convictions. One might perhaps say that at Chalcedon the Church preserved the vital parts, but the best it could do was to put them in a tidy pile, like the pieces of a jigsaw puzzle sorted out and neatly stacked, but not put together.

Such reservations about the achievement of Chalcedon will not be shared by all; the mystery with which we are concerned is such that it would certainly be extremely presumptuous to suppose that the puzzle can be completed here. But it may still be legitimate to look at the pieces again to see if some at least could be rearranged and fitted together in a way that will allow something more of the picture to emerge—a picture of which we ourselves and our evolutionary world are an integral part. With that assumption I shall now attempt to offer a brief outline of how the pieces might be handled on the basis of the approach which has governed this inquiry.

In the previous chapters it was argued that the 'Logos-Son' symbol played an invaluable role in pointing to the ultimate significance of Jesus; but at the same time we saw how the identification of Jesus with the Logos-Son, as if with a pre-existent spiritual being, generated a great many of the difficulties which confronted the Church in its earliest days and have done ever since. The problem of relating the Logos-Son to the Father, to the Holy Spirit, and to the human Jesus was and remains intractable.

The term 'Logos' itself admittedly fell out of use for a number of reasons, and was replaced by almost exclusive use of the symbol 'Son'. It is sometimes argued that the problems associated with the Logos-concept were removed when the term was relinquished. To some extent this may be conceded, inasmuch as the connotations of 'Son' can be derived more directly from the New Testament portrayal of Jesus, and are less tied to outside usage than was the case with

'Logos'. Nevertheless, we may say that by the time 'Son' displaced 'Logos' the damage had been done. 'Son' had by then acquired the connotations of a pre-existent spiritual subject. It was this spiritual being, the second person of the Trinity, descending 'from above', which was conceived of as taking flesh and so becoming incarnate in Jesus. So far from this being the truth by which membership of the Church should be defined, I would hold that this account not only creates an intellectual impasse, but obstructs the response of others to the ultimacy of Jesus and obscures its implications.

The way through this impasse lies in abandoning the identification of Jesus with the Logos, or with Wisdom, or with Son, *as if* with a pre-existent spiritual being, distinct from God. The symbols 'Logos', 'Wisdom', and 'Son' can then all be subordinated to the person of Jesus—as was the case with 'Messiah'—instead of their subordinating him to their connotations and logic. Logos may then be interpreted not as a personal being in itself, but as 'the principle of divine self- manifestation'[77] or, as I suggest, 'the form of God'. The word can then function in a positive sense, analogous to that of 'Messiah', pointing to the unique revelatory significance of Jesus, without implying a duality of selfhood in him any more than would be implied by calling him 'Messiah'. Thus, as Messiah, Jesus is the one who performs God's work. As Logos (or Wisdom), he is the one who brings God to light (John 1: 9) and renders the eternal truth of God visible, apprehensible, and communicable.

This interpretation allows us to recover the original significance and force of the symbol 'Son', which pointed to that relationship between Jesus and God which made it possible for him to reveal God and so to be for us the form of God. At last we can escape the problems posed by the merely quasi-filial relationship between God and the Logos, which could not be differentiated in a fully personal way without the risk of polytheism. We can abandon also the almost mechanical, impersonal relationship between the divine nature (Logos) and the human nature (flesh and perhaps soul) of Jesus, which could not be a personal relationship for fear

[77] Tillich, *Systematic Theology*, ii. 95.

of splitting Jesus in half. The impersonality of the latter view led only too easily to an impersonal view of the relationship between God and human beings. It lent itself to the idea of divine substance divinizing human substance,[78] in contrast to a personal understanding of the creative interactions of love between God and human selves. It was to these creative interactions that the New Testament bore witness; they have persisted among Jesus' followers despite doctrinal formulations rather than because of them. The recovery of the idea of sonship in the fully personal relationship of Jesus to the Father may disclose possibilities for Jesus' fellow human beings which have been rendered all too remote by metaphysical abstractions and mythological intrusions. At the same time, the designation of Jesus as the form of God would uphold his unique relationship to God and his distinction from all other human beings, without sacrificing his humanity.

Thus, by interpreting Logos in this way and not as a pre-existent being, we are free from the logical constraints which made it so hard for the Alexandrians to acknowledge a real human being to be the form of God. We are free to recover Jesus as a man whose life was woven into the fabric of creation, evolution, human history, and society, as much as any other human being's. Paradoxically, the recognition of this man as the form of God may be reckoned to impart a profounder significance to the ancient symbol of Incarnation than does the traditional view. The very word, 'enfleshment', gives itself away, isolating the physical from the social and historical, contrary to what we now recognize as constituting a human person. Despite professions to the contrary, the traditional view cannot represent Jesus coherently as of ultimate revelatory significance and yet at the same time fully implicated in all the many strands of human existence.[79]

The next question is whether the interpretation presented here, whatever its worth, parts company with the conclusions reached at Chalcedon to such a degree that no real connection or continuity can be claimed. Or does this resorting of the pieces in fact allow something more of the

[78] Ibid. 144, 'Popular piety did not want a paradox but a "miracle." By this kind of piety the way for every possible superstition was opened.'
[79] See above, p. 186 n. 15.

original picture to emerge? I would wish to defend the latter alternative. In order to do so, we must develop further a distinction which has already been implicit in what has been said, but which needs to be made explicit—the distinction between confessional and descriptive language, and the way each functions.

The traditional designations of Jesus—'Messiah', 'Lord', 'Logos', 'Wisdom', and 'Son of God'—as interpreted here, all emerge not as descriptive but as confessional symbols, that is, as expressions of faith in the unique revelatory significance of Jesus as the form of God. He was believed to have been in a right relationship with God and thus to have become for all human beings the norm of a right relationship with God, superseding all other supposed norms. It is the logic of this confession that must be explored.

If it is the truth of God that has appeared in Jesus, then it is a truth relevant to all things in every time and place, and no less valid for not being recognized as such in every time and place. This claim does not imply that the truth of God in Jesus can be fully and perfectly expressed in verbal form. This would contradict both the polar character of revelation, as outlined in Part I, and the account given in Part III of Jesus' revelatory significance. It is a judgement of faith that the truth of God was in Jesus, but this judgement is not and was not arrived at arbitrarily in a historical vacuum. Where it is made, it means that in principle Jesus is deemed to be (and so confessed to be) the criterion of truth, and that in practice the story of Jesus serves as the normative interpretative resource for the understanding of God, however tentative and contingent the conclusions drawn from the available evidence. On the basis of these observations we may now reconsider some of the central problems of Christology, in particular the sinlessness and eternal changelessness of Jesus.

No historical evidence can ever serve to prove (or disprove) that Jesus was sinless. We can, however, make sense of this traditional belief about Jesus on the basis of the distinction between descriptive and confessional language. Faith confesses Jesus to be the criterion of truth. He cannot be my criterion and not my criterion of truth simultaneously (even though I could be wrong). From the perspective of faith, then, it would be self-contradictory to confess that Jesus was and is the truth, the norm of right relationship with God, and *at the same time* to concede that he may have been wrong about God, or in a fundamentally wrong relationship, that is, a sinner. Hence, in confessional language, Jesus must be sinless; in this language his sinlessness is logically necessary. It is a way of saying that he is the criterion of truth.

The eternal changelessness of Jesus can similarly be seen to have a place in the language of confession. It would be incompatible with the conviction that Jesus was the truth of God to suppose that the truth which Jesus bodied out only became true during his ministry, as if the truth of God only came into being then. This would be absurd. The truth of God is conterminous with God, but was bodied out in time in the person of Jesus, not as a third person, but as eternal truth made visible.

Thus, the terms 'sinless', 'changeless', 'eternal', belong to Jesus confessed as the form of God, as the *locus* of revelation. But such terms cannot, without confusion, be transposed from the confession of Jesus as the form of God to descriptions of Jesus as the man he was. Some description is necessary, or else the confession would be devoid of content, but what can be said of a genuine human being, and of Jesus in particular, is not to be confused with the language and logic of commitment to Jesus as the form of God.

This claim, that Jesus is the form of God, can of course be challenged by anyone at any time, and even those who respond to him as such may well entertain doubts. But our concern thus far is with the logic or function of confessional language, not with the psychology of the confessor, or even at this point with the problems of the historian. When, however, we turn to consider Jesus as the man he was, our fellow human being, we can readily acknowledge in him the same conditions of human existence as are found in all of us, the experience of changing, growing, learning, loving, meeting temptation, and exercising human responsibility.

To describe Jesus as sinless in this context is simply to report the conviction of his followers that he remained faithful to his vocation in the face of real temptation (Heb. 4:

15) and that his vocation was indeed God's calling. This triumphant sinlessness of Jesus is the foundation of the confession; it is not nullified by the necessary sinlessness which belongs to confession. Very serious problems arise when the logical necessities of confessional language are transposed into descriptive language. Tension between confession and psychological description was the problem for the early Church. Tension between confession and historical description has been added to this in the last century and a half.

When ideas which have their roots in unconditional commitment are treated on the plane of empirical observation, they result in a demand for certainty in historical terms where historical judgement cannot reach beyond probabilities at best. Thus, the confusion of languages undermines the integrity of historical inquiry. The product of the confusion of languages in the case of Jesus is the contradiction of a non-historical being living historically. One-sided resolutions result in an account of Jesus as just one man among others, or in a portrayal of him as incapable of growing in wisdom and understanding (Luke 2: 52), immune to temptation and unable to sin. If that were so, he was not free and was therefore subhuman.

Having, then, the distinction between confession and description in mind, we may recognize that the early Fathers were necessarily concerned with both, but with different emphases, depending in part on their different understanding of human nature, of what Jesus had done, and how he had effected salvation. In very general terms it might be said that the Alexandrians tended to subordinate everything to the logic of confession. Given their Platonic presuppositions, the tensions of which we have spoken would not have seemed as acute to them as to us. Salvation was won by the Logos-Son taking humanity to himself. The Antiochenes, on the other hand, with their different presuppositions, were more concerned to preserve the content of the New Testament description of Jesus as a human being, as well as to confess him as the truth of God. Salvation was won by Jesus' genuine obedience to the Father. When at Alexandria the necessary sinlessness of Jesus as the form of

God (Logos) was applied to Jesus as a man, he ceased to be truly human (as far as their account went, if not their intentions). But at Antioch, as we have seen, the real human Jesus could not quite be presented as the form of God (even if that was intended).

Thus, as we have argued, Chalcedon in affirming both traditions preserved the essentials of confessional language and the description of Jesus as a historical human being, but failed to resolve the apparent contradictions. By removing from the symbol 'Logos' the connotation of a pre-existent personal being, and by interpreting it as synonymous with the form of God, we can see the possibility of resolving the contradictions of Chalcedon and reconciling the concerns of Alexandria and Antioch. We may reinterpret the Alexandrians' identification of the second person of the Trinity with the subject of Jesus' life, seeing it as an expression of faith in the ultimacy of Jesus in the most unequivocal terms open to them. The phrase 'Jesus is Logos-Son' can then be seen to be confessional rather than descriptive, echoing the New Testament confessions 'Jesus is Lord' and 'Jesus is Messiah', but introducing even higher connotations of ultimacy. Jesus, the man who lived a real human life in history, would be that, as against something else momentarily appearing in a historical figure. Arius' emphasis on the reality of Jesus' moral freedom and the Antiochenes' insistence on his genuine humanity would be vindicated, and would be no more incompatible with the confession of his ultimacy than recognizing Jesus as the carpenter from Galilee was incompatible with acknowledging him to be Messiah and Lord. But the supposed failure to distinguish Jesus unequivocally in terms of his unique revelatory significance from all other human beings would be overcome.

It is not being suggested here that the interpretation given above is all that the early Fathers really intended and meant. That would be almost certainly untrue, and very different interpretations of them can be given today. However, whatever their intentions, our case is that the distinctions we have drawn can be discerned in the formularies of the early Church, and that the question of the *ultimacy* of the *man* Jesus can be seen as the fundamental issue over which the

Church was wrestling, both in its internal controversies and in relation to other religions and worldly powers. If these convictions are the pieces, then it can at least be argued that the picture we are trying to construct is essentially the same as that which preoccupied the early Fathers, even if it is being assembled in a somewhat different way. It remains for us to consider some of the practical implications of confessing God to be revealed in the form of Jesus and in the vitality of the Spirit.

V

IMPLICATIONS

INTRODUCTION

I HAVE attempted in the preceding pages to reinterpret the significance of Jesus, and the response of his followers to him, in the light of contemporary studies and a modern view of the world. If this interpretation has any validity, then precisely because it concerns the claim that Jesus is of ultimate and universal significance, it will have implications extending in every direction, both theoretical and practical. It would be impossible to explore all these, but I shall try to examine some of them under three main headings: first, in relation to those people who claim ultimacy for Jesus (i.e. Christians); secondly, in relation to those who claim ultimacy for someone or something else in religious terms; thirdly, in relation to those who claim it or pursue it in non-religious terms. It might be thought that the implications for those who deny ultimacy to anything should also be examined. But they have already been considered in chap. 1, sect. 4, and will not be pursued further, except with the remark that implicit in the denial of ultimacy there may be at least an admission of its theoretical possibility.

Perhaps some who deny ultimacy are in fact reacting against the frequently destructive consequences of pursuing it. But commitment to Jesus does not, or rather need not and should not, have such consequences. On the contrary, it is truly creative in effect, even if the abandoning of false ultimates and misconceived solutions to the questions of life can have painful repercussions. However, criticism should begin at home, and it has to be admitted that Christianity has all too often in practice displayed a demonic and destructive character. It is important to consider why this is so, and the aim in the first two sections of chapter 8 will be to identify, in terms of the present approach, some of the causes of Christian disorder. Some critical comments may sound extreme, but this corresponds to our treatment of the Torah in chap. 3, sect. 3. There, some theoretical implications of the 'extreme case' were explored, before the actual historical communities committed to the Torah were examined and were shown to cover a wide spectrum and to be very diverse in character. The second stage of examining particular Christian Churches will not be embarked upon here, except to illustrate a few key issues. It will be left to the reader to judge how far the critique of the theoretical 'extreme case' applies to any particular Christian bodies.

As remarked, the claims made for Jesus cannot help but have implications for those who do not make them as well as for those who do. This is not the place for a detailed evaluation of other religions, and it is certainly not the place to question the sincerity of their adherents. But if the universe is one, and humankind is one, and the ground and goal of existence are one, then those who presume to address themselves to the question of ultimacy cannot pretend that what they say will not have critical implications for the positions others hold. It is proper, therefore, at least to offer an outline of the positive and negative implications for other religions of what has been argued here. The same applies to those who have abandoned the explicit use of theistic or religious language or imagery, but who nevertheless implicitly or explicitly raise and attempt to answer questions of ultimacy.

However, the Church can only hope to remove the splinters in the eyes of others when it has removed the beams in its own eye (Matt. 7: 3). So it is with failures within Christianity that we begin. The main concern is with conditions today, but to understand certain specific problems better it will be necessary to trace a little further some particular strands of historical development, as well as looking at the issue in the context of the overall interpretation offered here. We may then begin to understand better why Christianity, so often with the best intentions, has defeated its own (God-given) purposes.

8. The Abolition of Idols

(a) Some causes of biblical fundamentalism

THAT there should be a visible witness to the revelation of God in the form of Jesus is one thing. That any such witness should be itself regarded as the direct revelation of God is very much another. It would obviously be a mistake to suppose that the factors we are about to consider determined the whole course of development in Christian thinking about the Bible, or that they operated everywhere uniformly.[1] Innumerable forces and influences would have interacted here as in any historical situation. But it may still be possible to see how certain factors that were central and specific to the original Christian experience could lead to a basically un-Christian view of the Bible as the direct revelation of God.

In the first place, the close assimilation of Jesus to the Holy Spirit, and his identification with Logos and Wisdom, could, as we have seen, undermine the revelatory significance of his earthly life. He could be regarded as a continuing source of revelation, inspiring the prophets in early Israel and the early Church, and the writers of the Old and New Testaments. Such ideas contributed to the emergence of a doctrine of biblical inspiration. However, the limits of inspiration, and hence the boundaries of revelatory authority, were not easy to define, as early controversies quickly proved.

The need to define these boundaries more carefully provided the main impetus for the creation of the canon of scripture. This leads to the second factor in the emergence of a distorted view of biblical revelation which will need more detailed consideration. We shall see how the language

---

[1] For a detailed critique, see J. Barr, *Fundamentalism* (London 1977). I agree strongly with his view that evangelical faith is not necessarily tied to fundamentalism; rather, 'Evangelical faith is betrayed by the fundamentalist apparatus of argument' (p. 339).

of commitment itself seemed to offer a way to secure the
authority of scripture against the threat of revelational anarchy; but, as so often in the Church's history, the attempt
to solve one problem created others. Once again we encounter the ambiguity of symbols with their positive and
negative potential.

The confession of Jesus as the Wisdom and Word of God
served, in the first instance, to exalt him above the Torah
and at the expense of the Torah (see above, chap. 6, sect. 1).
It was this that created Christianity out of Judaism. In the
same moment, the confession of Jesus raised the question of
the Torah's standing in relation to God, and also the question of what degree of continuity or discontinuity lay between it and Jesus. The problem is already to the fore in
the letters of Paul. His solution, reached after an anguished
struggle (see Galatians and Romans), was to affirm the Torah
as a gift of God and witness to God and as serving his
purpose (Gal. 3: 24). But Paul would not allow it in any
way to put the ultimacy of Jesus in question. This balanced
conclusion was capable of distortion in two directions: either
the discontinuity or the continuity could be overstated at
the expense of the other. The Gnostics stressed the radical
discontinuity. Their belief that Jesus was the revealer of
the ultimately true God was matched by their denial that
Yahweh, the God of the Old Testament, was really God at
all, though he may have foolishly supposed he was the supreme God. Marcion[2] somewhat differently posited two
Gods, with the God of Love revealed in Jesus purchasing
believers from the God of the Old Testament, who had
created the world and human beings and imposed the Law.

We can recognize an element of truth in these positions.
If it is accepted that God is truly portrayed in Jesus, then
other portrayals of God, in the Old Testament or elsewhere,
are indeed put in second place and in that sense superseded.
This can, however, be said without denying the continuing
value of the Old Testament as a witness to the one God
continuously at work in the world and in Jesus.

---

[2] A second-century heretic and schismatic who based his teaching mainly on
Paul. See E. C. Blackman, *Marcion and his Influence* (London, 1948).

The early Christians failed to draw this distinction between the *portrayal* of God in the Old Testament and God
in himself. Developments since Ben Sira, which had turned
the Old Testament into a book of revelation, would have
made it very hard for anyone standing in that tradition to
make such a distinction. This view of scripture was, it seems,
particularly strong in Alexandria, which was not only the
city of Philo, but the place where early Gnosticism appears
to have flourished.

It seems that all were agreed that the Old Testament was
indeed a book of revelation. The important issue was
whether the God revealed in it was the true God or a false
God. The implications of supposing the latter were serious.
They did not lead merely to the dismissal of a supposedly
false God, but to the rejection of his sphere of influence and
area of operation. In other words, if the God revealed in the
Old Testament had indeed created the world as it is and
given the Law to Moses, but was not after all the supreme
God, then dismissing him meant dismissing his world and
his Law.

Such a price was too high for many in the Judaeo-
Christian tradition to pay. Apart from problems of dualism,
the supposition that the ultimately true God had nothing to
do with creation, history, and the truly human physical life of
Jesus contradicted too much that was central to the tradition.
However, if the Old Testament was not to be rejected as
false, it must be received as true revelation of the true God.
Supporting evidence seemed to be immediately to hand. The
reader finds within it reference to the Word and Wisdom of
God. This is hardly surprising, as the book was the original
source of these symbols of transcendence for Jesus. There is
now a reverse flow. With the identification of Word and
Wisdom with Jesus soon well established, the Christian
reader would see in the biblical references to Word and
Wisdom (and also Lord) evidence of the revelatory activity
of Jesus himself. Thus the claim of the Old Testament to be
a book of revelation would be legitimated. It would seem
that Jesus was as much at work revealing God in the Old
Testament as he was in his earthly life. The wheel has turned
full circle and the revelatory claim for the Torah made by

Ben Sira is virtually re-established, except that the eternal Wisdom of God revealed in it has acquired the name 'Jesus'. This made a difference and influenced interpretation, but scarcely limited the revelatory authority now reclaimed for the Old Testament. The symbols originally derived from the Old Testament to confess Jesus' revelatory supremacy over it now in effect return to the Old Testament and elevate it alongside Jesus.

Not only is Jesus' revelational pre-eminence weakened by this development, but the Christian understanding of revelation is seriously affected. The old idea of revelation in the form of a book returns and all but swamps the revolutionary new idea of the supremely transcendent God revealed in the form of a real person. The Logos, revealing God in the book—first the Old Testament, and then by natural extension the New Testament—is all but detached from the historical life of Jesus and renders it more or less logically unnecessary.

It can be accepted that the Church was right to claim the Jewish Torah as scripture. Yet in receiving it as a book of revelation in terms that closely matched the Jewish understanding of it, the early Christians risked losing sight of the radically new character of God's revelation in Jesus, and bequeathed to later generations a distorted understanding of the revelatory significance both of scripture and of Jesus. We see, then, how the experience of Jesus in the spirit, and the confession of him as Wisdom and Logos, could lead all too easily to the view that scripture after all was the *locus* of God's self-revelation. Where that view arose, both the Old and New Testaments could be embraced with enormous relief as the permanently available and visible direct revelation of God, in short, as the form of God, when Jesus was no longer visibly to hand. A revived doctrine of 'enbibliation' offers a security which the doctrine of God in Jesus—incarnation—cannot match.

(b) Some consequences of biblical fundamentalism

It makes little difference to the overall argument what factors contributed to the view that the Bible itself is the direct self-revelation of God. Whether Jesus in the spirit, the Holy

Spirit, the pre-existent Logos, or God himself, is looked on as the source of biblical revelation, in each case the relationship of such a supernatural agent to the earthly Jesus would seem arbitrary and incidental. What such a divine agent could take up, it cóuld put down again. In its spiritual nature it would seem free in principle to reveal itself wherever it liked, in whatever form it liked, at whatever time it liked. The comment still to be heard in some quarters, that Jesus could have chosen to appear at another time or place, betrays this point of view. So does the claim that the God or Spirit at work in Jesus has since been or is still at work with equal (or greater) authority in someone else.

In contrast, a unique historical configuration shaped the context of Jesus' life and created its extraordinary revelatory potential. That historical moment not only made his life possible, but made a meaningful human response to its revelatory significance possible. The story of Jesus is given in history and yet is a story with unique revelatory power. Its unique quality is not slapped upon it by some arbitrary divine decree, which could equally well have been pronounced in favour of anyone else. It stems rather from the unique content of the story itself, its very historicity, the unrepeatable interactions of individuals, groups, nations, events, and meanings at that place at that time. As such, it stands out of history as a unique challenge to human self-understanding. Yet the story remains integrally woven into the wider story which encompasses the whole of humankind's evolutionary and historical development, and is the story of a real person able to address persons in a truly personal way. Thus, it can be received as revelation without violence to human freedom and responsibility. A revelation which could be thought of as dropping at random into history at any time or place or in any form would be arbitrary and subhuman in its character and implications. Such a revelation would imply a revealer totally unlike the God revealed in Jesus. Such an idea of revelation is incompatible with commitment to Jesus as the form of God.

The appeal to Jesus in the spirit, or to the Holy Spirit, or to the Logos, in order to legitimate the revelatory claim for scripture not only results in an un-Christian view of revelation and of God, and in the displacement of Jesus as the form of God, it also leads, as one might expect, to the loss of the polar dialectic. Ironically, the very symbol of God's freedom in relation to humankind—Spirit—is harnessed to the cause of tyranny. In other words, commitment to the Bible as the form of God absolutizes a fixed form which cannot be responsive to a changing world, and which entails the surrender of reason and moral responsibility in those committed to it. The Bible is indeed irreplaceable as the primary and almost exclusive source of the story of Jesus. It is thus for Christians supremely important as the authoritative witness to Jesus as the form of God. But the Bible itself is not the form of God, and does not pretend to be. Its self-proclaimed purpose to witness to Jesus (John 20: 31) is defeated if it is itself accorded the dignity which does not belong to it.

The reality of the shift from Jesus to scripture as the form of God is revealed in the doctrine of the inerrancy of scripture. Such a doctrine is closely analogous to belief in the sinlessness of Jesus. We saw that the affirmation of Jesus' necessary sinlessness belonged to the logic of confession, rather than functioning as a historical or psychological statement. He could not be received and confessed as the norm and criterion of truth against which all other truth must be judged, and at the same time be thought of as perhaps mistaken, at odds with God—a sinner.

The doctrine of scriptural inerrancy works in the same way. Its real function is as a confession of faith, rather than as a scientific or historical statement, though it is often presented in those terms and creates insuperable problems in consequence. As a confessional statement, it is logically intelligible, but by the same token it shows itself to be theologically untenable, at least for those who proclaim Jesus to be the form of God. To shift that claim to the book about him is to allow the servant to usurp the master's place, and to make a god of a human creation. It is, in short, idolatry and a source of alienation.

The same criticism holds good not only in relation to the Bible as a whole, but in regard to any attempt to treat any part of it as absolute and binding for all time. To take any

particular words or acts of Jesus and to attribute binding
revelatory authority to them, on the grounds that they come
from a revelatory figure, is intolerable for three reasons.

First, the problems of historical criticism prevent us
knowing exactly what Jesus said or did in any specific instance; to accord binding revelatory authority to particular
words or acts attributed to Jesus is to deify a historical judgement. Secondly, even if we knew exactly what Jesus said and
did in a given instance, it would not be of binding revelatory
authority for reasons already given. Jesus was a real man,
subject to the limitations of human existence in every aspect
of his being—physical, psychological, intellectual, and spiritual. Equally, he was subject to the cultural conditions of his
day. If this cannot be said, then he was not a human being
like us and is of no interest to us. If it must be said, then to
seize on any particular word or act of Jesus and to accord it
absolute revelatory value is to deify what is creaturely and
cultural, and a random sample at that. The alternative, maintained by some of the early Fathers, that Jesus sometimes
spoke or acted as Logos (revelatory) and sometimes as a man
(non-revelatory), is no longer tenable. Furthermore, we have
argued that it was Jesus himself in the totality of his life in
the context in which it was set who could be grasped as the
form of God. No single part or detail in isolation can ever
properly be abstracted from his story and given binding
revelatory authority. Logically, there are three possibilities.
Either every detail of Jesus' life, words, and work must be
binding (which Christianity has never maintained), or nothing is, or else the truth shines through the wholeness and
not in parts. Finally, it would be incompatible with everything we have argued thus far to suppose that Jesus laid
down binding rules for his followers on the basis of some
claim to supernatural authority or divine revelation, without
regard to their understanding or experience. In doing so he
would have imposed a new Law, and the tyranny of formal
revelation would not be broken. But in fact all the evidence
suggests that Jesus allowed his followers to discover the
implications of holy love for themselves in their relationship
to him and in the freedom of the Spirit. He left them free to
meet the future in a changing world. The price was and still

is bitter conflict; the gain was and still is the possibility for human beings to grow and learn in a genuinely human way.

If it can be said of Jesus that he dared to leave his followers free to pursue the truth, and did not bind them to external law, then it certainly cannot be maintained that Paul or any other early Christian had the right to bind Jesus' followers for all time. To suggest such a thing is to slander Paul. Despite his passionate convictions, and though he pleaded and encouraged, he was splendidly loyal to Jesus in refusing to bind his converts to unquestioning obedience.[3] All the New Testament writers witness powerfully to their belief in the universal and ultimate significance of Jesus. That message can transform the reader now as it did then; but particular issues have to be evaluated in the light of our knowledge of God as seen in the form of Jesus, in relation to the world we live in and the insights we now have, not by referring to isolated scriptural verses here and there.

If this argument is valid, it follows that controversial issues today cannot be settled merely by appeal to scripture. The problems of marriage, divorce, abortion, homosexuality, as well as those of genetic engineering, nuclear energy and nuclear weapons, the use of force, and so on, must be grappled with in the freedom of the Spirit and in the light of Jesus, in the context of our knowledge and responsibilities in the contemporary world.

To take one further issue currently being debated in the Church: to argue that women should not be ordained priests because Jesus himself was male, or because he chose only male disciples, is indefensible. Such arguments isolate and deify either a contingent biological factor or culturally conditioned elements of the story. At the same time, they betray an understanding of Jesus as a bearer of divine law binding for all time in all circumstances. Such a view implies an idea of God as arbitrarily intruding into the history and outworking of his creation, without regard to the emergence of authentic human insight. This is incompatible with an understanding of historical existence as creative and purposeful. It is equally incompatible with our understanding of Jesus as one who broke the tyranny of Law and restored

---

[3] G. Shaw's acerbic criticism of Paul's misuse of moral pressure is too extreme, though a valid reminder that the greatest saints are not free from fault or exempt from criticism: G. Shaw, *The Cost of Authority* (London, 1983).

the creative interaction of form and vitality, thereby enabling the creative potentials of historical existence to be realized in new ways in a constantly changing world.

2. CREEDS, DOCTRINES, AND CHURCHES

(a) Creeds and doctrines

Most of what was said in the previous section applies with equal force to the creeds and doctrines of the Church. We have seen how in the face of distortions of its message, of opposition to it and competition with it, the Church was bound to define with greater precision what it believed and taught. Its primary concern was to confess the ultimate and universal significance of Jesus. Its confessional formulae were forged in the heat of persecution and controversy. It is not surprising, then, that they came to be regarded as the binding criteria of true faith, and definitive for membership of the Christian community. Nevertheless, the critique above concerning the inerrancy of scripture applies here too. There is in any notion of credal or doctrinal inerrancy or infallibility the danger of a shift from Jesus as the form of God to the formulations of confession and faith in him, and beyond these to teachings about him.

The issue is complicated once again by the ambiguities of language. The distinction drawn in chap. 7, sect. 5 between confessional and descriptive language does not correspond to creeds and doctrines, but applies to both. There is a descriptive element in the creeds, and certainly a confessional element in doctrines. A further distinction needs to be borne in mind between confessional intentions and confessional formulae.

For a person to confess Jesus as Lord, and at the same time to admit he might not be, would, as we have already argued, be self-contradictory. Equally, a confessional formula itself cannot be combined with reservations as to its truth without being self-contradictory. But that does not mean that a given confessional formula in a specific verbal form can serve equally well in any time or place, whatever the prevailing cultural conditions or conceptual framework.[4]

[4] See N. Lash, *Change in Focus: A Study of Doctrinal Change and Continuity* (London, 1973).

Least of all can a confessional formula containing descriptive elements be regarded as a whole as unchangeable, regardless of circumstances; and in fact confessional formulae cannot be wholly isolated from descriptive elements. A confession of faith can only be formulated in relation to the language, symbols, and thought-forms of a given place and time and within an overall conceptual framework. The symbols— 'Messiah', 'Lord', 'Logos-Son', or 'the form of God'—all reflect different ways of picturing supremacy in different cultures. Even if they are employed to express Jesus' ultimacy, that ultimacy belongs to Jesus and not to the confessional symbols as such.

It can, then, be maintained that continuity within the Christian community in time and space is to be found in the intention of confession, rather than in the acceptance of specific confessional formulations. To require acceptance of any particular one as a condition of membership of the Christian community is to substitute commitment to formulae for commitment to Jesus as the form of God. Such a demand has been defended on the grounds that the Councils which formulated the creeds and doctrines were directly inspired by the Holy Spirit or Jesus in the spirit. But this is open to the objections already given. Such an appeal once again harnesses the symbols of God's freedom to the service of worldly forms. The polar dialectic is broken, and the confessions of a living faith are transformed into a life-denying law.

In contrast, the approach suggested here allows the confessional formulae which have been inherited from earlier generations to be evaluated positively and openly. It is possible to discern a confessional intention in what may now to us be unfamiliar symbolism. With this understanding, it may become possible to use ancient formulations without being guilty of hypocrisy or being forced into intellectual suicide. Thus, a phrase such as 'he came down from heaven' may be taken not as literal description but as symbolic expression of the ultimacy of Jesus. Even if such language was once taken descriptively and even intended descriptively, it can be argued that it also always had a confessional intention as well. Continuity is not lost where it matters. We can accept that

the descriptive element will not do for us now, without part-
ing company on the central issue of who is confessed. The
same may be said of 'born of the Virgin Mary', though the
descriptive connotations here are so strong and misleading
that a reformulation would seem more desirable.

It remains to be said that doctrinal elaborations have been
undertaken in the past on the assumption that credal statements are true in descriptive terms which are no longer
tenable today. It follows that much of this can now be jettisoned, or at least consigned to historical study, without
denying its value in its day. Some of the material may indeed
still prove to be of confessional value when interpreted. It
may also be rich in spiritual insights and of lasting devotional
value. But in no case can any works of doctrine be supposed
to be of such eternal and unquestionable value as to make
their acceptance obligatory on all Christians at all times.
Freed from such bonds, those committed to Jesus today
may be better able to turn their minds and their energies to
expressing that commitment in their own world and in their
own language and thought-forms, without being forced to
drag today's world into unintelligible language or obsolete
world-views.

(b) The Churches

Scripture, creeds, and doctrines can obviously not be divorced from the overall life of the Church. So what has been
said thus far applies implicitly to the Church in the broadest
sense. However, we need to examine various meanings of the
word 'Church'. Once again we are faced with ambiguities.
'Church' can stand for the whole community of Christians—
past and present—thought of ideally as constituting one
body whose head is Jesus Christ, from whom it derives its
holiness. In a narrower but still ideal way it may be used of
the 'body of Christ' in the world, thought of as an existing
reality, even if its limits are hard to define and its membership impossible to determine. More specifically, 'Church'
is used of concretely existing, more or less clearly defined
Christian communities, with their own traditions, organizations, structures of leadership, and symbols of
identity.

More needs to be said about symbols of identity and the 'ideal Church' *vis-à-vis* actual Churches. First, the very great importance of symbols of identity for any social group must be acknowledged. No community can perpetuate itself in time or extend itself geographically without such symbols. National flags are the most familiar illustration. But many things can serve a dual purpose, having a specific practical function and at the same time serving as symbols of identity. Uniforms most obviously serve a dual role of dressing and identifying. Many other things can acquire symbolic significance through their use and associations. Thus, within Christianity, the Latin Mass in the Roman Catholic Church and the Book of Common Prayer in the Church of England have both had the practical function of ordering worship and at the same time served, and not surprisingly still serve in some quarters, as major symbols of identity. The identity involved here is that of a community committed to Jesus as revealer and redeemer, and is therefore of fundamental importance to its members. At stake is not merely its social identity, but its self-understanding as a community which can be sure of God's presence with it. So to treat the Latin Mass or Book of Common Prayer at merely the functional, rational, or even aesthetic level is to miss the point, and to provoke understandable indignation.[5] What is said here of forms of liturgy is also applicable to scripture, creeds, and doctrines. This may help to show why particular translations of the Bible and specific credal formulations are so highly valued in some quarters. The older they are, the greater their value is likely to be as symbols of identity, but that is no proof of greater religious worth.

However, it is one thing to value forms of confession or vehicles of worship, to accept them as symbols of identity, and even to revere them as symbols of God's presence. It is very much another to treat any book, formula, object, rite, ritual, office, or institution as the concrete *locus* of God's presence or as signifying God's exclusive presence with the particular community which has inherited that symbol. That is idolatrous. The value of symbols of identity can be fully

---

[5] See Douglas, chap. 3.

affirmed; but the dangers of overvaluation are real and remain in the Church today, as may be seen in specific cases to be considered below. The danger is often associated with the premature claims of specific Churches to be the ideal Church, a matter to which we must now turn.

It is scarcely conceivable for any Church not to think of itself as at least a valid part of the ideal Church. It is not unusual for particular Churches, or even small groups of Christians, to suppose that they alone are the ideal Church, and that other Christian bodies are more or less distant from the true Church or excluded from it—depending, perhaps, on how many normative symbols they have in common.

However, the arguments used to defend exclusive claims for Churches are those we have already seen used to elevate scripture, creeds, and doctrines, and are equally untenable. The claim of any Church to exclusive revelatory authority, in effect to be the form of God in the world, effectively displaces Jesus. His displacement, where it occurs (as it does frequently), can almost invariably be blamed on the Holy Spirit, or even on Jesus himself (in the spirit). Or rather, to put the matter correctly, the inspiration of the Spirit has been invoked in order to legitimate the establishment of alternative *loci* of revelatory authority. In this way the vacuum left at the South Pole of formal revelation has been filled (see above, p. 222), paradoxically at the expense of subjective revelation. In other words, although we saw that in a sense subjective revelation was duplicated in the risen Jesus and the Holy Spirit, nevertheless the harnessing of God in the Spirit to substitute forms of formal revelation has, in the course of history, denied to Jesus' followers the freedom of the Spirit to respond to God and grow in Christian commitment and understanding. Given the revelatory claims made for Bible, Church, bishop, pope, general,[6] or other leaders, anyone who questioned or criticized them could be judged guilty of questioning and criticizing the Spirit of God, and hence guilty of blasphemy. Freedom to

---

[6] *'Confidence in God and in me are absolutely indispensable both now and ever afterwards'*—the conclusion of General Booth's address to the Conference of the Christian Mission in 1877, quoted by H. Begbie, *Life of William Booth, the Founder of the Salvation Army*, 2 vols. (London, 1920), i. 408 (emphasis original).

grow was stifled, the strength of the Church depended more and more on appeal to divine revelation formulated in a bygone age and remote from the changing world. With the passage of time, the possibility of understanding diminished and the proclamation of the Christian Gospel had to rely more and more on appeal to supernatural agency to fill the gap created by the loss of human meaning. Once the operation of the supernatural *deus ex machina* was conceded, anything could be accepted as revelation—even the 'literal truth' of the Bible—in defiance of scientific understanding and God-given reason. But to base claims to revelatory authority on the inspiration of the Spirit and the argument that the Spirit of God cannot be mistaken is as invalid here as when applied to scripture, creed, or doctrine.

There is no basis in the New Testament for holding that those who possess the Spirit are already perfect and in possession of all truth. Historically, it has usually been acknowledged that individual Christians are redeemed sinners on the path to glory but not yet perfect. The same applies to the Churches, and yet recognition of this fact has been strangely lacking.[7] Failure to recognize that actual Churches in their institutional and organizational form are social constructs represents, in sociological terms, a classic case of alienation. It can certainly be affirmed that they are the social constructs of a society of redeemed sinners, and hence can or should bear the marks of redemption. But it cannot be supposed that they are perfect or beyond criticism in any

---

[7] E. Troeltsch's classic analysis of the way in which the gifts of the Spirit came to be focused on the Church and its hierarchy, instead of upon Jesus, has received far too little attention since its publication over fifty years ago. See his *Social Teaching of the Christian Churches* (2 vols., London and New York, 1931), i. 111:

> Self-consecration in free obedience of conscience, with the goal of the infinite value of the soul, heart purity, and the love of God, become humility and meekness towards the Church, which involves the sacrifice of one's own will and of one's own knowledge, and is ethically most valuable when the renunciation is most difficult. Brotherly love, with the aim of the universal fellowship of love, becomes the collective consciousness of the Church, which has the right to claim every sacrifice of the individual will, and without which a man is like a withered leaf fallen from the parent stem. It is precisely in obedience to the Church, and in sacrifice for the unity of the Church, that the destruction of the ego and self-sacrifice for others is exercised, good works are acquired, and future salvation is assured . . . Now the chief emphasis is laid on the authority of the Church, charity consists in submission to the Church.

respect, any more than this could be claimed for any of their members. When this is forgotten, the Spirit, the symbol of God's freedom, is once again harnessed to the cause of tyranny—this time ecclesiastical tyranny. Jesus is displaced, the dialectic broken, and all too often the Devil's work is done in God's name.

If this represents the extreme case, it is certainly not far removed from actuality, as is apparent when the Crusades, Inquisition, or early missionary practice in South America are remembered; but neither does the charge stand against only one Church or only against ancient Churches. Wherever the Spirit has been appealed to, not in prayer but in argument, to guarantee the inerrancy of credal formulae, or the exclusive efficacy of particular sacraments, or the exclusive validity of certain orders of ministry, or the infallibility of councils or leaders past or present, then Jesus is effectively displaced as the form of God, or the Holy Spirit is enslaved. But no one can enslave the Spirit, and those who attempt to do so find themselves enslaved instead to revelatory forms which are not directly of God and not free from distortion. The outcome is inevitably destructive for themselves and for others on whom they impose themselves in God's name.

The power of the Spirit to work through different vehicles of revelation is in no way denied here. Nor is there any denial of the presence of the Spirit in the lives of those nurtured within different expressions of the primary revelation in Jesus. What we oppose is the closing of the gap between God, who is the ground and goal, and those worldly forms in which his power and presence are bodied out in his creation.

What has been argued of the Church in rather general terms applies equally to all forms of authority by which particular Churches are governed. They may serve a very necessary and creative purpose in witnessing to God revealed in Jesus, in guiding, defining, organizing, and even disciplining the communities who live in this faith. But no focus of ecclesiastical authority, past or present, should be too highly exalted or treated as the definitive criterion of Christian faith.

This has implications for particular Churches and for the

question of relationships between Churches, namely,
ecumenism. Only one or two issues can be explored further
here to illustrate what is at stake. First, it follows that the
doctrine of papal infallibility[8] cannot be accepted, any more
than a doctrine of scriptural or doctrinal inerrancy. Admittedly, the doctrine has always been subject to strict conditions, and in recent years has been carefully qualified by
Roman Catholic interpreters.[9] But the words at their face
value represent an untenable position, and should be abandoned. It is not the doctrine itself but the very difficulty
which any question of abandoning it presents which points
to the necessity of doing so. This is in no way to deny
that the doctrine has positive value in witnessing to God's
continuing living relationship with his world and with those
committed to him in the form of Jesus. Nor is it to deny the
valuable role of the pope in guiding the Roman Catholic
Church, or in acting as its spokesman, or in his function as a
symbol of identity and indeed of God's presence in the Spirit. But the over-exaltation of one particular symbol or witness to God's revelation displaces Jesus and places
constraints on the activity of the Spirit in other individuals
and communities committed to him.

The same criticism may apply when any particular Church
lays down non-negotiable conditions in discussing its relationship with other Churches. Here, however, important
distinctions need to be drawn to avoid confusion. The distinction lies between establishing the terms for mutual recognition and the terms for organic union.

In the former case, a Church which lays down any non-
negotiable conditions apart from the intention to confess
Jesus to be of ultimate and universal significance is in danger
of self-idolatry for reasons already given. To impose its own

---

[8] Defined in *Pastor Aeternus*, issued at the concluding session of the First Vatican
Council, 18 July 1870. See B. C. Butler, *The Vatican Council 1869-1870* (London,
1962), 385.

[9] See J. M. R. Tillard, *The Bishop of Rome* (London, 1983), 172–8; P. Chirico,
Infallibility: The Crossroads of Doctrine (London, 1977); H. Küng, *Infallible?* (London, 1971); A. Hastings, ed., *Bishops and Writers: Aspects of the Evolution of Modern
English Catholicism* (Wheathampstead, Herts., 1977), esp. chap. 7, 'The Forgotten
Council', and chap. 8, 'The Primacy: The Small Print of Vatican I'; H. R. McAdoo
and A. C. Clark, eds., *The Final Report* (The Anglican-Roman Catholic International Commission, London, 1982), 91–8.

tradition, practices, or symbols (liturgical or otherwise) as a condition for recognizing another community as Christian is to put itself in Jesus' place. Where any Church is willing to recognize others as Christian, but is unwilling to abandon its claims to be the ideal Church or to revalue its own symbols, it creates a contradiction. This may be preferable to the first alternative of maintaining an exclusive claim to truth, but no Church can leave such a contradiction unresolved indefinitely without sacrificing the intelligibility of its own witness to revelation.

Where the question arises of organic union, rather than of mutual recognition, various options lie open. Communities body themselves out in the world in different ways just as individuals do. Certain possibilities open to individuals are mutually incompatible without being any the less human. For example, a single individual could not easily become an all-in wrestler and a ballet dancer. Other roles may more closely relate or overlap, such as surgeon and musician. Commitment to Jesus can be lived out differently in each case without invalidating others. The same is true of corporate bodies—the Churches. Some corporate embodiments of Christian commitment may be mutually incompatible at the organic level, such as the Roman Catholic Church and the Salvation Army, or the Quakers. To achieve the widest possible expression of Christian commitment, the continuing of both may well be desirable. This is not incompatible with their mutual recognition as fellow Christians. In other cases, even if separate embodiments have served Jesus' cause in the past, changed conditions today may mean that that cause can be better served by a greater or lesser degree of organic union. Something might be lost—indeed, would have to be lost—but for a larger gain.

It is against these alternatives that the question of non-negotiable conditions must be evaluated. A particular Church might sincerely believe that it could not sacrifice the whole, or some feature, of its way of bodying out faith in Jesus without in consequence weakening his cause in the world. It might then identify conditions which make it what it is and which it could not sacrifice without ceasing to be what it is. In given circumstances it might count the loss too great, when set against the possible advantages (for Christian witness) of union with another Church. But to absolutize such conditions against all possible circumstances, or to suggest explicitly or implicitly that recognition of them is a necessary condition for belonging to the true Church and for recognition as a Christian, is indefensible, idolatrous, and blasphemous.

It follows, to take one important example, that for a particular Church to insist on acceptance of episcopacy as a condition for complete or partial integration *may* be justifiable. It would need to be shown that it was justifiable in relation to the particular tasks facing the Church. At present, its practical value can be defended, and the role of episcopacy as a symbol of identity is clearly important. However, to insist that episcopacy was non-negotiable simply because it was claimed to be God-given would be idolatrous; and to argue that Churches without episcopacy were in consequence non-Christian, or at best Christianly defective, would be to subvert the revelation of God in the form of Jesus. To appeal to scripture or to the Spirit in the Church to 'prove' otherwise would be inadmissible, as we have seen. Episcopacy may well continue to serve larger Churches in particular, but can never rightly be used to define the Church (least of all can a particular understanding of episcopacy— or priesthood, for that matter—be treated as definitive for all time). It is not just the case that commitment to Jesus *can* be expressed in other forms of non-episcopal Church; it cannot be expressed in its full and varied potential *without* these Churches.

What is right in certain circumstances for particular Churches on earth cannot be regarded as universally and eternally binding. To argue that if such things are not eternally binding, then Jesus was wrong, or the Holy Spirit has misled the Church for two thousand years, is absurd, and betrays an understanding of God's revelatory activity which, I suggest, is incompatible with commitment to Jesus as the form of God.

Turning from relationships between Churches, we can see that the polarity model also has a bearing on developments within particular Churches. The question of the ordination of women has already been touched upon. Another example may be taken from the Church of England. It is quite often observed these days that a remarkable convergence is occurring between the Anglo-Catholic and Evangelical movements in the Church, despite their history of mutual suspicion and antagonism. This is seen by some as the growth-point of the future, which will leave liberal theology and the broad Church behind as a passing digression.

However, while any evidence of the spirit of reconciliation at work is welcome, it should occasion little surprise to see movements which tend towards the same wing of the polar axis, that of form, finding common ground. For 'High Church' and 'high Bible' movements to converge is rather to be expected. To see this as the growth-point of the future is to betray a combination of complacency and blindness. Such a trend witnesses rather to the strengthening of formal revelation, perhaps in fearful reaction to the uncertainties of the age and the heavy burdens of responsibility placed on human beings today. But the resulting imbalance and loss of the polar dialectic can only further frustrate the Church's true and God-given purpose. This, it may be suggested, is to open the way to the realization of the highest human potentials, which were present as potentials from the beginning of creation but which can only be actualized when men and women live in a right relationship with God and hence with each other. In this relationship, human responsibility is enhanced and not denied. It offers a way forward in creative freedom within a changing, disordered, and alienated world.

Surrendering responsibility to divine revelation in any existing concrete form, Church or Bible, will provide no solutions to the world's problems, only illusory escape. The tyranny of form is no remedy for anarchy. In fact the Spirit cannot be chained to form. It follows that though the way of commitment to God in Jesus represented by liberal theology runs the risk of anarchy, and cannot on any account lay claim to final truth, it is nevertheless one place in which the freedom of the Spirit is not repressed. However inadequately it is expressed, this side of the polar axis can never become obsolete. A Christianity without it would not represent the

revelation of God in the form of Jesus and in the vitality of
the Spirit; it would not be truly Trinitarian or creative.

It might be argued at this point that the vitality of the
Spirit is indeed expressed in many Churches today in the
Charismatic movement. Since this is flourishing among
evangelical Christians and Roman Catholics, the argument
above in defence of liberal theology may appear irrelevant.
There is no need to deny the genuine spirituality and commitment of many in the Charismatic movement, or to deny
the value of their experiences to themselves and the value of
what they have to offer the Churches. However, it presents
curious anomalies. On the one hand, freedom of the Spirit in
the Charismatic movement verges on the extreme of anarchy
when it breaks through the form of language, and certainly
abandons forms of conventional behaviour. On the other
hand, this phenomenon is usually associated with a dominant
formal revelation. In other words, the Charismatic movement is as a matter of fact often associated with biblical and
ecclesiastical fundamentalism. This correlation is interesting, even if not a matter of necessity. It might serve as
evidence that God's relationship to human beings cannot be
restricted to the mode of form, but must break through in
the Spirit. However, if this occurs in a context where the
absolute claims of a given form are not qualified, tensions
and potentially destructive consequences may result.

The real dangers must be carefully identified and not simply misconstrued from a wrong perspective. For example,
from the point of view of someone committed to ecclesiastical form, as shaped by tradition and authority, the
Charismatic movement may appear totally and dangerously
anarchic. In fact, many Charismatics may have recovered
the vitality of the Spirit in a way that is truly creative. On
the other hand, far from being anarchic, many professed
Charismatics are, it seems, merely committed to a different
form, the Bible. To put it in extreme terms, many Charismatics are, as biblical fundamentalists, not really free but
enslaved to a book, which, even though it is the primary
witness to Jesus, is still a human creation and not the form
of God. Given the intolerable constraints which biblical li-
teralism imposes on the God-given human mind and intellect, it is perhaps not wholly surprising that the Spirit,

when it breaks through this form of commitment, is denied the use of words and reason. In this situation, whatever gifts it confers on those who experience its coming, neither it nor they can say anything new to the world. They can only offer a share in the excitement of an 'other-worldly' experience and the comfort of fellowship with others whose love may indeed be real and Christlike, but whose minds have abandoned full responsibility in and for this world.

In short, the Charismatic movement in general points to the recovery of the Spirit; it may well serve to revitalize individuals and Churches from various backgrounds and traditions. But it cannot of itself restore the polar dialectic, or ensure the primacy of Jesus as the form of God. Indeed, paradoxically, it runs the risk of reinforcing the claims of false absolutes, whether seemingly Christian or blatantly anti-Christian. Thus, the Charismatic movement cannot answer the world's needs as they really are, but tends either to be driven into privacy or into attempting to force today's world into the mould of first-century Palestine. The right-wing character of some Charismatic movements in the United States of America is fearful evidence of this. It is when the dynamic interaction of God's revelation in the form of Jesus and the vitality of the Spirit is recovered that one may hope to see the gifts of the Spirit put to effective use in the Churches and in the world, creating a redeemed future out of an alienated past.

In conclusion, it may be recognized that there are many who fear that if the revelation which a Church claims to represent—through its leaders, doctrines, or interpretation of the Bible—is qualified or compromised in any way, then the door is at once opened wide to anarchy. If, as it appears, every individual, let alone so-called Church, is free to decide for himself what is true, the truth would be lost. Those who fear this will react in uncompromising defence of what they have inherited.

On the other hand, there are those who welcome this anarchy, seeing it rather as the freedom of the promised Spirit, in whose name they are free to abandon the structures and ethical traditions, doctrines and interpretations, and all forms inherited by their respective Churches. Even in the extreme case, the Bible may be retained, especially if there is a wish to preserve the name of 'Christian'; but when it is open to 'inspired' interpretation so that anything can be read into it, the connection is tenuous.

In the first case, the dangers of formalism arise and need no further elaboration. In the latter case, the opposite dangers are equally real, of Churches fragmenting into formless groups or ultimately isolated individuals, moved only by emotion and excitement, and liable to fall victim to the first dominant leader (and potential tyrant) who comes their way.[10] Deification of the individual in the name of the Spirit is no answer to the deification of Church, Bible, or doctrine in the name of the Spirit. Either way Jesus is displaced and the Spirit abused.

The solution does not lie on one side or the other, or in attempting to work out compromises between different claims to absolute truth.[11] It lies rather in denying all claims to absolute truth whether in the formal or subjective mode. To do so accords with the doctrine of justification by faith, inasmuch as it extends not only to human individuals, but to human social organizations and human conceptual constructions; *all* fall short of the glory of God. It is as falling short and not as claiming perfection that they are acceptable to God. This means that every Church should relinquish its claims to be the true Church, in effect, the form of God. Each will then be free to reaffirm Jesus as the form of God, and so to confess God revealed in the form of Jesus and the vitality of the Spirit. Each Church will then be free to hear and accept valid criticism coming from its own members, or from others who share the same commitment but body it out in a different way. It will also be able to recognize the strength and weakness of those others, and to offer valid criticism of their attempts to body out the common conviction. In the last resort, it is as forgiven sinners that all Christians are equal and united before God. So too, Christian Churches are equal and united as forgiven sinners.

[10] See P. Tillich, *The Courage to Be* (Glasgow, 1962), 150, for the failure of 'the courage to be as oneself' and 'the longing for authority and for a new collectivism'.

[11] This may be judged to be the fault of many ecumenical discussions, where no Church, it seems, can actually admit it might have been wrong. Cf. The ARCIC Report, above, n. 9.

It remains the case that the Holy Spirit cannot in fact be successfully harnessed to worldly forms. In the Spirit, what is new continually breaks through what is given, with or without ecclesiastical permission. The Church, or rather the Churches, cannot remain unchanged or unchanging any more than can the world. Yet where the polar dialectic is broken, change is potentially destructive. If a given form cannot bend, it is bound to be broken. This may lead to an equal or even greater dominance by another form, or result in anarchy. Both possibilities were realized at the time of the Reformation. Perhaps Luther restored the polar dialectic more adequately than anyone else, but his achievement did not last long, as the formalism of Protestant orthodoxy took hold. The self-contradiction of Protestant totalitarianism came into being and in some quarters remains a fact of life. The danger and futility of reacting to the opposite pole of subjective revelation had already been demonstrated by the Anabaptists. In contrast, the withdrawal into quietism avoided conflict, but also let the world at large avoid the challenge of faith in Jesus.

The application of the polarity model to that and other periods of the Church's history will not explain all that happened, but may shed some light on the course of events, not least on those in which the Church manifestly went badly wrong, and where it is still going badly wrong. If these conclusions hold good, the Churches will be free, without necessarily falling into chaos, to recognize each other and to shed trunkfuls of outworn symbols and obsolete practices. These may well have served a valid purpose once, or still have some value as symbols of identity, but if they now hamper the Churches in their task they can be given up, or be kept only in particular places where they still have a use. It can hardly be denied that there are places in the world today where the Churches need to travel light, especially when, like Abraham, they venture into new territories. It is absurd to saddle them with the trappings of sedentary life, so long as they remain, like him, committed in faith.

Just as importantly, time need no longer be wasted discussing unity and trying to achieve compromises between mutually exclusive absolutes. It can be better spent by all

Churches, whether in mutual recognition or active unity, getting down to the job they are there for. This is to witness to the disclosure of the ground and goal of existence in the personal form of Jesus and in the continuing vitality of the Spirit.

3. CHRISTIANITY AND OTHER RELIGIONS

The general case argued here, and applied in particular to Judaism and Christianity, must apply in principle to all religions, large or small, new or old. The question of the proper definition of religion is much debated and not easily answered. It will be understood here simply on the basis of the position developed in Part I, as having to do with the question of being and meaning. It arises out of the encounter of human beings with the wider reality within which the reality of their own being is set, and within which the question of the meaning of their own existence arises—the question of origin, goal, and place in life.

Religions in their manifold variety offer 'answers' to these questions even where the questions themselves are not explicitly or clearly articulated. The 'answers' certainly need not be presented in narrowly intellectual or logical terms. As often as not, religions help to create a meaningful social context where the answer to the question of existence is experienced rather than spoken. Religions may vary in the extent to which they tolerate or encourage individual pursuit of the religious quest, but a social context can never be entirely lacking. That fact does not of course of itself preclude the possibility that the meaning found there is grounded in something real beyond the reality of individual and society.

Religions are distinguished from social groupings and individual pursuits generally by a concern for what is ultimately real and of ultimate value[12]—that which transcends the contingencies of ordinary everyday life as the source of being and meaning. Whether the word 'God' is used or not, the sense of the transcendent may still be present as a sense of the 'out of the ordinary' which bears powerfully on the

[12] See Tillich, *Systematic Theology*, i. 14 and *passim*.

ordinary. The widespread phenomenon of a sense of the sacred may be interpreted in this light. Thus, the concern of religion may be brought into focus as the concern of human beings with transcendent, sacred, ultimate reality, in relation to which the meaning of human existence is to be found. The ground of meaning and being is commonly called God.

I have argued that God is disclosed in the form of Jesus and in the vitality of the Spirit. The question that immediately arises is whether he can be known outside this particular revelatory constellation or whether, in the light of it, all other claims to know God are proved to be false.

Today, as in the past, views diverge. At one extreme, the possibility of any knowledge of God outside Christianity is denied; at the other, the view that God is as fully known in other religions and cultures is affirmed. Between the extremes various ideas can be found which allow for a partial knowledge of God outside Christianity.[13] On the basis of the polarity model and the account of Jesus presented above, I shall argue that the two extremes are untenable, and that the uniqueness of God's revelation in Jesus can be upheld without denying a true knowledge of God in other religions.

(a) Formal revelation

In the first place, we consider claims to a knowledge of God in the formal mode: in the form of a book on the one hand, in the form of a person on the other. The critique already directed against various kinds of Christian fundamentalism must be applied with equal force against all forms of religious fundamentalism. Questions of sincerity, loyalty, spirituality, and courage are not at stake here, but questions of truth. The contemporary analysis of alienation helps us to see why the overestimation of the revelatory value of human verbal constructs—books—can be disastrously destructive. In so far as absolute revelatory value is attributed to the time- and culture-bound expressions of past religious insight, the religious vitality of the present is placed under the constraints of the past.

[13] For an anthology of different points of view, see J. Hick and B. Hebblethwaite, *Christianity and Other Religions* (Glasgow, 1980).

Hence, to take one example, we may better appreciate the strength and the tragedy of the Iranian revolution in these terms. However varied, or secular, the forces interacting within it may be, we may allow that a genuine spirituality— a vital awareness of God—was and is at work there, reacting against anti-religious elements in Western technological civilization. However, that spirituality is of necessity channelled through and shaped by the Koran directly, or by an Ayatollah, whose own spirituality is under the constraint of revelation in the form of the Koran. Islam as a whole is not to be judged by the form it has acquired in Iran; but Iran is now the inspiration of Islamic fundamentalism on a widening front. Our case is not against Muslims, but against every kind of fundamentalism.

The Koran will always remain a powerful witness to human awareness of God. It is likely to remain a formative resource and symbol of identity in a continuing religio-cultural tradition. It remains the case that the absolute revelatory authority attributed to it as a whole, and to the equally binding traditions based on it, continues to obstruct the appropriation of later ethical or religious insight. To take one important example, submission to the Koran makes it very hard indeed to acknowledge the dignity and social status of women to the degree that is now beginning to be recognized as just in Western society, for all its faults. This is something unimagined in Muhammad's day, even though he himself may have contributed to the raising of women's status at that time.[14] Many Muslims in the past century have campaigned for the emancipation of women;[15] their problem

[14] P. M. Holt, A. K. S. Lambton, and B. Lewis, eds., *The Cambridge History of Islam*, 4 vols. (Cambridge, 1970), vol. iiB, 541 f., 'The reasons for Quranic legislation on all those matters were, in the first place, the desire to improve the position of women, of orphans and of the weak in general . . .'. For Muhammad's own somewhat depreciatory attitude to women, see R. Levy, *The Social Structure of Islam* (Cambridge, 1957), chap. 2, 'The Status of Women in Islam'.

[15] Cf. 'The Universal Islamic Declaration', iv. 4 (c), drawn up by the Islamic Council of Europe, which affirms a policy of 'Ensuring that women enjoy the full rights—legal, social, cultural, economic, educational and political—which Islam has guaranteed to them', quoted in S. Azzam, ed., *Islam and Contemporary Society* (London and New York, 1982), 263. For earlier campaigners for women's rights (e.g. Quasim Amin, Khalid Muhammad Khalid), see K. Cragg, *Counsels in Contemporary Islam* (Islamic Surveys, 3; Edinburgh, 1965), 91, 100 f.

lies in reconciling this objective with the absolute authority of the Koran and Koranic tradition.[16]

The consequences may differ, but the implications are in principle the same wherever any particular book is accorded absolute revelatory authority. Where such a book appears to provide sanction for political claims, the risk of destructive conflict is extreme.

We cannot here embark on a detailed examination of contemporary Judaism, with its very diverse forms of expression.[17] Still less is it possible to go into the rights and wrongs of the Middle East conflict. But one clear implication of the present argument is that to appeal to the word of God revealed in scripture to legitimate historically contingent territorial claims is totally invalid.[18]

It can indeed be argued that the perpetuation of absolutist revelatory claims from the past in the changing modern world poses one of the greatest threats to world peace. Revelatory absolutisms of various kinds reveal in practice the destructive consequences of alienation and idolatry. The answer on the part of Christianity is not to interpose its own alternative fundamentalism. The consequences of doing so in Northern Ireland are sufficient warning of the dangers of this supposed solution. The rising tide of fundamentalism in the United States of America, with its right-wing, backward-looking, intolerant character, may give even greater cause for anxiety.

The next question is whether these problems could be met simply by locating revelation in the form of a person rather than a book. The answer must be no. The case argued in chap. 2, sect. 2 may be briefly summarized; subject-dependent formal revelation does not of itself re-establish the polar dialectic. A person hailed as 'revealer' may release his followers from book-bound revelation or ancient tradition and allow them to relate more or less appropriately to conditions in the world around them. But by becoming the

---

[16] Cf. Levy, 134.

[17] For an account of Judaism, see I. Epstein, *Judaism* (Harmondsworth, 1959). See also Marmur.

[18] See Marmur's criticism of the use of the Bible 'to legitimize extremist actions' (p. 17)—though not of the Jewish right to 'the land'. See also above, pp. 76 f., for the contingent factors behind the exaltation of Jerusalem's status.

definitive *locus* of revelation for others he impedes the realization of their truly human potential. On the one hand, the responsible and dynamic interaction of revelatory experience and revelatory authority is inhibited or eliminated. On the other hand, any genuine spiritual insight which a supposed revealer may actually have becomes destructive rather than creative when its worth is overvalued. Any such insight in a living human being is necessarily contingent, conditioned, and partial. By being absolutized it is itself distorted and so distorts the understanding of those who regard it as absolute (see above, p. 2 n. 4, and chap. 1, sect. 3). This criticism applies to any religious leader for whom infallible revelatory authority is claimed, though much will depend on how that authority is exercised in practice and the extent to which individual freedom of response is in fact denied.

With the death of any such revealer, the way is open to a continuation of the same problem, with the added complication of unresolvable conflict between persons claiming to represent his revelatory authority; or else the attempt may be made to perpetuate the authority of dead revealer, through preserving the tradition about him. This, of course, leads back to revelation in the form of a book or tradition which falls under the criticism already offered.

If there is an answer to these problems, it is not to be found in supposing that God is revealed in the form of a book, any book at all. Nor is it to be found in supposing that God can be revealed in the form of *any* person at all at any place or time. Yet in and through a particular person, at a particular place and time, an answer may be found—in other words, in the personal response of Jesus to the givenness of his world. He himself stands out in the story handed down as a person who did not impose his revelatory authority on others. He appeared to be free from the destructive consequences of self-alienation,[19] and yet was willing to bear the consequences of alienation himself,[20] without retaliating against or rejecting those responsible. He left both his enemies and his friends free to allow their own experience to interact with the vision of God which came to expression

---

[19] Cf. Tillich, *Systematic Theology*, ii. 125 f.
[20] Ibid. 175 f.

in the totality of his life. Those who freely responded to this vision were thereby freed from book-bound (and indeed person-bound) revelation. By the same token, their sacred book, the Torah, was freed from claims made for it which were too great for it to bear. Thus freed, the Torah and the tradition associated with it could still serve, but no longer dominate, the spiritual life of human beings in a continually changing world. Within this freedom, the way was open for new and valid spiritual insights to emerge and be recognized and accepted, whatever the source.[21] What seeing God in the form of Jesus can do for the Torah it can do for any book of revelation.

It is a mistake, therefore, to posit either the alternative of accepting any supposed book of revelation as absolutely true, or that of rejecting it as absolutely false. The answer lies in denying absolute revelatory authority to any book of revelation. Those who claim such authority for the Christian Bible in fact play, without realizing it, into the hands of those who claim it for other books, and leave themselves with little alternative but to shout more loudly and impose themselves more aggressively. It is very much in reaction to this kind of behaviour and to the exclusivist claims of some Christians, not only to all truth but to all hope of eternal salvation, that many religious people have abandoned the Christian religion and many Christians have swung to the opposite extreme of arguing that knowledge of God is as fully available in other religions as in Christianity. However, this view creates its own logical as well as theological problems.

(b) Subjective revelation

Religions teach a great many different and often contradictory things about God, humankind, and the world. If knowledge of God is to be looked for in what religions say about him, it would seem absurd to suppose that all religions are equally right (unless they are all equally wrong—but this is not the conclusion intended). In fact, the intelligibility of the claim that God is known in all religions depends on

---

[21] This offers a basis for inter-faith dialogue. The Christian can expect to discover new insight and truth, but the criterion of judgement will be God as seen in Jesus.

laying much greater emphasis on the possibility of knowing
God in the Spirit—in the immediacy of personal experience—than on what can be known about him. In other
words, the emphasis will be on subjective rather than on
formal revelation. This can be maintained as much by down-
grading formal revelation as by upgrading subjective
revelation.

In the first place, advantage can be taken of the now widely
recognized symbolic character of religious language and the
changed understanding of its function which accompanies
this shift. Different symbols carry different weight and
meaning in different cultures and traditions. Differences in
talk about God may therefore be more apparent than real,
and a basic knowledge of the same God may be supposed to
underlie the seemingly diverse representations of him.

With the playing down of the revelatory value of objective
propositional language about God, there can be a corresponding emphasis on subjective revelation. The Christian
tradition itself can provide support for this. It has always
recognized a knowledge of God in the immediacy of experience. With the constraints of formal revelation and verbal expression relaxed, it is much easier to allow that God
in the Spirit is present or able to be present to the experience
of human beings of whatever culture or tradition, in whatever place or time. The limitations of language about God are
matched here by the limitations of the language of personal
knowing as such. If personal knowing can never be adequately verbalized, it would be absurd to expect to speak
literally of a personal knowledge of God. At most such an
experience can only be described partially or poetically. The
different accounts of God in different religions are therefore
scarcely surprising, and the claim to a knowledge of God in
one is certainly not proof that God is not known elsewhere.[22]
To say of two poems that one must be right and the other
wrong is to misunderstand poetry.

Thus, the case that God is known in the immediacy of
experience in other religions is not easily refuted (except on
a priori dogmatic grounds). It can be reinforced by evidence

---

[22] Cf. Hick, 140 f.

of godliness and seemingly genuine spirituality and grace-
fulness in persons nurtured in other religions independently
of Christianity. It would seem harder to attribute this to
what is not God (the Devil?) than to God himself. Finally,
the Christian doctrine of God's love would seem to count
against the view that God is only known in Christian experience, or that only Christians have the knowledge of God
sufficient for eternal salvation. It will be argued here that
this positive regard for other religions can be reinforced by
the acknowledgement of Jesus as the form of God, but that
without this acknowledgement the position, however generous and well motivated, collapses into anarchic
subjectivism.

The problems arise out of the premiss on which this positive evaluation of other religions rests. That God is known
in the Spirit (subjectively) may be true and something the
members of other religions would wish to claim. But to
affirm this at the expense of the objective claim to truth
which many religions make is to affirm such religions at the
expense of what they claim to be. A welcome on these terms
may not in fact be very welcome to them.

The Christian faith which acknowledges God revealed in
the form of Jesus and in the vitality of the Spirit is able in
principle to comprehend every dimension of human experience and understanding. It is able to affirm the creative
power of God within every culture and religious tradition,
without lapsing into an all-embracing sentimentality with no
cutting edge. On the contrary, in the story of Jesus Christians find the criterion of every ethical decision and of every
claim to truth. They discover also what it is possible for
men and women to become, and what they cannot become
without losing their humanity. In the light of Jesus, they can
recognize godliness in other religions; they can also discern
what is godless or contrary to God's purpose. Such positive
claims do not evaporate the ultimate mystery of God. The
story of Jesus as the symbol of God carries within itself its
own negation, in the crucifixion of Jesus. It is as given and
taken away that Jesus reveals God. In the dialectic of affirmation and negation, Jesus, the supreme symbol of God,

points through himself to the reality beyond language, the ultimate ground of meaning and life, the goal of all religion.

Under the symbol of Jesus on the cross it is possible to affirm all symbols of God in every religion and culture, but only as symbols which must be broken through if the reality of God is to be grasped. The failure of all fundamentalisms— Christian or otherwise—is the failure to let symbols be broken.[23] Unbroken symbols, even the most treasured symbols of scripture or tradition, are idols which bring destructive consequences not only upon those who acknowledge them as such, but on others, not least on those who refuse to acknowledge them. It is the mark of those committed to Jesus as the form of God to bear those consequences without hatred or retaliation, and in so doing to point the way to the truth that cannot be fully concretized in history. When the truth is grasped in the form of Jesus and the vitality of the Spirit, the power of idolatry and alienation is broken in principle, the demonic forces of tyranny and anarchy collapse. Within that confession, the presence of God with the adherents of other faiths is affirmed. Equally important, the creative potential to witness to God is recovered for sacred books and traditions, for Churches and religions, and for all the great spiritual leaders in human history. The redemption of religions is vital for the redemption of persons and the world.

4. POLITICAL LIFE

Christianity, with its concern for the world and history, cannot help but have implications for political life. It may even be said to have as much affinity with political ideologies which deny God, but are deeply concerned for the world, as with religions which affirm God, but often at the expense of the world. It is therefore as important to consider the implications of Christian faith in the sphere of politics and ideology as in its relation to other religions. Once again, this

---

[23] Tillich, *Dynamics*, 52, 'Faith, if it takes its symbols literally, becomes idolatrous! It calls something ultimate which is less than ultimate. Faith, conscious of the symbolic character of its symbols, gives God the honour which is due to him' (see also pp. 50 f. for 'broken' and 'unbroken' myth).

can only be done in general terms, without dealing with particular movements or political systems except by way of illustration.

The way the present interpretation of Christianity bears on political life will be explored in two parts. First, the implications for ordinary political life will be considered, where politics is conceived of as the art of the possible and is concerned with the management of national and international affairs, without engaging directly in questions of ultimacy. Secondly, the implications will be considered in relation to political movements and ideologies which implicitly or explicitly raise the question of ultimacy and purport to answer the fundamental questions of life.

(a) Politics

Politics is almost as hard to define as religion, but a full definition is no more necessary here than in the last chapter. Our concern is simply with the ordering of society, in respect of its internal and external relationships, conflicting interests, and divergent goals. Just as the possibilities of being human can be bodied out individually in an infinite variety of ways, so also with the structuring and bodying out of society. It would seem as foolish to ask which is right and which is wrong of the latter as of the former. The variety is simply a fact of life and the product of a whole range of interacting forces—geographical, climatic, dietary, economic, military, and so on.

The first point to be made, then, is that it is not the task of religion as such to establish or legitimate particular forms of political structure. Religion, as concern for the ultimate, is not engaged directly with the penultimate. Where political parties or policies do not lay claim to ultimacy, to engage with them directly in the name of religion, whether in support or opposition, is an offence against God and humanity. To treat the penultimate explicitly or by implication on the same plane as the ultimate is to idolize it. Hence, to support any party or movement as the direct agent of God is to be guilty of idolatry. Equally, to oppose any party or movement as the agent of the Devil, especially when it has no such pretensions to self-deification itself, is to be guilty of inverted idolatry.

However, the question of meaning and purpose which arises over individual life arises equally over political and cultural life. Any answer arrived at will help to determine not only what a society is, but what it seeks to become. It will also influence what an individual in a given society will support or oppose. So to deny the direct engagement of religion and politics on the same plane is not to deny indirect engagement. On the contrary, while the distinction remains important, total disengagement is ruled out.

The task here, therefore, is to state as briefly as possible some of the ways in which the interpretation of Christianity which has been offered will bear on political life and thinking. In the first place, it will serve to identify the primary aim of political activity. This will be to create conditions in which the creative potential of all human life can be realized as far as possible, and in which those things which impede its realization will be removed. This aim will hold good in principle, however great the problems created by a pluralist society, by class and economic, racial and cultural divisions, and by the often seemingly irreconcilable clash of sectional interests. Secondly, the possibility of realizing a perfect political structure is in principle ruled out on traditional theological grounds, with the doctrine of human fallenness and the impossibility of perfection on earth. In terms of the polarity model, the concrete existence of any perfect, unchanging form, political or otherwise, is excluded. Thirdly, the affirmation of ultimate meaning and purpose, of a goal to be pursued though never to be fully realized on earth, will confer meaning and purpose on all aspects of life, including the political, however imperfectly the goals of individual and corporate human life are actually realized.[24]

The second and third factors create the dynamic basis for political engagement. On the one hand, affirmation of ultimate meaning and purpose prevents a slide into apathy, or despair, or the cynical manipulation of political systems for short-term selfish interests. On the other hand, with the

---

[24] See J. Moltmann, *Theology of Hope* (London, 1967), 26 ff., para. 4, 'Does Hope Cheat Man of the Happiness of the Present?'

possibility of perfection in history rejected, the validity of criticism can be accepted, and with it the possibility of moving nearer to the goal is kept open. When existing political conditions are measured against the transcendent ideal of human existence, as discerned in and through the story of Jesus, then both the strength and weakness of existing political systems can be recognized, and attention can be given to reinforcing what is good and rectifying faults. How drastic any remedial action may need to be will depend on the particular conditions revealed.

The policies of different political parties can be judged in the same way. Support can be given where the objectives pursued appear most likely to create conditions in which the transcendent ideal is more rather than less capable of realization. Pursuit of the ideal may involve strengthening or changing existing political structures. In practice, choices may be difficult to make. The ambiguities of life are such that the best policies invariably have harmful and unjust consequences for some. In the present political situation in the United Kingdom, it is possible to discern aspects of the Christian ideal right across the political spectrum. These can still be acknowledged even if they are found in the company of motives and interests which are far removed from the ideal. On one side, the freedom and responsibility of the individual is affirmed; the attendant risk is that this is pursued at the expense of social justice. On the other side, concern for social justice is affirmed, with the risk of undermining individual freedom and responsibility. In the centre, we see a renewed attempt to hold the balance, which is inevitably threatened by the inescapable tension between these polar aspects of the ideal.[25]

It is not the task of a theologian or Christian to decree to others, Christian or non-Christian, which political party should be supported. To do so would mean claiming an authority one does not possess and would run the risk of idolatry already mentioned. It is, however, proper to try to

[25] The polarity model does not of itself legitimate only the central position (see above, pp. 2 f., for the analogy of different kinds of sport which do not invalidate each other), nor (to repeat) is the religious criterion ever to be identified with particular policies or a particular party.

identify the transcendent ideal as far as possible, and to offer it as a basis upon which to examine the intentions of political parties and the methods employed in pursuit of their goals. The recognition that neither goodness nor wickedness is the exclusive property of any political party makes it possible to weigh up which one in given circumstances can do most to correct imbalances and pursue the ideal. Given the fact of continuously changing conditions, and also changing political personnel, it is clear that judgement as to where support is due may also have to change. This does not necessarily mean that a Christian must be a floating voter. Long-term commitment to a political party may well be justified in pursuit of desirable long-term political objectives that accord with the transcendent ideal. What is ruled out is unconditional commitment, to which only the unconditional itself is entitled.

It is in matters where political parties or policies lay claim to unconditional commitment that the relationship between Christianity and politics is radically transformed. It may in practice often be difficult to distinguish between the legitimate claims for political commitment and loyalty and the illegitimate demand for unconditional commitment. Once again, a critique of the extreme case will be attempted, and the question of its applicability in particular circumstances will be left open.

(b) *Ideologies*

The claim to ultimacy on the part of political movements or ideologies may or may not be made explicitly, and may be indicated in various ways. A major clue is provided by reaction to internal criticism and external opposition. As already suggested, openness to criticism implies a readiness in principle to acknowledge a transcendent ideal. The critic can be recognized, if not welcomed, as a prophet. Where the critic—any critic—is treated and denounced as if a blasphemer, a totally different situation is disclosed. Implicit in the refusal to accept criticism is a claim to possess the whole truth, the ideal itself, because only the ideal can be beyond criticism. To admit criticism would be to undermine that claim; while the critic on his part discloses himself as the enemy of the ideal, an agent of the Devil. In the name of the supposed ideal and for the sake of this truth, such an enemy must be destroyed or expelled. Perhaps the only concession is to allow that the critic is mad rather than bad. The commitment of critics to mental hospitals in certain countries is one logically effective way of preserving the plausibility of prevailing claims to possess the ideal.

Reactions to external opposition may in a similar way disclose claims to ultimacy. Opposition and even resort to violence and war to protect specific interests is one thing.[26] The desire to destroy or totally transform the social and political structures—the individual and corporate self-understanding of others—is very much another. The latter intention can only make sense (though not be justified) in the name of some ideal, which those who claim to possess it believe to be realizable on earth and of universal and ultimate significance, and hence for the good not only of themselves, but of all humankind. That would be the positive motive. The negative motive would correspond to the attitude to internal criticism. The external opponent reveals himself as the enemy of the claimed ideal, and hence in the service of the Devil. The greater the threat posed by external enemies to the bearers of the ideal, the greater justification there would seem to be for seeking their destruction by any means, not for their sake but to ensure that the ideal itself not only survives but triumphs in the end.[27]

Thus far a distinction has not been clearly drawn between the claims of small minorities and the claims of States to be bearers of the ideal, because what has been said applies in principle to both. Each group, large or small, has to exist with the possibility of internal criticism and external opposition, and in its reactions will disclose how far it lays claim to ultimacy.

However, certain points need to be made about minority claims to be bearers of the ideal. The first point is that not all criticism within a given society is necessarily prophetic;

[26] This is in no way to justify the option of nuclear war, since in that case *no* human interest could be served.

[27] Those who identify the communist State, or the capitalist State, with 'the kingdom of darkness', or use similarly emotive religious language are guilty of inverted idolatory; see above, p. 314.

it may be idolatrous. Paradoxically, it can be received as prophetic even when it is offered idolatrously. It may come from those, however few, who claim to possess the ideal already in principle, and who believe it to be capable of full actualization on earth. The basis of their criticism may appear to be a transcendent ideal, since it is not yet actualized, but it is not a truly transcendent ideal when the possibility of actualizing it fully on earth is entertained at all. It is then at best merely an as yet unrealized expression of the ideal. When and if such an ideal is realized, it may indeed be good, but it cannot escape the historically and culturally conditioned and ambiguous character of all historically realizable expressions of the transcendent ideal. To regard it as free from such limitations is to render it demonic.

To treat any projected political structure or world order as perfect may have even more deadly consequences than claiming perfection for an existing structure. In the name of the projected perfect true order of society, which is supposedly realizable on earth, it will seem reasonable and even obligatory to work for the overthrow of all existing political and social structures. The imperfect can be condemned for not being perfect. In fact, however, since the perfect can never be actualized in history, the loss of the less than perfect is followed not by the arrival of the perfect, but by disorder and chaos, which the less than perfect had at least helped to keep in check. The threat of chaos is likely to generate the creation of *ad hoc* intermediate structures, very imperfect themselves, but which for the sake of the imagined perfect to come must eliminate criticism and opposition. In practice, for the sake of the unrealizable perfect order, small minorities can justify their attempts to destroy existing political structures. These structures will all inevitably be imperfect, deserving of criticism, and in need of change. Yet many will have developed over centuries not only in response to factional interests, but often in response to a transcendent ideal. While never immune to criticism in the light of the ideal, they may nevertheless create conditions within which the potentials of human life may be realized to a very high degree. The oak that has taken long to grow can easily be destroyed by vandals overnight. When the acorn they offer in its stead proves to be rotten, the loss is great.

The discussion, however, is not about oaks, or even about impersonal political structures, but about people. In the name of various claims to the ideal, bombs are planted to cause random death and injury, or else armies overrun whole nations and attempt to bring all actual or potential critics to heel. What we have described as idolatry is of course equally well described as alienation, which arises when human beings worship their own creations. When that happens, all suffer.

It is one of the supreme ironies of history that the genius who analysed alienation so profoundly, and who was so concerned to see it overcome, has become the inspiration behind the most alienated and alienating political systems and ideologies that the world has ever seen. The tragedy may be located in Karl Marx's elimination of God.[28] The God of nineteenth-century belief, harnessed as he so often was to class interest, may well have deserved radical criticism. But the loss of the reality of God behind the contingent portrayal of him had perhaps unexpected consequences. In the absence of God, man has in effect made himself God and laid claim to the divine attributes—omniscience, omnipotence, the right to judge, to consign blasphemers to hell, and to decide who merits heaven. With the disappearance of the kingdom of God as a transcendent ideal, human beings claim absolute value and attempt to secure the eternal reign of their own man-made systems. In the face of nineteenth-century injustices, the experiment might have seemed worth making. It has been made, and has failed disastrously.[29] The remedy does not lie in attempting to destroy Marxist-inspired political systems, but in restoring them to their proper place in

[28] K. Marx, *A Contribution to the Critique of Hegel's* Philosophy of Right: *Introduction* [c.1843], in *Critique of Hegel's* Philosophy of Right, ed. J. O'Malley (Cambridge, 1970), 131, 'Man makes religion; religion does not make man. Religion is, in fact, the self-consciousness and self-esteem of man who has either not yet gained himself or has lost himself'. See D. McLellan, *Karl Marx: His Life and Thought* (London, 1973), 89.

[29] L. Kolakowski, *Main Currents of Marxism*, iii, *The Breakdown* (Oxford, 1978), 530, 'The self-deification of mankind, to which Marxism gave philosophical expression, has ended in the same way as all such attempts, whether individual or collective: it has revealed itself as the farcical aspect of human bondage.'

relation to the transcendent ideal. What seeing God in the form of Jesus can do for the Torah and for great world religions, it can do for Marxism,[30] and equally for capitalism and all other overburdened ideologies.

In conclusion, it seems that the question of ultimacy and the yearning for an answer cannot be wished out of existence as readily as God himself. With the loss of God, it may seem that the only answer left to man's question is himself—his conceptual systems, social structures, and projected ideals. But if the proof of the pudding is in the eating, enough of this pudding has been eaten to prove that it cannot satisfy. There is still a hunger in the spiritual depths of human life. Where the polarities of existence are not held in creative tension, grounded in God, the claim to possess the ideal breaks out in the anarchy of individualistic self-assertion, or the tyranny of group-claims to revelatory authority, whether in terrorist cells, military dictatorships, or the Russian empire.

In the West, the sense of God and of the transcendent ideal still serves in some measure, perhaps, to hold in check the absolutist claims of individuals and States. But, on the one hand, the sense of the transcendent is fading fast under the impact of a materialistic, scientific, technological culture; on the other hand, in reaction to this, there is desperate recourse to a wide range of supposed guaranteed sources of revealed truth. The very guarantees they claim disclose their idolatrous character. Their destructive consequences, above all their attacks on human reason, confirm their impotence to enable the potential of human life to be fulfilled. Human potential cannot be realized where human reason is enslaved or despised, however real the sense of God's presence may seem to be.

It remains to be said that Christians have a full part to play in political life. Precisely because they do not lay claim to absolute truth on earth or presume to possess the ideal here and now, and precisely because they do not recognize perfection in any individual, party, or movement, they may be found in or supporting parties across the whole political

[30] For an illustration of how this might be done, see J. L. Segundo's rigorous analysis in his *Faith and Ideologies* (London, 1984).

spectrum. However, their commitment will not be unconditional, and because of that they will themselves be open to criticism, and also free to criticize, in the light of the transcendent ideal that is shaped in the light of Jesus.

It may be that Christian criticism will itself be treated as blasphemy. In that case, the story of Jesus shows clearly what is required of his followers when they themselves are at risk: it is to accept the consequences of the rejection of God without reacting in hate, but instead with the love of God. It may be that the sacrificial acceptance of the destructive consequences of alienation will provide the alienated themselves with a vision of transcendence, and so freedom from their own enslavement. What Christians are not free to do is to *impose* their answers or transcendent ideal on others.

The problem is far more acute when followers of Jesus see others falling prey to human godlessness and to the self-idolatry of party or ideology. Resort to violence may in the extreme case be justified as the lesser evil, but the greatest care would need to be taken to avoid the mistake of inverted idolatry alluded to above, and to avoid damning the imperfect for the sake of an unrealizable ideal. An alliance between those who uphold a truly transcendent ideal and those who act for a pseudo-transcendent, not yet realized, ideal is full of danger. It can drive the upholders of existing political systems to such extremes of self-defence that their creative potential is all but eliminated, or else they are replaced by something worse.

Finally, those who are open to the transcendent ideal will always be open to the possibility of seeing the transcendent ideal itself in a deeper and truer light, precisely because they do not claim to possess it in its perfection. Paradoxically, they may be helped to grasp the ideal more adequately by those who deny its very existence. It needed the freedom of atheists to enable Christians to break through the false absolutes of their own religion. If so, atheists need Christians to liberate them from the false absolutes of their own making, with their appallingly destructive consequences. Such an interaction in the context of history and political life would demonstrate once again how the ground of meaning and

being discloses itself continuously in the outworking of evolutionary and historical existence. It broke through dramatically and definitively in the interaction of Jesus with his
world. It will continue to break through in the interaction
of Christians with their world as long as they do not lose
themselves in their beliefs, traditions, and institutions, or
scatter in the incoherent freedom of purely personal opinion.

In short, those who know God in the form of Jesus and in
the vitality of the Spirit have a positive role to play in enabling human political societies, as well as individuals, to find
meaning and purpose, and so to realize as fully as possible the
creative potentials of life in the world. Because this never
can be realized absolutely in history, the path will never be
closed to new discovery and the excitement and pleasure of
achieving it. Because perfection on earth is not envisaged,
failure and falling short will never be grounds for despair.

Conclusion

THIS book has addressed those who share an assumption and ponder a question. The assumption is that, in general terms, the modern scientific understanding of our world and its evolutionary character is valid; the question is whether life has meaning.

The first task was to spell out some of the implications of an evolutionary understanding of existence, since the question of meaning can only be raised in relation to existence as we now envisage and experience it. Our world does not seem to carry its meaning unambiguously within itself. Yet there may be that which confers meaning on existence, which in itself transcends the limitations and ambiguities of our finite being.

To raise the question of meaning in these terms is to pose the question of ultimacy. That in which the true being, character, and purpose of things is grounded must be ultimate. It must not only be real, but be knowable somehow; otherwise the question of ultimacy would remain unanswered and unanswerable. That question can scarcely be raised even today without resort to the supreme symbol of ultimacy available in our language, namely 'God'. If the word 'God' was merely a symbol of ultimacy, and did not signify that which in fact is the ground of meaning and being, the discussion would disclose little more than subjective attitudes and speculations, without claim to any foundation in reality and so not deserving to be taken seriously.

The existence of God cannot be proved, but one of the aims here has been to show that belief in the reality of God as the ground of meaning and being is not unreasonable. It would only be unreasonable, and indeed nonsensical, if the reality of God was affirmed at the expense of the reality of the world—in other words, in terms that are incompatible with our world as we now perceive it. To misrepresent the world in order to match some theory of meaning would be futile, or worse.

I have argued that the evolutionary understanding of existence gives rise to the concept of polarities; and central

to the present account has been the concept of life and existence set within the polarities of form and vitality. On this
premiss, only a concept of God able to embrace the whole
of life within its polar dimensions can measure up to the
demands of the symbol of God as creator and ground of all.
Such a concept began to emerge within the Israelite–Jewish
tradition. What emerged was not merely an isolated intellectual concept, but an understanding of God bound up
with a sense of his presence. I have tried to outline the
historical conditions within which this sense of God developed, but which also threatened to distort it. I have argued that Jesus' execution was a consequence of this
distortion, and yet without it he himself could not have been
perceived as the ultimate symbol of God. This recognition,
when it came, had radical, life-transforming effects.

Within the milieu of Judaism the conviction that Jesus
was of ultimate and universal significance could arise in a
humanly intelligible way. Where it arose, a new community
was constituted, the Christian Church. I have suggested that
the same conviction has continued to constitute the identity
of the Christian Church, despite the divisions, bitterness,
and crimes into which it has been thrown in its attempt to
articulate its beliefs and work out their practical
implications.

The final question, namely the truth of the Christian confession, is by no means settled by such an account of its
origins and development, or by any demonstration of its
internal logical coherence. However, two practical and interrelated tests can be applied by which we can measure the
plausibility of its claims. The first is whether the Christian
confession generates an understanding of reality which can
do justice to the deepest spiritual yearnings of all human
beings. The second is whether it opens up a path through
the distortions, evils, failures, and frustrations of life which
constantly threaten disaster on an individual, communal,
and planetary scale. The conclusion advanced here, on the
basis of the case made in the previous pages, is that the
Christian confession measures up to these tests to a remarkable and perhaps unique extent.

Christianity is certainly not the only religion in which

spiritual hunger is satisfied. It is itself heir to a great spiritual tradition. But there are degrees of satisfaction. In perceiving unconditional love at the heart of reality, as the ground of meaning and being, Christianity is in a position to meet the profoundest needs of all human beings. It undergirds the experience of goodness and value; it deals with the problems of guilt, failure, and despair, and creates conditions within which humans can grow truly as persons in relationship with each other. This central conviction of God's love arises out of the confession that Jesus is the form of God. This means that the self-sacrificing love of Jesus is the truth of that which is the ground and goal of existence—God.

But Christians have never identified God with Jesus without remainder. To do so would be nonsensical and contrary to the witness of Jesus himself. The confession that Jesus is the form of God leads on, as we have seen, to the confession that God, who *is* eternally, and who is present in the Spirit, is revealed in the form of Jesus. More concisely, we may say 'God is revealed in the form of Jesus and in the vitality of the Spirit'. So far from being an irrelevant metaphysical puzzle, the doctrine of the Trinity interpreted in this way is of enormous practical significance.

Both the content and the dialectical polar structure of this confession enable it to meet the demands of the tests we proposed, not only in respect of individuals or small groups, but in relation to humankind as a whole. In virtue of the polar character of God's revelatory outreach, he can be seen to embrace the polarities of existence and hence the totality of evolution and history within the dimensions of time and space. If nothing is excluded or divorced from God, then the response to God should never lead to exclusivist negative dualisms, and certainly does not entail them. God thus conceived is not, however, contained within the limits of finite existence. This means that while God's presence in the Spirit is not excluded anywhere, he is not exclusively present anywhere. Hence nothing finite, no worldly form, nor the universe as such, can claim or rightly be accorded ultimate value.

The power of the Christian confession to overcome the demonic distortions that now threaten the whole planet lies

precisely here. Its bearing on particular issues was explored
in Part V, but the present crisis is such that the basic case
needs to be re-emphasized, not least because the Christian
Churches have generally dwelt too much on the troubles and
needs and often rather unimportant failings of individual
human life, at the expense of corporate human life and its
deep-seated disorder.

To confess God to be revealed in Jesus is to acknowledge
Jesus as the supreme symbol of God. To confess God revealed in Jesus *on the cross* is to acknowledge God revealed
at the point where the supreme symbol of God is itself
broken and negated. If this holds for the supreme symbol of
God, it holds equally—if not more so—for all other symbols
of truth and ultimate reality. All fundamentalisms, all claims
to absolute value or truth, whether political or religious,
Christian or otherwise, are at this point exposed in their
falsehood. But the exposure of their falsehood and demonic
character is not after all their destruction, but their redemption. Paradoxically, in acknowledging the ultimacy of
Jesus, the truth which all religions and ideologies bear in
some measure is validated, not negated. The true creative
power of worldly forms is released, not lost, when the premature claim to ultimacy is disavowed.

Liberated from such presumptuous claims, the various
forms of human self-understanding and world-ordering are
free to adapt, grow, and develop, within the changing conditions of life on earth and in interaction with other traditions
and cultures. They can even be left behind without all seem-
ing to be lost and without their proper value in the past
being denied. They are validated not as perfect in themselves,
but as creating conditions and mapping the various routes
within which and along which human beings in all the diversity of their traditions, cultures, and environments can move
towards the transcendent goal. Because the goal is transcendent, no worldly form has the right to monopolize life
on earth or to claim absolute value. This applies as much to
the diverse worldly forms of Christianity as to anything else;
and certainly to acknowledge the ultimacy of Jesus on the
cross will not entail becoming a Christian in a narrowly
institutional or Westernized cultural sense. But wherever the

confession is made, it will open up a new and shared vision of the transcendent goal of human life. In its light will be disclosed whatever in one's own life or religious or cultural tradition is incompatible with true human being and destiny.

It is, then, only in response to someone who accepted the total rejection and denial of all his claims that other human beings are asked to surrender their claims to ultimacy. Such surrender is a kind of sharing in his death, and yet, as the story tells, the outcome from the start was life, not death, and life even in the face of physical suffering and death. The power of death, its power to impose meaninglessness on life, was and is overcome. The power of false gods to divide humankind and to frustrate our highest aspirations was and is defeated in principle. In practice, the forces of division and the tempting lure of security and meaning offered by false gods remain. They must be repeatedly overcome, and *can* be overcome in the name of Jesus on the cross, and of God revealed in the form of Jesus and the vitality of the Spirit.

We conclude, then, that this confession opens up the way forward between the distorted, demonic, and destructive extremes of tyranny and anarchy. In its hopeful realism the deceits of Utopianism are stripped away and the despair of cynicism is overcome. The most serious cause of human conflict, the sincere and passionate devotion to false gods, is removed. Thus, the conditions are created within which, without loss of variety or spontaneity, and without denying the significance of the past, human life can look to the re-alization of its highest potentials on earth, while still re-maining open to the mystery and reality beyond.

Three things remain to be said. First, if the confession is true, what must reality as such be like? In technical language, what is the ontological corollary of the Christian confession? What must be the case with God, with Jesus, with the Spirit, with the world, and with humankind, for it to be possible for this confession to be true, not merely in theory, but in actuality? It has not been the aim of this book to answer that question, but to show how such a confession could be made, how it can measure up to the demands of intellectual inquiry without being dissolved into relativism, and what some of

the practical implications will be. Such an undertaking can
be described as apologetic theology.

It is the task of what is sometimes called fundamental
theology to make the Christian confession its starting-point,
and from there to attempt to spell out the true nature of
things and their relationship to each other. Such an analysis
of reality (ontology) may be a valid and valuable undertaking,
but is not the starting-point for faith; nor should it be mistaken for an argument that can, with the force of logic, lead
to faith. It rather speaks from faith to faith; it asks in the
light of faith how Jesus himself in his own being related to
the being of God. If the confession that God is revealed in
the form of Jesus is true, the relationship must have been
unique in the strongest sense. We can accept here that one
of the functions of traditional incarnational language has
been ontological (Christological in a strict sense) in its intention to say something about the being of God and Jesus.
It has thus served not only as a confession of faith, but also
as a pointer to the underlying ontological relationship which
faith discerns, and on which it must rest if it is valid. But
such language, though it may be adequate to the intention
of faith, is far from adequate as an explanation or description
of the ontological relationship.

This brings us to the second point, which is the importance of distinguishing the different functions and limitations of theological language. Human language and
symbols can definitively express the intention of faith. This
is proved by the act of a confessor in accepting whatever
consequences his confession brings upon him, even death.
Human language is also adequate to describe earthly things.
But such language cannot measure up descriptively to the
reality of God's being. We must therefore recognize the
distinction between the confessional, the physically descriptive, and the ontologically descriptive functions of language. Not only may different languages perform different
functions, but the very same word or symbol may be functioning in more than one way at the same time. In one
respect it may function far more adequately than in another.
Undiscriminating approval and condemnation are in that
case equally misguided.

The failure to make the necessary distinctions leads to the premature or improper literalization of theological symbols. This has been perhaps one of the most serious causes not only of conflict and confusion in the Christian Church, but of its demonic perversion. It has also resulted in the erection of unnecessary obstacles to faith itself. The language of incarnation may again be drawn upon to illustrate. If accounts of the virgin birth or representations of Jesus as a pre-existent, personal, quasi-human subject are intended to express faith in his ultimate and universal significance, they may still serve a valid purpose. If taken literally in descriptive terms, such language is liable to obscure precisely what it is intended to convey, the content of faith. It makes the response to the ultimacy of Jesus depend on descriptions of him which are incompatible with the generally accepted scientific, biological descriptions of humans as evolutionary beings.

Intellectual integrity would rightly deter many from responding to Jesus on such conditions. To accept them would involve either surrendering such truth as has yielded itself to scientific inquiry, or submitting to a dualistic way of thought that divorces religion from the real world. Any denial of the fact that Jesus was completely human and as much a product of evolution, culture, and history as anyone else divorces him from our world and our world from God. A response to Jesus on such terms is distorted inasmuch as it is a response to what he was not. Equally, the view of God arrived at through the distorted form must itself be distorted, with all the implications that follow from that.

An equally serious consequence of the laying down of such conditions is the transformation of the commitment of faith into unquestioning acceptance of supposedly divinely revealed propositions or historical (or quasi-historical) facts. The case has already been made against revelation by proposition on the grounds that it is incompatible with the revelation of God in the form of Jesus. Historical knowledge for its part cannot by its very nature become certain fact, and, as we have argued, to force certainty on to history in the name of faith perverts both faith and intellect. Faith as response to Jesus as the form of God involves decision, however complex and mysterious the factors that make a genuine decision possible. The decision of faith is the orientation of the whole personality—heart, mind, and will—on the story of Jesus as the clue to the truth of God. Through that decision the possibility of knowing God in the form of Jesus and in the vitality of the Spirit is opened up. Such commitment is compatible with continuing doubts and uncertainties of every kind. Without them, the possibility of growth and deeper understanding would not exist. Faith as confession and commitment takes doubt into itself;[1] it does not offer the false security of absolute certainty, least of all at the expense of such knowledge as we do have of our world.

The presence of God with Jesus and his role in bodying out the truth of God are here affirmed. What is opposed is treating the language of confession as the description of being in a way that distorts the response of Christians to God and prevents others responding. It would be the task of fundamental theology to wrestle with these difficulties in order to express the truth of God in Jesus and of Jesus being the form of God in a way that did not raise insuperable barriers to faith, but helped to disclose what must be true about God and Jesus, humankind, and the world, if the Christian confession is true. It is a task of faith, not a precondition of faith.

The last thing to be said can be briefly stated. If the confession is true, and the far-reaching claims based upon it have any validity, then the Christian message is far too important to be left to Christians, least of all to clergy and theologians. It must be made public to the widest possible extent, because it is a matter of life and death here and now. The threat of disaster is all too real, but in the confession that God is revealed in the form of Jesus and the vitality of the Spirit lies the possibility of life.

---

[1] P. Tillich, *The Protestant Era* (London, 1951), p. xxix; id., *The Courage to Be*, 56, 168 ff.

Select Bibliography

[The Bibliography contains books available in English and referred to in the text.]

ACKROYD, P. R. , and EVANS, C. F. , eds., *The Cambridge History of the Bible*, vol. i, *From the Beginnings to Jerome* (Cambridge, 1970).

ARMSTRONG, A. H., *An Introduction to Ancient Philosophy* (3rd edn., London, 1957).

——, ed., *The Cambridge History of Later Greek and Early Mediaeval Philosophy* (Cambridge, 1970).

AZZAM, S., ed., *Islam and Contemporary Society* (London and New York, 1982).

BANKS, R., *Jesus and the Law in the Synoptic Tradition* (Cambridge, 1975).

BARNES, J., *Aristotle* (Oxford, 1982).

BARR, J., *Fundamentalism* (London, 1977).

BARRETT, C. K., *The Gospel according to St. John* (2nd edn., London, 1978).

BEGBIE, H., *The Life of William Booth, the Founder of the Salvation Army* (2 vols., London, 1920).

BERGER, P. L., *A Rumour of Angels* (Harmondsworth, 1970).

——, *The Social Reality of Religion* (London, 1969).

——, and LUCKMANN, T., *The Social Construction of Reality* (Harmondsworth, 1967).

BLACKMAN, E. C., *Marcion and his Influence* (London, 1948).

BOWKER, J., *The Sense of God: Sociological, Anthropological and Psychological Approaches to the Origin of the Sense of God* (Oxford, 1973).

——, *Jesus and the Pharisees* (Cambridge, 1973).

——, *The Targums and Rabbinic Literature: An Introduction to Jewish Interpretations of Scripture* (Cambridge, 1969).

BROWN, R. E., *The Community of the Beloved Disciple* (London, 1979).

——, *The Virginal Conception and Bodily Resurrection of Jesus* (New York, 1973).

——, *The Birth of the Messiah: A Commentary on the Infancy Narratives in Matthew and Luke* (London, 1977).

BROWNLEE, W. H., *The Midrash Pesher of Habbakuk* (Missoula, Mont.,1979).

BULTMANN, R., *Faith and Understanding: Collected Essays* (Eng. trans., London, 1969 (6th edn.); 1st edn., Tübingen, 1966).

BUTLER, B. C., ed., *The Vatican Council 1869-1870* (London, 1930; rev. edn., Glasgow, 1962).

CAMPENHAUSEN, H. VON, *Ecclesiastical Authority and Spiritual Power in the Church of the First Three Centuries* (Eng. trans., London, 1969; 1st edn., Tübingen, 1953).

CHADWICK, H., *The Early Church* (Harmondsworth, 1967).

CHARLES, R. H., ed., *The Apocrypha and Pseudepigrapha of the Old Testament in English* (Oxford, 1913).

CHIRICO, P., *Infallibility: The Crossroads of Doctrine* (London, 1977).

CLEMENTS, R. E., *Prophecy and Tradition* (Oxford, 1975).

COGGINS, R. J., *Samaritans and Jews: The Origins of Samaritanism Reconsidered* (Oxford, 1975).

CRAGG, K., *The Call of the Minaret* (New York, 1964).

——, *Counsels in Contemporary Islam* (Islamic Surveys, 3; Edinburgh, 1965).

CRENSHAW, J. L., *Old Testament Wisdom: An Introduction* (London, 1982).

DANBY, H., *The Mishnah* (London, 1933).

DANIÉLOU, J., *Origen* (Eng. trans., London, 1955; 1st edn., Paris, 1948).

DAVIES, W. D., *The Setting of the Sermon on the Mount* (Cambridge, 1964).

DILLON, J., *The Middle Platonists: A Study of Platonism 80 BC to AD 220* (London, 1977).

DOUGLAS, M., *Natural Symbols: Explorations in Cosmology* (London, 1970).

DUNN, J. D. G., *Christology in the Making: An Inquiry into the Origins of the Doctrine of the Incarnation* (London, 1980).

DRIVER, G. R., *The Judaean Scrolls* (Oxford, 1965).

ELLIS, E. Earle, *Prophecy and Hermeneutic in Early Christianity* (Tübingen, 1978).

EPSTEIN, I., *Israel: A Historical Presentation* (Harmondsworth, 1959).

GODFREY, L. R., ed., *Scientists Confront Creationism* (London and New York, 1983).

GRANT, R. M., *From Augustus to Constantine* (London, 1971).

GREEN, W. Scott, ed., *Approaches to Ancient Judaism*, 3 vols. (Chico, Calif., 1978-81).

GREGG, R. C., and GROH, D. E., *Early Arianism: A View of Salvation* (London, 1981).

GRILLMEIER, A., *Christ in Christian Tradition*, vol. i, *From the Apostolic Age to Chalcedon (AD 451)* (2nd, rev. edn.; Eng. trans., London and Oxford, 1975).

GUTHRIE, W. K. C., *A History of Greek Philosphy*, 5 vols. (Cambridge, 1962–81): vol. iv, *Plato the Man and his Dialogues: Earlier Period* (1975); vol. v, *The Later Plato and the Academy* (1978); vol. vi, *Aristotle: An Encounter* (1981).

HARDY, E. R., ed., *The Christology of the Later Fathers* (The Library of Christian Classics, 3; London and Philadelphia, 1954).

HARE, R. M., *Plato* (Oxford, 1982).

HARRÉ, R., ed., *Personality* (Oxford, 1976).

—— and SECORD, P. F., *The Explanation of Social Behaviour* (Oxford, 1972).

HARVEY, A. E., ed., *God Incarnate: Story and Belief* (London, 1981).

——, *Jesus and the Constraints of History: The Bampton Lectures, 1980* (London, 1982).

HARVEY, V., *The Historian and the Believer* (London, 1967).

HASTINGS, A., ed., *Bishops and Writers: Aspects of the Evolution of Modern English Catholicism* (Wheathampstead, Herts., 1977).

HAYES, J. H., and MILLER, J. M., eds., *Israelite and Judaean History* (London, 1977).

HEATON, E. W., *The Hebrew Kingdoms* (New Clarendon Bible, Old Testament, 3; Oxford, 1968).

HEIDEGGER, M., *Being and Time* (Eng. trans. (of 7th edn.), Oxford, 1962; 1st edn., Tübingen, 1927).

HENGEL, M., *Judaism and Hellenism* (2 vols., Eng. trans., London, 1974; 1st rev. edn., Tübingen, 1973).

——, *The Son of God* (Eng trans., London, 1976; 1st edn., Tübingen, 1975).

HENRY, P., *New Directions in New Testament Study* (London, 1980).

HERRMANN, S., *A History of Israel in Old Testament Times* (Eng. trans., London, 1975; 1st edn., Munich, 1973).

HICK, J., *God and the Universe of Faiths: Essays in the Philosophy of Religion* (London, 1973).

—— and HEBBLETHWAITE, B., *Christianity and Other Religions* (Glasgow, 1980).

HIGGINS, A. J. B., *The Son of Man in the Teaching of Jesus* (Society for New Testament Studies, Monograph Series, 39; Cambridge, 1980).

HOLT, P. M., LAMBTON, A. K. S., and LEWIS, B., eds., *The Cambridge History of Islam*, 4 vols. (Cambridge, 1970).

JAGERSMA, H., *A History of Israel in the Old Testament Period* (Eng. trans., London, 1982; 1st edn., Kampen, 1979).

KÄHLER, M., *The So-called Historical Jesus and the Historic, Biblical Christ* (Eng. trans., Philadelphia, 1964; 1st edn., Leipzig, 1892).

KELLY, J. N. D., *Early Christian Doctrines* (5th, rev. edn., London, 1977).

KITCHER, P., *The Case against Creationism* (Milton Keynes, 1983).

KOLAKOWSKI, L., *Main Currents of Marxism*, 3 vols. (Oxford, 1978).

KÜMMEL, W. G., *The New Testament: The History of the Investigation of its Problems* (Eng. trans., London, 1973, of 2nd, rev. edn., Freiburg and Munich, 1970).

KÜNG, H., *On Being a Christian* (Eng. trans., Glasgow, 1976; 1st edn., Munich, 1974).

——, *Infallible?* (Eng. trans., London, 1971; 1st edn., Cologne, 1970).

LAMPE, G. W. H., *God as Spirit: The Bampton Lectures, 1976* (Oxford, 1977).

LASH, N., *Change in Focus: A Study of Doctrinal Change and Continuity* (London, 1973).

LEE, D., trans., *Plato*, Timaeus *and* Critias (Harmondsworth, 1965).

LENNEBERG, E. H., 'Brain Correlates of Language', in F. O. Schmidt, ed., *The Neurosciences Second Study Program* (New York, 1970).

LEVY, R., *The Social Structure of Islam* (Cambridge, 1957) [2nd edn. of *The Sociology of Islam*].

LIDDELL, H. G., and SCOTT, R., *A Greek-English Lexicon*, 7th edn. (Oxford, 1883); 9th edn., rev. H. S. Jones (Oxford, 1940).

LIETZMANN, H., *A History of the Early Church*, vol. iii, *From Constantine to Julian* (*Eng. trans., 2nd, rev. edn., London, 1953; 1st edn., Berlin, 1938*).

LINDARS, B., *Jesus Son of Man: A Fresh Examination of Son of Man Sayings in the Gospels in the Light of Recent Research* (London, 1983).

LINDBLOM, J., *Prophecy in Ancient Israel* (Oxford, 1962).

McADOO, H. R., and CLARK, A. C., *The Final Report* (The Anglican-Roman Catholic International Commission, London, 1982).

McKANE, W., *Prophets and Wise Men* (London, 1965).

McLELLAN, D., *Karl Marx: His Life and Thought* (London, 1973).

MACQUARRIE, J., *Principles of Christian Theology* (2nd edn., New York, 1977).

MARMUR, D., *Beyond Survival: Reflections on the Future of Judaism* (London, 1982).

MARSHALL, I. Howard, *The Gospel of Luke* (Exeter, 1978).

MARX, K., *Critique of Hegel's* Philosophy of Right, ed. J. O'Malley (Cambridge, 1970).

MAYES, A. D. H., *The New Century Bible Commentary: Deuteronomy* (Grand Rapids and London, 1979).

MOLTMANN, J., *Theology of Hope: On the Ground and the Implications of a Christian Eschatology* (Eng. trans., London, 1967; 1st edn., Munich, 1965).

MUSAPH-ANDRIESSE, R. C., *From Torah to Kabbalah: A Basic Introduction to the Writings of Judaism* (Eng. trans., London, 1981; 1st edn., Baarn, 1973).

NEUSNER, J., *A Life of Rabban Yohanan ben Zakkai, ca. 1–80 C.E.* (Leiden, 1962).

——, *Development of a Legend: Studies on the Traditions concerning Yohanan ben Zakkai* (Leiden, 1970).

——, *From Politics to Piety: The Emergence of Pharisaic Judaism* (Englewood Cliffs, NJ, 1973).

——, 'The Use of later Rabbinic Evidence for the Study of First Century Pharisaism', in W. Scott Green, ed., *Approaches to Ancient Judaism*, vol. i (Missoula, Mont., 1978).

——, 'The Use of Rabbinic Sources for the Study of Ancient Judaism', in W. Scott Green, ed., *Approaches to Ancient Judaism*, vol. iii (Chico, Calif., 1981).

NIEBUHR, R., *The Nature and Destiny of Man*, 2 vols. (New York, 1964; 1st edn., 1941 and 1943).

NINEHAM, D. E., *Saint Mark* (The Pelican Gospel Commentaries; Harmondsworth, 1963).

NORRIS, R. A., *God and the World in Early Christian Theology* (London, 1966).

PAGELS, E., *The Gnostic Gospels* (London, 1980).

PANNENBERG, W., *Jesus: God and Man* (Eng. trans., London, 1968; 1st edn., Gütersloh, 1964).

PEACOCKE, A. R., *Science and the Christian Experiment* (London, 1971).

PHILLIPS, A. J., *Deuteronomy* (The Cambridge Bible Commentary; Cambridge, 1973).

POLLARD, T. E., *Johannine Christology and the Early Church* (Cambridge, 1970).

RICHES, J., *Jesus and the Transformation of Judaism* (London, 1980).

ROBINSON, J. A. T., *The Human Face of God* (London, 1973).

ROHDE, J., *Rediscovering the Teaching of the Evangelists* (London, 1968).

RUDOLPH, K., *Gnosis: The Nature and History of an Ancient Religion*, Eng. trans. and edn. R. McL. Wilson (Edinburgh, 1983; 1st edn., Leipzig, 1977).

RUSSELL, D. S., *The Jews from Alexander to Herod* (The New Clarendon Bible, 5; Oxford, 1967).

SANDERS, E. P., *Paul and Palestinian Judaism* (London, 1977).

SCHÜRER, E., *The History of the Jewish People in the Age of Jesus Christ (175 BC-AD 135)*, vol. ii, rev. and ed. G. Vermes, F. Millar, and M. Black (Edinburgh, 1979).

SCHWEITZER, E., *The Good News according to Matthew* (London, 1975).

SEGUNDO, J. L., *Faith and Ideologies* (Eng. trans., London, 1984; 1st edn., Madrid, 1982).

SHAW, G., *The Cost of Authority: Manipulation and Freedom in the New Testament* (London, 1983).

STENDAHL, K., *The School of St. Matthew, and its Use of the Old Testament* (Philadelphia, 1968; 1st edn., Copenhagen, 1954).

STEVENSON, J., ed., *Councils, Creeds and Controversies: Documents Illustrative of the History of the Church AD 377-461* (London, 1966).

SYKES, S. W., *Christian Theology Today* (London and Oxford, 1971).

THEISSEN, G., *The First Followers of Jesus* (Eng. trans., London, 1978; 1st edn., Munich, 1977).

TILLARD, J. M. R., *The Bishop of Rome* (Eng. trans., London, 1983; 1st edn., Paris, 1982).

TILLICH, P., *Systematic Theology*, 3 vols. (London, 1978; 1st edn., Chicago, 1951-63).

——, *Christianity and the Encounter of the World Religions* (New York, 1963).

——, *The Courage to Be* (Glasgow, 1962; 1st edn., London, 1952).

——, *Dynamics of Faith* (London, 1957).

——, *The Protestant Era* (London, 1951).

TROELTSCH, E., *The Social Teaching of the Christian Churches*, 2 vols. (Eng. trans., London and New York, 1931; 1st edn., Tübingen, 1912).

VAUX, R. DE, *Ancient Israel, its Life and Institutions* (Eng. trans., London, 1961; 1st edn., Paris, 1958-60).

VERMES, G., *The Dead Sea Scrolls: Qumran in Perspective* (London, 1977).

——, *The Dead Sea Scrolls in English* (2nd edn., Harmondsworth, 1975).

——, *Jesus the Jew: A Historical Reading of the Gospels* (London, 1973).

WALLACE-HADRILL, D. S., *Christian Antioch* (Cambridge, 1982).

WEBER, M., *The Sociology of Religion* (Eng. trans. (of 4th edn.), London, 1963; 1st edn., Tübingen, 1921).

WEINGART, R. E., *The Logic of Divine Love* (Oxford, 1970).

WHYBRAY, R. N., *The Intellectual Tradition in the Old Testament* (Berlin and New York, 1974).

WICKHAM, L. R., ed., *Cyril of Alexandria: Select Letters* (Oxford, 1983).

WILES, M. F., *The Making of Christian Doctrine* (Cambridge, 1967).

——, *Working Papers in Doctrine* (London, 1976).

WILKEN, R. L., *The Christians as the Romans saw them* (New Haven and London, 1984).

WILSON, R. McL., *The Gnostic Problem: A Study of the Relations between Hellenistic Judaism and the Gnostic Heresy* (London, 1958).

YOUNG, F. M., *Sacrifice and the Death of Christ* (London, 1975).

——, *From Nicaea to Chalcedon: A Guide to the Literature and its Background* (London, 1983).

General Index

Ecclesiasticus (Wisdom of ben Sira), book of 79, 236
ecumenism 296, 302 n.
Edom 129
Egypt 59, 75, 77, 119, 245
El Elyon 66
Elephantine 75
enbibliation 284, cf. 182 n.
Enoch, 1st book of 149
episcopacy 298 f.
eschatology 107; see also hope
Essenes 98 n., 105 f., 108, 160, 179; see also Qumran
eternity 44, 204 f., 238
ethical concern, see Judaism
evangelical movement 299 f.
evil 32
evolutionary existence/world 1 ff., 7–12, 23–8, 54 f., 92, 94, 100, 138, 218, 221, 271, 322 f., 325
  Jesus' life set within 140 ff., 175, 200, 207 f., 273, 285, 329
  see also God and the world
exile (Babylonian) 59, 68–72, 74, 83, 113, 115, 147
existence 29, 215, 280; see also evolutionary ~/world
existentialist 30
exodus 59, 107, 226
experience 199, 308, 310 f.
  of God 48, 102, 310 f.; in Judaism 88, 137; through Jesus 191 ff., 201–4, 214 n., 215, 221 ff., 225, 232
  see also interpretation; revelation in subjective mode; Jesus' human life and ministry

failure 97 n., 175, 178, 217, 302 n., 312, 322, 325
faith 114, 172 f., 250, 255, 259, 266, 274 f., 281 n., 286, 302 f., 311, 312 n., 328 ff.
  definition/criteria of 270, 289, 295
  judgements of 168, 195, 274, cf. 277 f.
  justification by 302, cf. 330
Father 135, 138, 244; see also Abba; God in the light of Jesus
Father, Son, Holy Spirit 222, 271
Fathers of the Church 222, 256 f., 269, 276 ff., 287
  Cappadocian 264
femininity 238

followers of Jesus 170 f., 173, 175, 192, 199, 201, 205, 221, 223, 225 f., 287 f., 293, 321; see also Christians; Church
force, use of 288
foreigners/gentiles 91, 95, 98, 131, 133 n., 154, 158, 160, 172 f.
forgiveness 161, 167, 302
form and vitality 2–4, 9 f., 17, 24, 27, 35 ff., 47, 53 ff., 119, 175, 201, 203, 204 n., 232, 236, 289, 324
  in Christianity 191, 216, 218 f., 229 f., 247, 267
  of God 191, 202–6, 211–20, 229, 244, 267
  in Judaism 83, 86, 101, 112, 125
  see also form of Jesus and vitality of the (Holy) Spirit; polar dialectic/dynamic; polarity model
form of God 171, 187, 197 ff., 217, 223, 263, 272 f., 277, 290
  Bible as 284, 286, 299 ff.
  Church as 293, 302
  see also Jesus and the response of faith; Torah
form of Jesus, see God in the light of Jesus
form of Jesus and vitality of the (Holy) Spirit 214, 218, 232, 278, 299–305, 311 f., 322, 325, 327, 330
forms:
  of book/person 182, 210 f., 264, 284, 300, 305, 307 f., cf. 88
  concrete 10, 36 ff., 44, 126, 183, 187, 299
  human 184, 187
  Platonic 240
  symbolic (written/verbal) 16, 18, 21–4, 27 ff., 29, 38–41, 44 f., 53, 91, 155, 183, 188, 191, 198 ff., 225 f., 274, 289
  worldly 295, 303, 325 f.
  see also revelation in formal mode
Fourth Gospel 192 f., 229, 243 f., 257, 260, 263
'fourth philosophy' 130
freedom 2 f., 12, 16, 84, 137, 164 f., 191, 193 ff., 216, 287 f., 293, 299, 308 f., 321 f.
  of atheists 321
  of God 164–7, 188, 266, 286, 290, 295
  of interpretation 46, 54, 110
  of Jesus 56, 153, 158 f., 166 f., 171 ff., 175, 194, 252, 257, 267, 269, 277

Index of Proper Names

Index of Modern Authors

[Italics indicate a reference to the main text. All other references are to the footnotes]

Index of References to the Bible and Other Ancient Sources

BIBLE AND APOCRYPHA

JEWISH SOURCES

OTHER ANCIENT SOURCES

DATE DUE

HIGHSMITH 45-220